EVALUATION

EVALUATION
A SYSTEMATIC APPROACH

Second Edition

Peter H. Rossi
Howard E. Freeman
with the collaboration of
Sonia Rosenbaum

SAGE PUBLICATIONS
Beverly Hills / London / New Delhi

For information address:

SAGE Publications, Inc.
275 South Beverly Drive
Beverly Hills, California 90212

SAGE Publications India Pvt. Ltd.
C-236 Defence Colony
New Delhi 110 024, India

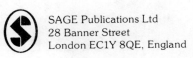

SAGE Publications Ltd
28 Banner Street
London EC1Y 8QE, England

Printed in the United States of America

Library of Congress Cataloging in Publication Data

Rossi, Peter Henry, 1921-
   Evaluation.

   Bibliography: p.
   Includes indexes.
   1. Evaluation research (Social action programs)
I. Freeman, Howard E. II. Rosenbaum, Sonia. III. Title.
H62.R666 1982   361.6'1'072   81-21350
ISBN 0-8039-1784-8   AACR2

FIRST PRINTING

To

Don Campbell, Lee Cronbach,
and Fred Mosteller,

*whose net impacts upon the
field of evaluation are beyond
assessment*

CONTENTS

EVALUATION

*T*here are several reasons behind the decision to revise this book: Progress in a field requires an updating; we have found better ways to communicate concepts and technical methods; and syntactical and printing errors in the first edition require corrections.

Evaluation is a swiftly changing field, and new concepts, techniques, and empirical examples needed to be included in our volume. Our own experiences in teaching from the book and our readers' helpful criticisms have stimulated us to do a better job pedagogically. Further, we have worked harder this time to minimize typographical errors and ones of syntax as well, and to simplify the writing style as much as possible. Finally, the authors, in addition to having grown a few years older, have continued to participate actively in applied social research. Our thoughts, views, and knowledge of the field have changed, grown, and perhaps deepened. At least we think so, and we hope our readers will too.

This book has a cosmopolitan past. Its beginnings go back more than five years, when we presented independently written but remarkably similar papers (Freeman, 1977; Rossi and Wright, 1976) on the state of evaluation research, at an international meeting sponsored by UNESCO in Washington, D.C. While the authors were hardly strangers to each other, the convergence of ideas in the two papers was so close that, throughout the conference, we jokingly accused each other of plagiarism, a charge that upset our non-American colleagues, who were afraid that we were about to run each other into court. The consistency of views, bibliographic references, and terminology suggested to us and to others at the conference that there was considerable structure and consensus within the field of evaluation, at least as practiced in the United States. Evaluation appeared to have grown out of a feeble childhood and through a clumsy adolescence, finally achieving some adult dignity.

Staff of the Organisation for Economic Cooperation and Development (OECD) attending the conference urged us to expand our papers into a survey of evaluation methods that could be employed in lesser developed countries with relatively limited resources and without highly trained specialists. The manuscript went through several revisions and lengthy reviews at two international working conferences in Paris. It was finally published in both English and French (Freeman, Rossi, and

Wright, 1979). We hope that it has met at least some of the needs of evaluators in lesser developed countries.

Our experience in writing the OECD book inspired us to try writing a similarly organized volume for a North American (and, if possible, European) audience. The two resulting books are siblings but not clones. Both volumes attempt to describe and explain in an organized fashion the current frameworks and technical procedures in the field. They differ because of the nature of the audiences and because, at least in the United States, evaluation fits more closely in the larger context of social policy development and program implementation. We can also expect that the audience for this volume will have the greater technical knowledge that is needed to appreciate more sophisticated approaches to evaluation. The books differ further in the depth with which specific topics are handled and in the examples given.

The joy, conflict, and work that went into this volume were shared equally by the two authors. Age and notoriety were the major determinants of the order of authorship. Our co-author of the first edition, Sonia Rosenbaum (formerly Sonia R. Wright), has shifted career interests and did not participate in the revision. Her earlier contributions, particularly as author of the chapter on efficiency evaluations, which appears in the present edition with our modifications, merit continued acknowledgment.

There are many other individuals who have played significant roles in the development of this volume and its revision. Our enthusiasm and motivation have been maintained by the steady support and subtle influence of our friends at Sage Publications. Marian A. Solomon of the Lutheran Hospital Society of Southern California advised us on federal evaluation policy and evaluability assessment. For their part in manuscript preparation, we are grateful to Cynthia Coffman, Adrienne Porema, Jeanne Reinle, and Nancy Sturge.

A continuing source of learning, upon which we have drawn heavily, is our own research experiences. We are grateful to the Agency for International Development, the California State Department of Rehabilitation, the Centers for Disease Control, the Department of Housing and Urban Development, the Department of Labor, the Educational Testing Service, the Ford Foundation, the National Center for Health Services Research, the National Academy of Science, the National Institute of Mental Health, the National Science Foundation, the National Institute of Justice, the Office of the Secretary of Health and Human Services, the Pan American Health Organization, the Robert Wood Johnson Foundation, and the Russell Sage Foundation for supporting our various research endeavors. Currently, and in the recent past, these agencies and others have provided us with support and consequently opportunities to accumulate working experiences with the processes and problems of evaluation. In addition, our universities have provided congenial environments for our work.

We have tried to write a volume useful to both the practicing evaluator and the student of applied social research. We are gratified that the first edition was used by students in over two hundred universities. The book is not discipline-oriented in its approach, and we would be most happy if the reader is unable to determine from the text itself the social science disciplines from which we originate. We will be pleased if we continue to reach the growing audience of practitioners and students. But truthfully, that would not entirely satisfy us. We aspire in this edition, as before, to bring about a closer relationship between persons in positions of policy development and social program implementation and those in evaluation research.

January 1982   *— P.H.R., H.E.F.*

Programs, Policies, and Evaluations

Systematic evaluations of purposive organized-action programs are now commonplace. Evaluation research is a robust area of activity devoted to collecting, analyzing, and interpreting information on the need for, implementation of, and impact of intervention efforts to better the lot of humankind by improving social conditions and community life. Evaluations are undertaken for different reasons: to judge the worth of ongoing programs and to estimate the usefulness of attempts to improve them; to assess the utility of innovative programs and initiatives; to increase the effectiveness of program management and administration; and to meet various accountability requirements. Evaluations may also contribute to substantive and methodological social science knowledge.

In planning social intervention programs, the focus of research is on the extent and severity of problems requiring social intervention, and on the designing of programs to ameliorate them. In the conduct of ongoing and innovative programs, there is concern that programs are reaching their intended target populations and are providing the resources, services, and benefits envisioned. As interventions are implemented and continued, there is interest in whether they are effective to any degree and, if so, the magnitudes of their impacts. For accountability and future planning, it is important to consider costs in relation to benefits, and to compare an intervention's cost efficiency to that of alternative resource allocation strategies.

Some evaluations are comprehensive and consider all these questions; others are directed at only some of them. In all cases, the aim is to provide the most valid and reliable findings possible within political and ethical constraints and the limitations imposed by time, money, and human resources.

KEY CONCEPTS

Comprehensive Evaluation:	Analysis covering the conceptualization and design of interventions, the monitoring of program implementation, and the assessment of program utility.
Conceptualization and Design Analyses:	Studies of (1) the extent and location of problems for intervention, (2) ways targets can be defined in operational terms, and (3) whether the proposed intervention is suitable.
Cost-Benefit Analyses:	Studies of the relationships between costs and outcomes of social projects, usually expressed in monetary terms.
Cost-Effectiveness Analyses:	Studies of the relationship between project costs and outcomes, usually expressed as costs per unit of outcome achieved.
Delivery System:	Organizational arrangements, including staff, procedures and activities, physical plants, and materials, needed to provide program services.
Formative Research:	Design and development testing to maximize the success of intervention.
Impact Assessment:	Evaluation of the extent to which a program causes changes in the desired direction in the target population.
Intervention:	Any program or other planned effort designed to produce intended changes in a target population.
Monitoring:	Assessment of whether or not an intervention is (1) operating in conformity to its design, and (2) reaching its specified target population.

Program Utility Assessment:	Study of the effectiveness (impact) and efficiency (costs to benefits or effectiveness) of programs.
Target Population:	Persons, households, organizations, communities, or other units at which interventions are directed.
Target Problem:	Conditions, deficiencies, or defects at which interventions are directed.

• With support from the U.S. Department of Justice, a number of communities have developed programs to increase the visibility of the police, on the assumption that crimes against both property and persons will be reduced by community perceptions of increased police presence. One program provides police officers with marked cars to use as personal automobiles as well as on duty; another increases the number of hours of police "beat-walking." These efforts have had a modest influence on crime rates.

• In four major cities in the United States, a large private foundation is providing the operating costs for community health centers in low-income areas. These centers are designed to reduce costly ambulatory-patient care now provided by hospital outpatient clinics and emergency rooms, and to offer an alternative to lengthy and expensive in-hospital care. A variety of other efforts to provide economical medical care to the poor and to contain the costs of health care are being undertaken throughout the United States. Evaluations suggest that community health centers are cost-beneficial in comparison with hospital clinics.

• In a large Latin American country, educational television is used to raise the low literacy levels of the population. An educational television program, *Plaza Sésamo,* was created by modifying a U.S. television program, *Sesame Street,* and showing it at times when schoolchildren would have opportunities to view it. Similar educational television programs have been attempted in many other countries. The utility and efficiency of these efforts in terms of costs to benefits is open to question.

• A community mental health center in a medium-sized New England city has developed an extensive program using local community members to counsel teenagers and adults about emotional, sexual, and educational problems. Compared with persons treated by psychiatrists and social workers, the clients of the indigenous workers seem to do as well in terms of need for hospitalization, maintaining treatment, and self-reports of satisfaction with the center. This finding holds even when the clients' psychological and social characteristics are taken into account.

• CETA (the Comprehensive Employment Training Act) allocates federal funds to local governments to provide jobs in public service projects for chronically unemployed persons. Many of the jobs and work settings are "unusual" compared with the ordinary opportunities available to longtime out-of-work persons. However, periods of employment for CETA workers are usually short, lasting not more than one year. Whether or not CETA jobs lead to careers of gainful employment is a key evaluation question for the U.S. Department of Labor.

• Fully two-thirds of the world's rural children suffer mild to severe malnutrition resulting in documented negative consequences for their physical growth, health status, and mental development. A major demonstration of the potential for improving the health status and mental development of children through diet supplementation is being undertaken in Central America. Pregnant women, lactating mothers, and children from birth through age 12 are provided daily with a high-protein, high-calorie food supplement. Results show major gains in physical growth and modest increases in cognitive function.

• A large manufacturing company, in an effort to increase worker productivity and product quality, has reorganized its employees into independent work teams. Within the teams, workers designate and assign tasks, recommend productivity quotas to management, and vote on the distribution of bonuses for productivity and quality improvements. Although long-term impact results are not yet available, information obtained in monitoring the program suggests it reduces days absent from the job, turnover, and similar measures of employee inefficiency.

These are but a few illustrations of the diversity of human resources programs that are undertaken and evaluated with the support of local, state, and federal governmental groups, international organizations, private foundations and philanthropies, and both nonprofit and for-profit associations and corporations. Evaluation research, by any standard, is a large enterprise. It is estimated conservatively that the U.S. government alone spends annually between $.5 billion and $1 billion for program evaluations. There is no way to estimate international expenditures. Just in the family planning area, however, the World Bank has identified over one hundred social action programs of varying size, utilizing strategies that have been tried since the 1960s, and in which citizens of over twenty-five different nations have participated.

There is no need to belabor the obvious — that many human beings suffer serious deficiencies in their lives, defects that exist both in industrialized countries and in lesser developed nations. The challenge to improve existing purposive, organized-action efforts (generally referred to as either human service or social action programs) and to create new ones is rooted in the realization that, all too often, programs designed to improve the human condition — regardless of their geographical location and sponsorship — have been misguided, misconceived, badly implemented, and ineffective. In order to distinguish useful current programs from ineffective and inefficient ones, and to plan, design, and implement innovative efforts that impact effectively and efficiently on community members and their environments, it is critical that policymakers, funding organizations, planners, and program staffs obtain answers to a range of questions, including:

- What is the nature and scope of the problem requiring actions?
- What interventions may be undertaken to ameliorate the problem significantly?
- What is the appropriate target population for the intervention?
- Is the intervention reaching that target population?
- Is the intervention being implemented in the ways envisioned?
- Is it effective?
- How much does it cost?
- What are its costs relative to its effectiveness and benefits?

Answers to such questions are necessary not only for broad, complex programs — such as nationwide family planning or income maintenance efforts — but also for local, specialized projects — such as those offering occupational training in a rural village or increasing public safety in a large city. Providing those answers is the heart of evaluation research.

WHAT IS EVALUATION RESEARCH?

We can begin this volume with a simple definition of evaluation, or evaluation research (and we will use the terms interchangeably): *Evaluation research is the systematic application of social research procedures in assessing the conceptualization and design, implementation, and utility of social intervention programs.* In other words, evaluation research involves the use of social research methodologies to judge and to improve the planning, monitoring, effectiveness, and efficiency of health, education, welfare, and other human service programs.

Note that this definition does not imply that evaluation studies follow either one or another or some particular combination of the different social research styles currently employed. Evaluation research is a social science activity; its practitioners are recruited from the broad spectrum of the social sciences; and its methods cover the gamut of social research paradigms. Evaluations are *systematic* to the extent that they employ the basic approaches to gathering valid, reliable evidence.

It is the commitment to the "rules" of social research that is at the core of our perspective on evaluation.

In describing evaluation activities, Cronbach et al. (1980) make the following points:

1. The intention of an evaluation is to influence social thought and action during the investigation or in the years immediately following. (It is reasonable to hope for long-term influences as well.)

2. Evidence is collected on experience with an already existing program or one installed for research purposes. After the analysis, the investigators set forth just how they reached their conclusions. They document their observations and reasoning so that readers can judge the plausibility of each conclusion.

3. Evaluators aim to give a comprehensive and disciplined interpretation. The account is intended to impress fair-minded persons, including those whose preconceptions or preferences run counter to the findings. Furthermore, the information collected is made available for others to scrutinize and interpret independently.

A BRIEF HISTORY

Systematic, data-based evaluations are a relatively modern development, coinciding with the growth and refinement of social research methods, as well as with ideological, political, and demographic changes during this century in our nation. Commitment to the systematic evaluation of programs in such fields as education and public health can be traced to efforts at the turn of the century to provide literacy and occupational training by the most effective and economical means, and to reduce mortality and morbidity from infectious diseases. As far back as the 1930s, there were social scientists who advocated the application of rigorous social research methods to the assessment of programs (Freeman, 1977): Dodd's attempt to introduce water-boiling as a public health practice in Middle East villages forms part of the pre-World War II empirical sociological literature; Lewin's field studies and Lippitt and White's work on democratic and authoritarian leadership have been well known to psychologists for decades; and the famous Western Electric study that contributed the term "Hawthorne Effect" to the social sciences was undertaken half a century ago. (See Bernstein and Freeman, 1975, for a more extended discussion, and Cronbach et al., 1980, for a somewhat different historical perspective.)

The Rise of Evaluation Research

Over forty years ago, an Arkansas sociology professor pleaded for evaluations of President Roosevelt's New Deal social programs (see

Exhibit 1-A). From such beginnings in the 1930s and earlier, applied social research received considerable impetus. Its employment increased during World War II: Stouffer and his associates worked with the U.S. Army (Stouffer et al., 1949) to develop continual monitoring of soldier morale as well as to evaluate personnel and propaganda policies. The Office of War Information used sample surveys to monitor civilian morale. At the same time, a host of smaller studies assessed the efficacy of price controls and campaigns to modify American eating habits. Similar social science efforts were mounted in Britain and elsewhere (see Exhibit 1-B).

The period immediately following World War II saw the beginning of large-scale programs designed to meet needs for urban development and housing, technological and cultural education, occupational training, and preventive health activities. It was also during this time that major commitments were made to international programs for family planning, health and nutrition, and rural community development. Expenditures were huge, and consequently were accompanied by demands for "knowledge of results."

By the end of the 1950s, large-scale evaluation programs were commonplace. Social scientists were engaged in evaluations of delinquency-prevention programs, felon-rehabilitation projects, psychotherapeutic and psychopharmacological treatments, public housing programs, and community organization activities. Such studies were being undertaken not only in the United States, Europe, and other industrialized countries, but also in lesser developed nations: Increasingly, programs for family planning in Asia, nutrition and health care in Latin America, and agricultural and community development in Africa included evaluation components (Levine et al., 1981; Freeman et al., 1980). Knowledge of the methods of social research, including the survey and complex statistical procedures, became widespread. Computer technology made it possible to conduct large-scale studies and undertake sophisticated statistical analyses.

During the 1960s, papers and books on the practice of evaluation research also grew dramatically. Suchman's (1967) review of evaluation research methods, Hayes's (1959) monograph on evaluation research in lesser developed countries, and Campbell's (1969) call for social experimentation are but illustrations. By the late l960s — in the United States and internationally — evaluation research, in the words of Wall Street, had become a "growth industry."

In the early 1970s, a variety of books on evaluation appeared, including a text (Weiss, 1972), collections of readings (Caro, 1971; Rossi and Williams, 1972), critiques of the methodological quality of various

(text continued on p. 26)

Exhibit 1-A: The New Deal and Social Research

No one can deny the progress in the social sciences. But with all the exacting methods developed, the economists, sociologists, and political scientists have suffered from a lack of large-scale experimental set-ups to match the everyday resources of the scientists in the laboratory.

The current enthusiasm over planning schemes now being devised by the alphabetical corporations of the federal government furnishes some hopes that this deficiency may be partially remedied. The blueprints of these agencies and the carrying out of their plans may well be looked upon as the creation of experimental laboratories for the social scientists, and for the social workers, educators, and administrators who may profit from their research.

These laboratories, set up by the planning agencies of the New Deal, permit a more effective use of the experimental method in the research projects of the social scientists. This research, in turn, would not only be an addition to science but would also be a form of social auditing for the planning authorities in noting and accounting the changes wrought by the programs.

Do slums make slum people or do slum people make the slums? Will changing the living conditions significantly change the social behavior of the people affected? The public housing projects may furnish the made-to-order test-tubes to help in answering these fascinating and bewildering questions.

The accumulating studies of the sociologists reveal the slums as the sore spots of our modern industrial civilization. In the slum areas of our urban centers are found high rates of delinquency, adult crime, dependency, tax delinquency, sickness, malnutrition, insanity, and similar conditions, together with such characteristic groups as delinquent gangs and institutions of vice. These institutions and conditions epitomize the so-called viciousness of the slum. The implication is that if these people lived under more wholesome conditions there would not be as much delinquency, dependency, sickness among them. No doubt — but how much less delinquency, dependency, sickness? Compare a slum group with the people living in a suburb. Less delinquency, dependency, and sickness? To be sure. But the people living in the suburbs are not similar to the people living in the slums in terms of certain significant factors. They are usually wealthier, better educated, healthier than the slum dwellers. The layman would call this an unfair comparison. The best way we can answer this problem, perhaps, is to compare the social indices (rates of delinquency, dependency, adult crime, sickness, and similar factors) characteristic of a given population while living in the slum, with the social indices of the same or a similar population after living in the changed environment of a model community. This would mean a "before and after" study. In other words we would have to employ the exacting techniques of an experimental approach. This would permit controlled observation and enable us to know with more precision the difference which may occur in social behavior accompanying a change in social environment brought about by the altering of living conditions. Graphically, it would be like transferring a population mass from Test Tube 1 of Liquid A to Test Tube 2 of Liquid B and finding out what happens.

Certain of the social indices may be reduced to monetary items in terms of costs to the government (costs of delinquency, adult crime, dependency, police protection, sickness, and similar factors) and a comparison made of the costs to the government preceding and following slum clearance of the transference of a slum population to a model community on more open land. Specifically, such a program may reduce delinquency and adult crime. The cost-per-delinquent and the cost-per-adult-criminal may be computed and the differential in lower costs to the state that may result from the housing program calculated. A computation may be made of the social cost differential in favor of the new communities, which may be logically considered a governmental and social saving. Such a body of data may even serve as a basis for recruiting financial support to future housing programs.

SOURCE: Adapted, with permission, from *Social Forces,* 13 (May, 1935): 515, 518. "Prospects and Possibilities: The New Deal and the New Social Research" by A. S. Stephan. Copyright © The University of North Carolina Press.

Exhibit 1-B: Early Experiments in Mass Communication

In designing Army orientation programs, an issue that was frequently debated was this: When the weight of evidence supports the main thesis being presented, is it more effective to present only the materials supporting the point being made, or is it better to introduce also the arguments of those opposed to the point being made?

1. The Two Programs Used

At the time the experiment was being planned (early 1945), the war in Europe was drawing to a close and it was reported that Army morale was being adversely affected by overoptimism about an early end to the war in the Pacific. A directive was issued by the Army to impress upon troops a conception of the magnitude of the job remaining to be done in defeating Japan. This furnished a controversial topic on which arguments were available on both sides, but where the majority of experts in military affairs believed the preponderance of evidence supported one side. It was therefore chosen as a suitable subject for experimentation.

2. The Study Groups

The preliminary survey was administered during the first week of April 1945 to eight quartermaster training companies. One week later eight platoons, one chosen at random from each of the eight companies, heard Program I (which presented only one side) during their individual orientation meetings. Another group of eight platoons, similarly chosen, heard Program II (which presented both arguments). Immediately after the program the men filled out the second questionnaire, ostensibly for the purpose of letting the people who made the program know what the men thought of it. Included in this second questionnaire, with appropriate transitional questions, were some of the same questions that had been included in the earlier survey, asking the men how they personally sized up the Pacific War. A third group of eight platoons served as the control, with no program. They filled out a similar questionnaire during their orientation meeting, which, in addition to asking the same questions on the Pacific War, asked preliminary questions about what they thought of their orientation meetings and what they would like in future orientation meetings. For the control group, the latter questions—in lieu of the questions about the transcriptions—were represented to the men as the main purpose of the questionnaire.

3. Summary of Results

- Presenting the arguments on both sides of an issue was found to be more effective than giving only the arguments supporting the point being made, in the case of individuals who were *initially opposed* to the point of view being presented.
- For men who were *already convinced* of the point being presented, however, the inclusion of arguments on both sides was less effective, for the group as a whole, than presenting only the arguments favoring the general position being advocated.
- Better educated men were more favorably affected by presentation of both sides; less well educated men were more affected by the communication which used only supporting arguments.

SOURCE: Adapted, with permission, from Carl I. Hovland et al. *Experiments in Mass Communication. Volume III: Studies in Social Psychology in World War II.* Princeton, N.J., Princeton University Press, 1949 (copyright 1949; © 1977 by Princeton University Press): pp. 201-225.

studies (Bernstein and Freeman, 1975), and discussions of the organizational and structural constraints on the successful conduct of evaluation research (Riecken and Boruch, 1974; Wholey et al., 1970). Guttentag and Struening's two-volume *Handbook of Evaluation Research* was published in 1975. *Evaluation Review,* started in 1976, is widely read by evaluation researchers, and now there are other journals as well, such as *Evaluation News, Evaluation and the Health Professions,* the *Journal of Evaluation and Program Planning,* and *New Directions for Program Evaluation.* The proliferation of publications and conferences, the formation of a professional association — the Evaluation Research Society — and special sessions on evaluation studies at the meetings of academic and practitioner groups are testimony to the rapid development of the field. These efforts to improve, refine, and reform evaluation activities continue today. As Cronbach and his associates (1980: 12-13) put it, "evaluation has become the liveliest frontier of American social science."

But history can obscure as well as illuminate: While there is continuity in the development of the evaluation field, a qualitative change has occurred. Even as late as 1967, Suchman's definition of evaluation research as the application of social research techniques to the study of large-scale human service programs was a useful and sufficient delineation of the field. Now, however, it is clear that evaluation research is more than the application of methods. It is also a political and managerial activity, an input into the complex mosaic from which emerge policy decisions and allocations for the planning, design, implementation, and continuance of programs to better the human condition. In this sense, evaluation research also needs to be seen, at least in the United States, as an integral part of the social policy and public administration movements.

Social Policy and Public Administrative Movements

A full treatment of the development of the overlapping social policy and public administration movements would require not only tracing the remarkable growth of population and industrialization in the United States during the first part of this century, but also detailing the changing social values related to the shift of responsibility for community members' welfare from volunteers and family members to public groups. At least a few highlights are important here.

Emergence of the Government Role

First, as Bremner (1956) has noted, obtaining human services before World War I was seen primarily as a personal responsibility. Poor people, physically and mentally handicapped persons, and troubled families were the clients of local charities staffed mainly by volunteers drawn from the ranks of the more fortunate. Our image of these volunteers as little old ladies or wealthy matrons toting care baskets is only somewhat exaggerated. Along with civic associations and locally supported "charity hospitals," county and state asylums, locally supported public schools, state normal schools, and sectarian old-age homes, volunteers were the bulwark of our human service "system."

Second, government — particularly the federal government — was comparatively small before the 1930s. There were few national health, education, and welfare initiatives and therefore no need for an army of federal employees. The idea of annual federal expenditures of billions of dollars for health research would have completely bewildered the government official of the 1920s. Federal support of public education was infinitesimal; for public education alone, more dollars now flow from Washington in six months than were spent in the entire first decade of this century. The scope and utilization of social and economic information mirrored the sparseness of government program operations. Lynn (1980) records that even in the late 1930s, federal expenditures for social science research and statistics were between $40 and $50 million, as opposed to *forty times* that amount today.

Finally, the human services field and government operate with different norms. Key government officials and even ordinary staff members once were selected without consistent regard to objective competence criteria; indeed, there were few ways of objectively determining competence. The professional civil service was a fraction of the size it is today, most jobs did not require technical know-how, and formal training programs were rarely available. Moreover, since its activities and influence were comparatively small, there was relatively little interest in what went on in government — at least in terms of human service programs. The ways the government bureaucracies operated made it much less possible to find out anyway. For example, the Federal Freedom of Information Act, which allows public access to government documents, is comparatively recent.

Growth of Programs

Human services grew at a rapid pace with the advent of the Great Depression, and of course so did government in general during the period surrounding World War II. In part because of the unwieldiness that accompanied this accelerated growth, there was strong pressure to apply the concepts and techniques of so-called scientific management, which were well thought of in industry. These ideas first took hold in defense and then filtered to other government organizations, including human services agencies. Concepts and procedures for planning, budgeting, quality control, and accountability, as well as later, more sophisticated notions of cost-benefit analysis and system modeling, became the order of the day in the human resource area.

At the same time, persons with social science training, particularly in political science, began to apply themselves to understanding the political, organizational, and administrative decision-making that took place in executive departments and other governmental agencies. Economists were simultaneously perfecting models for planning and decision-making and refining macroeconomic theories (Stokey and Zeckhauser, 1978). In part, the interests of social scientists in government were purely "academic." They wanted to know how government worked and to explain the direction of its activities. But more than that happened: Some recognized that their concepts and methods could facilitate and improve the governmental operations and actions they were documenting.

Likewise, persons in leadership positions in governmental agencies, groping for ways to deal with their large staffs and full coffers of funds, recognized the critical need for orderly, explicit ways to deal with their policy, administrative, program, and planning responsibilities. They became convinced that concepts, techniques, and sometimes principles from economics, political science, and sociology could be useful. The study of the public sector grew into a specialty that most commonly is termed "policy sciences," or "policy analysis."

Moreover, as the federal government was becoming increasingly complex and technical, it could no longer be managed and conducted by persons hired either as intelligent generalists or because of their connections with political patrons, relatives, or friends. Most mid-level management jobs and many senior executive positions required specific substantive and technical skills, and those who filled them needed either training or extensive experience to do their work competently (see Exhibit 1-C). State and local counterparts of federal agencies expanded at a similar rate, in part stimulated by federal initiatives and funding, and they too required skilled staffs.

As we noted, university social science departments provided some of the needed humanpower for government positions, training new researchers as well. Now, in response to the demand for government "technocrats," graduate schools of management, public health, and social work began programs to meet the need for executives and technicians, and special schools, generally with "public administration" in their titles, were organized or expanded. In short, a new army of professionals emerged.

The institutionalization of policy analysis and public administration programs in universities has maintained the momentum of the intertwined policy science and public administration movements. Concepts and methods from the social sciences have become the core of the educational programs from which many of our public officials and program managers are drawn, and these programs stress training in evaluation research. The importance of evaluation is now acknowledged by those in political as well as executive roles. For example, the General Accounting Office, Congress's "watchdog," established a special evaluation institute in 1980 in response to congressional interest in the conduct of program assessment. Evaluation research has become

Exhibit 1-C: The Rise of Policy Analysis

The steady growth in the number, variety, complexity, and social importance of policy issues confronting government is making increasing intellectual demands on public officials and their staffs. What should be done about nuclear safety, teenage pregnancies, urban decline, rising hospital costs, unemployment among black youth, violence toward spouses and children, and the disposal of toxic wastes? Many of these subjects were not on the public agenda twenty years ago. They are priority issues now, and new ones of a similar character emerge virtually every year. For most elected and appointed officials and their staffs, such complicated and controversial questions are outside the scope of their judgment and previous experience. Yet, the questions cannot be sidestepped; government executives are expected to deal with them responsibly and effectively.

To aid them in thinking about and deciding on such matters, public officials have been depending to an increasing extent on knowledge derived from research, policy analysis, program evaluations, and statistics to inform or buttress their views. More often than in the past, elected and appointed officials in the various branches and levels of government, from federal judges to town selectmen, are citing studies, official data, and expert opinion in at least partial justification for their actions. Their staffs, which have been increasing in size and responsibility in recent decades, include growing numbers of people trained in or familiar with analytic techniques to gather and evaluate information. Increasing amounts of research, analysis, and data-gathering are being done.

Because the power to influence policy is widely shared in our system of government, public officials seeking to influence policy — to play the policy game well — must be persuasive. Because of the changing character of policy issues, it is probably harder to be persuasive than it used to be. Seniority, affability, and clever "wheeling and dealing" may be relatively less influential than being generally knowledgeable and tough-minded, having the ability to offer ideas and solutions that can attract a wide following, or having a reputation as a well-informed critic. Increasingly, officials from the President on down lose influence in policy debates when they cannot get their numbers right or when their ideas and arguments are successfully challenged by opposing experts. Indeed, thorough and detailed command of an issue or problem is often mandatory. Legislatures are requiring executives to be experts in the programs and issues under their jurisdiction. Judges are requiring detailed proof that administrative decisions are not arbitrary and capricious. Budget officials demand positive program evaluations. The public demands accountability. Thus the dynamic processes whereby our political system confronts social problems are perceptibly, if not dramatically, raising the standards of substantive and managerial competence in the performance of public responsibilities.

SOURCE: Adapted, with permission, from Laurence E. Lynn, Jr., *Designing Public Policy.* Copyright © 1980 by Scott, Foresman and Company.

more than an isolated academic concern; it thrives in the context of the social policy and public administration movements.

Finally, it should be noted that the last few years have seen serious questioning of the continued expansion of government programs, resulting in increased requirements for effectiveness and efficiency (Freeman and Solomon, 1979) and detailed audits of governmental expenditures. Referenda such as California's Proposition 13, which limits local tax revenue, and sunset laws, which require the automatic shutdown of ineffective programs, have increased the demand for systematic evaluations (Adams and Sherman, 1978). Paradoxically, fiscal and political conservatives, often skeptical about social science methods, share with advocates of expanded social action programs a need for the types of information evaluations can provide.

The evaluation enterprise must acknowledge the importance of the changing mood and times of the country. Efforts continue to control inflation and revive a faltering economy by restricting federal expenditures, including, of course, those for social programs. A similar posture is manifest in many states and cities; local and state reactions to inflation are often particularly severe. This is not simply a consequence of the distrust, hostility, and political actions of community members dismayed with the burdensome and growing bite of income and property taxes. It also results from disenchantment with a large share of programs advocated by public officials, planners, and politicians since World War II. It is clear that Reagan's election to the presidency is widely seen as a mandate for reduced or at least rearranged human and social program efforts. Recent elections in a number of Western European countries suggest this is a widespread phenomenon.

Given the tenor of the times, it can be expected that there will be increased scrutiny of existing programs, accompanied by pressure to curtail or dismantle those for which there is limited evidence of program efficacy and efficient delivery of services. At the same time, however, evaluations will be needed to assess economical alternatives to programs that are curtailed and forsaken, as well as revised means of delivery.

**Current Status of
Evaluation Research**

The flourishing of evaluation research certainly is rooted in the efforts of social scientists undertaking technically sophisticated studies aimed at achieving progressive social change (Berk and Rossi, 1976). But it is those on and close to the firing line — the legislator, the planner, the program manager, and the foundation executive — who form the "evaluation research lobby" that is primarily responsible for the widespread growth of evaluation activities. Their commitment to orderly policy development and implementation will continue to be the major influence on the direction of work in the evaluation research field.

Nevertheless, whatever the social values, goals, and objectives of those in influential positions, information on program efficiency, efficacy, and accountability is indispensable to the elusive decision-making processes that direct the design and implementation of social policies and programs. It is the products of evaluation research — their pragmatic worth — that have encouraged the field's remarkable growth.

AN OVERVIEW OF EVALUATIONS

Evaluations may be undertaken for a variety of reasons (Chelimsky, 1978): for management and administrative purposes, to assess the appropriateness of program changes, to identify ways to improve the delivery of interventions, or to meet the accountability requirements of funding groups. They may be undertaken for planning and policy purposes, to test innovative ideas on how to deal with human and community problems, to decide whether to expand or curtail programs, and to support advocacy of one program as opposed to another. Finally, they may be undertaken to test a particular social science hypothesis or a professional practice principle (the particular program studied in this case may be mainly a matter of convenience). For all these purposes, the key is to design and implement an evaluation that is as objective as possible — that is, to provide a firm assessment, one that would be unchanged if the evaluation were replicated by the same evaluators or conducted by another group.

Foci of Evaluations

The scope of each evaluation, of course, depends on the specific purposes for which it is being conducted. Furthermore, the ways the evaluation questions are asked and the research procedures undertaken depend on whether or not the program under evaluation is an innovative intervention, a modification or expansion of an existing effort, or a well-established, stable human service activity.

Evaluation in our sense encompasses several related sets of activities. It is useful to distinguish between three major classes of evaluation research: analysis related to the conceptualization and design of interventions, monitoring of program implementation, and assessment of program utility. Although it is not always possible to do so fully, the evaluation of most social programs needs to include all three classes of activities. Evaluations that do so are termed *comprehensive evaluations*. *[handwritten margin notes: design, implementation, utility]*

An expanded discussion of the variations in evaluation strategies in relation to types of programs is the central topic of Chapter 2. Here we discuss the three foci of evaluations in general terms, listing the major questions adhering to each.

Program Conceptualization and Design

Interventions, particularly during their planning but also throughout their existence, can be seen as responses to either perceived or incipient communal problems. The origin of a social program is the recognition of a "social problem" — by which we mean a diverse set of defects in the human and social condition — and a resolve to take purposive, organized action to remedy the problem. The impetus for a program to raise educational skills, for example, is usually the recognition that a significant number of persons in a given population are deficient in reading and mathematics skills. An ongoing program may be justified by the persistence of a social problem: Driver education in high schools receives public support and is subject to evaluations because of the continuing high rates of automobile accidents, particularly among adolescent drivers. Chapter 2 discusses the relationships among problem identification, program design and planning, and evaluation activities. In Chapter 3, we examine "diagnostic" evaluation activities, that is, concepts and procedures to allow the specification of a social problem in ways that enhance both the design of appropriate interventions and their evaluations.

Program Conceptualization and Design Questions

- What is the extent and distribution of the target problem and/or population?

- Is the program designed in conformity with intended goals; is there a coherent rationale underlying it; and have chances of successful delivery been maximized?

- What are projected or existing costs and what is their relation to benefits and effectiveness?

Monitoring and Accountability of Program Implementation

There are many reasons for monitoring programs. First, proper management and administration of human resource programs require empirical evidence that what presumably was paid for and deemed desirable was actually undertaken. Increasingly, there is concern with the lack of accountability of programs, particularly public programs.

Second, there is no point in being concerned with the impact or outcome of a particular project unless it did, indeed, take place and served the appropriate participants in the way intended.

Many programs are not implemented and executed according to their original design. Sometimes personnel simply are not available or equipment is in disrepair; sometimes project staffs may be prevented by political or other reasons from undertaking what they intended. Some project staff members may not have the motivation or know-how to carry out their tasks as outlined. In still other instances, either poor budget estimates or inflation leads program staffs to modify their efforts.

There are also instances in which the intended project participants do not exist in the numbers required, cannot be identified precisely, or will not be cooperative. For example, in certain communities, funds have been provided for projects in which the participants are identified as children with congenital heart conditions. For some of these projects, locating potential participants has been so costly that funds are short for supporting the treatments intended.

Monitoring can alert project personnel to such problems by providing a systematic assessment of whether or not a program is operating in conformity to its design and reaching its specified target population. As a result of such an evaluation, staff of the New York City School Lunch Program discovered some serious deficiencies in their services (see Exhibit 1-D). Monitoring and accountability undergo detailed discussion in Chapter 4.

Exhibit 1-D: A Monitor's Report on a Free Meal Program

A monitoring committee consisting of volunteers with expertise in education, nutrition, research and children's services conducted visits to New York City schools to describe the free lunch program. Twenty-four schools in nine districts were selected, and school staffs were interviewed informally. Monitors also observed lunchroom and cooking facilities. In addition, 1,322 mailed questionnaires from lunchroom workers were analyzed.

In March 1975 in New York City, there were 1,292 schools and institutions serving an average of 537,359 meals daily. Of these, 90 percent of the meals were free, the remainder full price. Until the end of 1975, New York City had no reduced-price school meal program. It is currently being introduced in response to federal legislation that mandates it. About 57 percent of the children registered in elementary and junior high schools are eligible for free meals. Of these, 87 percent participate in the School Lunch Program. If reduced-price meals were available, the monitors estimated that based on 1970 Census data, at least 250,000 additional children would be eligible for them.

As of June 1975, twenty-two of the thirty-two community school districts served an average of 63,838 daily breakfasts in 365 schools. Only 13 percent of the eligible children in New York City received free breakfasts. At least 400,000 others who now eat a free lunch are eligible for a free breakfast, but are not being served.

Program Administration

The monitors found that centralized food distribution is not necessarily the cheapest or most efficient way of getting food to children in school. Monitors observed during visits to schools that food purchased in bulk through the Bureau of School Lunches frequently was more expensive than it would have been at a local market. For instance, chicken bought through the Bureau was $.67 a pound, while the price at the local market was $.47. In addition, school officials complained that the Bureau often paid for larger produce deliveries than were ordered or could be used.

Quality of Meals

In general, the monitors were dissatisfied with both the appearance and the taste of the food served in these programs. They rated the food in only three of the fourteen breakfast programs and twelve of the thirty lunch programs visited, as "appetizing in appearance"; the food in four breakfast and ten lunch programs tasted good. They observed greenish hot dogs and tasted cloyingly sweet baked beans, unidentifiable mixtures of rice and meat, stale rolls, soggy vegetables, and other unappetizing dishes. Most of the lunch programs and nearly all the breakfast programs offered no choice of food. Some monitors reported overly small portions for older children, although when the meal is disliked, even small portions may remain uneaten.

Menu Planning and Distribution

Schools do not distribute menus regularly or widely. Neither parents nor children know the menus in advance, nor are they consulted in menu planning, even though the parents have requested it in some schools. The monitors noted that in one school on the Lower East Side, parents are involved in menu planning with the result that the school is serving appetizing and nutritious meals. No provisions are made for special dietary needs or problems. Although lunchroom workers said they frequently knew children's preferences — such as extra peanut butter with a meal-pack or frozen meal; beans instead of sauerkraut which the children will not eat; one extra slice of bread so children can make sandwiches — they were unable to influence menu planning to reflect them.

Lunchroom Atmosphere

Many schools are ill-equipped to feed large numbers of children. Lunchrooms are small and lunch sometimes is served in shifts from 10 a.m. to 2 p.m. The monitors found many lunchrooms very crowded, and in more than half of the schools visited, children eat with their coats on and books in their laps. Times for meals and times for recreation are not separated in most schools with the result that in some lunchrooms, children rush through their food or skip it entirely so that they will have an extra few minutes to play and talk, making the atmosphere extremely noisy and unsettled for those still eating.

There is a significant amount of waste, and several schools were described as having an insufficient number of garbage cans. Tables and floors, and the areas around the garbage cans, were often strewn with leftover food.

Separation of Free-Lunch Recipients from Other Students

There was evidence that children who receive free lunches and those who pay for lunch or bring their own were separated. Of the schools visited that served both free and paid lunches, half separated non-paying children by maintaining different waiting lines, separate tables, and/or by the use of tickets instead of money.

SOURCE: Adapted, with permission, from Trude W. Lash and Heidi Sigal, *State of the Child: New York City.* New York: Foundation for Child Development, 1976.

Program Monitoring Questions

- Is the program reaching the specified target population or target area?
- Are the intervention efforts being conducted as specified in the program design?

Assessment of Program Utility

It obviously is critical to know both the degree to which a program has an impact and its benefits in relation to costs. The former is referred to as the program's *effectiveness* or *impact* and the latter as its *efficiency* (its cost-effectiveness and cost-efficiency, to be discussed in more detail in Chapter 8).

Unless programs have a demonstrable impact, it is hard to defend their implementation and continuation; hence the need for impact assessments. But knowledge of effectiveness simply is insufficient in most cases; outcome or impact must be judged against input costs. Some programs may not be supportable because of their high costs in comparison to their impact. For example, some universities, in the face of budget problems, have terminated their student counseling programs because costs are high and benefits slight. Others may be expanded, retained, or terminated on the basis of their comparative costs. For instance, findings about the impact of institutional versus community care for adolescent offenders suggest that community programs are preferable because of their markedly lower costs. The need to determine the relation of such costs to effectiveness necessitates efficiency assessments.

Impact Assessments

An impact assessment gauges the extent to which a program causes change in the desired direction. It implies that there is a set of specified, operationally defined goals and criteria of success. A program that has impact is one that achieves some movement or change toward the desired objectives. These objectives may be social-behavioral ones, such as lowering functional illiteracy or nutritional deficiencies among children; they may be community-related, such as reducing the frequency of certain crimes; or they may be physical, such as decreasing water pollution or increasing the number of bus trips that conform to a time schedule.

To conduct an impact evaluation, the evaluator needs a plan for data collection in order to demonstrate in a persuasive way that the changes are a function of the intervention and cannot be accounted for in other ways. Specific impact assessment plans may vary considerably: Sometimes it is possible to use classic experimental designs in which there are control and experimental groups that receive different treatments and are constructed through randomization. Basic strategies for impact analysis are found in Chapter 5; random experiments are discussed in Chapter 6.

For practical reasons it is often necessary, however, to employ statistical approaches rather than true experiments. Nonrandomized experiments and nonexperimental methods are commonly employed in impact assessments. With proper safeguards and appropriate qualifications, such nonexperimental designs can provide reasonably firm estimates of effects. These designs are found in Chapters 6 and 7.

Impact evaluations are essential when there is an interest in either comparing different programs or testing the utility of new efforts to ameliorate a particular community problem. An illustration is the evaluation of a program to maximize psychosocial development in children (see Exhibit 1-E).

Efficiency Assessments

Because resources present a constant and increasing problem, programs demand efficiency assessments. Interventions compete with

Exhibit 1-E: Infant Day Care

The question that provoked the work can be put in deceptively simple form. Do infants attending a well-run, nurturant, responsible group-care center five days a week for a little over 100 weeks display different patterns of psychological development during or at the end of that period when compared with children of the same sex and family background who are being reared in a typical nuclear family context in the northeastern United States?

A longitudinal investigation was designed to assess the psychological effects of an experimentally conducted day-care program on children ages 3.5 to 29 months. The subjects were Chinese and Caucasian children from working and middle-class families who were cared for at a special group-care center five days a week; the major control group consisted of children reared totally at home and matched with the experimental children in terms of ethnicity, social class, and sex.

The central question that provoked the investigation can be answered with some assurance: Attendance at a day-care center staffed by conscientious and nurturant adults during the first 2.5 years does not seem to sculpt a psychological profile very much different from the one created by total home rearing. This conclusion is based not only on our formal assessments but also on our informal observations of the children over the 2.5-year period. These data did not confirm several popular notions about early group care. Although it is reasonable to assume that daily encounter with other children during the first two years might speed up the maturation of the social interaction sequences usually seen in 3- and 4-year-olds, our data did not provide dramatic support for that prediction. The 20- and 29-month-olds were simply not very social and did not often initiate play with other children. Both cooperative and aggressive play occurred infrequently among both groups. There were as many shy children among the day-care groups as there were among the home controls. Indeed, on one occasion we satisfied our curiosity about a particular girl who was inordinately shy with a strange peer in our 20-month assessment by bringing an unfamiliar peer to the day-care center. The girl retreated at once to her day-care teacher, even though she was in her territory. The day-care children were neither more cooperative nor more aggressive than home controls. In brief, the evaluation revealed a remarkably similar growth function for both day-care and home controls.

SOURCE: Adapted from J. Kagan, R. B. Kearsley, and P. R. Zelazo, "The Effects of Infant Care on Psychological Development." *Evaluation Quarterly*, 1 (February 1977): 109-142.

each other for funds from foundations, international organizations, and the various levels of government. Similarly, specific interventions within programs often compete for funds and resources. Choices continually must be made between funding or not funding, continuing or discontinuing, and expanding or contracting one program as opposed to another.

At least some of the considerations that go into such choices concern economics: Is a program producing sufficient benefits for the costs incurred? Is it intended to produce a particular benefit at a lower cost per unit of outcome than other interventions or delivery systems designed to achieve the same goal? The techniques for undertaking evaluations to answer these types of questions are found in two closely related approaches: *cost-benefit* and *cost-effectiveness* analyses. (See Exhibit 1-F for an illustration of cost-benefit analysis.) The ideas underlying the two approaches and further illustrations of them are presented in Chapter 8.

Program Utility Questions

- Is the program effective in achieving its intended goals?
- Can the results of the program be explained by some alternative process that does not include the program?
- Is the program having some effects that were not intended?
- What are the costs to deliver services and benefits to program participants?
- Is the program an efficient use of resources, compared with alternative uses of the resources?

PROGRAM STAGES

As we have just discussed, evaluations are conducted to answer a variety of questions related to what we have listed as the three *foci* of

Exhibit 1-F: Ambulatory Surgery in an HMO

In recent years the subject of ambulatory surgery has become one of great interest in the health-care field. Interest in it has been stimulated by the opening of free-standing surgical care centers throughout the country and by the increasing efforts of health regulatory agencies to contain the rapidly rising costs of health care.

This study is a retrospective examination of data taken from a self-contained medical care system that introduced a change in surgical services in its hospital. The ambulatory surgery services it provides are similar to those offered in free-standing surgical care centers. Surgeons of the Kaiser-Permanente Medical Care Program (KPMCP) in Portland, Oregon, have been performing ambulatory surgery for more than 20 years. As early as 1961, 10 percent of their patients having surgery performed in the hospital operating rooms were not admitted either before or after the surgery. As of 1977, about 41 percent of operating-room surgical patients in the Kaiser-Permanente Medical Care Program were not admitted to the hospital.

Analysis of Cost Savings

The study investigated the process differences between the inpatient and ambulatory modes and found that the only significant differences were that ambulatory patients were not admitted (thus saving inpatient costs) but required longer recovery-room time than inpatients. These differences were then priced out as follows, to find the cost savings. The savings made from shifting certain procedures from inpatient to ambulatory mode were calculated based on the assumption that (except in a few cases noted in the cost analysis of selected procedures), had the ambulatory mode not been available, the patient would have been admitted. Therefore, when the procedure is performed as an ambulatory case, inpatient costs are saved. Inpatient costs include routine service per-diem costs and costs of physician inpatient visits. They are partially offset by the extra costs for ambulatory patients' recovery-room time, which is longer than for inpatients.

Cost Savings Per Ambulatory Case for Selected Procedures
(based on 1974 ambulatory procedures applied to 1977 dollars)

Procedure	Total Routine Inpatient Costs ($)	Subtracted Recovery- Room Costs ($)	Total Cost Saved Per Ambulatory Case ($)
Dilation and curettage of uterus	210.45	28.91	181.54
Excision and destruction of lesion of skin and subcutaneous tissue	274.00	7.45	271.16
Bilateral ligation and division of fallopian tubes and bilateral salpingectomy	147.02	24.97	122.05
Myringotomy	147.02	12.70	134.32
Biopsy of breast and partial mastectomy	210.45	25.84	184.61
Excision of lesion of muscle tendon and fascia	274.00	17.96	258.74
Exploration and neurolysis of peripheral nerve	274.00	18.83	255.17
Circumcision	147.02	37.67	109.35
Partial excision of bone	274.00	7.45	271.02
Trachelectomy (conization)	147.02	25.40	121.62
All selected procedures (weighted average of all cases for 1974)			192.19

Conclusions

This study found that ambulatory surgery can save a great deal of money for health-care consumers. If implemented nationally at a rate similar to the rate of ambulatory surgery in the Oregon Region of the Kaiser-Permanente Medical Care Program, approximately three-quarters of a billion dollars would be saved annually (based on 1977 figures). The study also found that both patients and providers of care were very satisfied with ambulatory surgery and that the quality of care was very high.

The results of the study clearly indicate that a widespread program of ambulatory surgery would be beneficial to the entire health-care system. The study also gives indications that such a program could be implemented easily.

SOURCE: Adapted, with permission, from Sylvia D. Marks et al., "Ambulatory Surgery in an HMO." *Medical Care,* xviii (February 1980): 127-146.

evaluation research: program conceptualization and design, program implementation (monitoring and accountability), and program utility (impact and efficiency assessments). Beyond dealing with these questions, an evaluation must be tailored to the *stage* of development of the intervention being addressed. This may be found by locating the program on a continuum whose poles are "innovative" programs and "established" programs, with those in need of "refinement," "modification," or "fine-tuning" lying somewhere between. While the same generic procedures characterize all evaluations, the state of the program's development — what we shall refer to as the program stage — determines the level of effort and technical procedures undertaken during the evaluation.

Evaluations of Innovative Programs

Completely new interventions are relatively rare. Most programs introduced as "new and innovative" are ordinarily modifications of existing practices. What makes an intervention innovative in our sense is that the "treatment" has never been applied to the population specified. It may have been tried as a small-scale, impressionistically judged demonstration, but never with the realistic intent of having it implemented on a broad scale.

In our terms, a program is innovative if it has not been subject to implementation and assessment in the following ways:

1. The intervention itself is still in an emerging or research and development ("R and D") phase. That is, there is no, or very limited, evidence that it has an impact as an installed program. For example, hospices, which are nonmedically oriented settings for terminally ill patients, are now being evaluated as an innovative alternative to long-term hospitalization. While hospices have been operating for some years, only recently have they been seen as a widespread initiative possibly meriting governmental and national foundation support.

2. The delivery system or parts of it have not been adequately tested. Such a program would be one that includes the untested idea of having high school students provide nutritional education and information to the elderly.

3. The targets of the program are markedly new or expanded. An intervention of this type might offer casette-recorded language training to immigrant schoolchildren who are not present in large enough numbers to justify bilingual educational programs in individual schools.

4. A program originally undertaken in response to one goal is continued or expanded because of its impact on another objective. For instance, a program providing marked automobiles to police

for their personal use may have been initiated to cut the crime rate, but is continued to curtail job instability and keep police living close to their precincts.

Evaluations for Fine-Tuning

Once programs are under way, it is often important to test variations in the ways they operate. The major reason to do so is to improve either their efficacy of their efficiency — that is, to increase the magnitude of their impact or to decrease their costs per unit of impact. An example of the former would be a weekly tutoring program for economically disadvantaged children that is improving educational skills to a fair extent, but that program staff feel could be more effective if the children were provided learning opportunities beyond once-a-week tutoring sessions. Accordingly, a supplemental "homework" program is introduced and evaluated. An example of the latter is a program that involves three months of daily counseling for discharged, previously hospitalized alcohol addicts. Because the costs of the program are high, reducing the program's duration from three to two months may become the subject of an evaluation.

There are other reasons to undertake fine-tuning evaluations. One is to provide equitable service delivery — that is, to see that a program's services are delivered to its target population just as these services are delivered to persons in the general population. In a health-care clinic, this may involve putting in an appointment system, thereby cutting down on waiting time. Here the issue would be whether or not patient satisfaction with the delivery system is increased without loss of efficiency. Another basis for fine-tuning a program is to reduce dropouts from the target population. In our hypothetical clinic, this might be a second rationale for putting in the appointment system.

It should be emphasized that there is no clear-cut dividing point between innovative and fine-tuning or modification efforts. Sometimes the changes being tested are minor and clearly modificatory. Other times, however, they are costly and may have broad ramifications for human service networks. For example, fine-tuning that integrates formerly free-standing community health centers with teaching hospitals does not change the basic concept underlying delivery of medical care to low-income persons. However, it may have major consequences for the costs of such care on a national basis and may markedly alter the quality of services received.

Evaluations of Established Programs

Programs mandated by legislation and even those in existence for decades may also be subjected to evaluation for a series of different reasons. First, a program may have been instituted for a complex set of political and other external reasons, and it is important in order to justify its continuation, expansion, or termination to have hard data on its impact and the ratio of benefits to costs. Changes in resources available, political outlooks, community members' priorities, and real or asserted declines in the extensiveness or severity of the target problem may provoke evaluation activities. Perhaps most important in stimulating evaluations of an established program is evidence of or suspicion that programs are either ineffective or inefficient. Moreover, as mentioned, many state and local and a growing number of federal programs must meet the requirements of sunset legislation, which provides for regular program reviews and "automatic" termination of programs failing to demonstrate utility. Evaluations of established programs may focus on impact and costs-to-benefits ratios. Often, however, the assessments are limited to examinations of service delivery. In such cases, the evaluation centers on monitoring questions: whether or not appropriate target groups are served, and the extent to which program staff and management are meeting commitments with respect to the quality and quantity of services delivered. The human service area is highly vulnerable to serious, responsible questioning of the ways programs are conducted, as well as to political or publicity-related attacks. Evaluation results, both from monitoring program implementation and from assessing impact and efficiency, can influence decisions on the expansion, continuation, or termination of programs and the organizations that are responsible for them.

HOW EVALUATIONS ARE USED

Not only do evaluations differ according to states of program development; the uses to which they are put also vary. The scope and design of evaluations must take into account these varying uses. Again, no clear-cut distinctions are possible. But the range of uses nevertheless can be described with some degree of specificity. One can do this by considering evaluation uses in terms of decision-making modes. Use can also be examined in terms of the consequences or ramifications of the evaluation effort. Both perspectives are relevant to how evaluators go about their work.

Modes of Decision-Making

Evaluations, as is the case in all applied research, are undertaken to influence the actions and activities of individuals and groups who have or are presumed to have an opportunity to tailor their actions on the basis of the results of the evaluation effort. In the simplest case, the results are directed at an individual executive, such as a key public official who has the authority and responsibility to allocate resources and shape a human service program. For example, within limits police chiefs can decide on how to assign their officers, how to structure communication between various divisions, and how to deal with emergencies and other unforeseen occurrences.

In other cases, of course, the situation is more complex; a variety of parties influence the ways human resource programs are designed and implemented. For example, a national health insurance initiative would require agreement on program outlines by both the congressional and the executive branches of the federal government, and would involve attention to the views and interests of a variety of stakeholders, including health professionals and their organizations, labor and management groups, insurers, and consumer aggregates. The various permutations and combinations of stakeholders and the range of influences and decision-making processes encountered across human resource activities are subject to both speculative and systematic inquiries. There are three modal alternatives; we discuss them below.

Go/No-Go Decisions

At various points in programming human services, decisive actions are required. For example, the Secretary of Health and Human Services must recommend to either Congress or the White House whether or not to provide training for different categories of health practitioners, what types of patients to admit into federally supported hospitals, eligibility requirements for welfare programs, and so on. At a local level, a school superintendent and board may have to decide whether or not to impose standards of classroom size, to establish a work-study program for high school students, or to terminate kindergarten instruction.

There are probably relatively few instances wherein decisions are made solely on evaluation findings, although if they are strong enough and the studies are defensible from the standpoint of rigor, they may dominate decision-making.

Developing a Rationale for Action

More often, evaluations influence the determinants of decisions: political, practical, and resource considerations, and the wisdom and personal experience of those with influence. Sometimes evaluations directly affect the underlying rationale of a program and consequent professional, political, and legal decisions about it. For example, the pressure to deinstitutionalize the treatment of mentally ill and retarded persons is accompanied by a large number of political, legal, and practical issues. The first court-ordered deinstitutionalization of a state facility for mentally retarded persons was accompanied by a federally supported evaluation to determine the consequences of deinstitutional- ization on the severely retarded, their families, and community mem- bers living close to where they would reside. The results may have important consequences for future legislative and legal decisions in various states and at a national level.

Other times, evaluations have an indirect or delayed effect. Those conducted either to develop knowledge or for a particular program purpose may have subsequent impact. This type of evaluation impact is sometimes referred to as the *conceptual use* of evaluation results. For example, some years ago a carefully controlled study examined the impact of psychotherapy in prisons. Findings suggesting that psychotherapy had limited, if any, utility were available for a number of years prior to the surge of concern about the efficacy and efficiency of prison rehabilitation programs (Kassebaum et al., 1971). Efforts to expand psychotherapy in prisons, including court actions, were thwarted by the evidence of inefficacy provided by the previously conducted evaluation. In this sense, although difficult to gauge, evalua- tions may make important contributions to the human service area. Likewise, evaluations serve to "discipline" program decision-making. As we will discuss later, the emphasis of evaluations on explicit goals, criteria, and specification of intervention activities may influence how much weight other decision determinants are given.

Legitimation and Accountability

Evaluations also may serve either program advocates or opponents as inputs into the oversight of programs. Information on how well interventions are implemented, the extent to which they reach targets, their impact, and their costs may help advocates of a particular program to ward off their adversaries, or vice versa. Legitimation may be re- quired at different levels. For example, the board of a foundation supporting a school health program may be concerned with whether or not the activity is providing treatment to a sufficient number of children, and with the per-child costs of care. The state administration of such a program may use regular reports on such information to judge the production and performance of the school health teams that are located in local school systems throughout the state.

Evaluations for legitimation purposes need not be used, of course, to justify the status quo with respect to programs. Rather, they alert program sponsors and managers to "soft spots," serving as the basis for the modification, expansion, or reduction of interventions. For example, different district rates of disabled persons returning to the labor force may suggest to a state agency director the need either to reallocate staff resources or to redraw the boundaries of districts to shift the attention to population groups with the greatest needs.

Policy and Administrative Studies

The literature on evaluation research, indeed much of the commentary on all of applied research, refers to the "policy-relevance" of work in the field. Policy evaluations may generally be described as those that either have potential impact on large segments of the population, or result in major organizational changes in the structure and activities of groups delivering interventions, or are critical to the allocation of monetary, staff, and other resources. At the margins it is easy to separate policy from administrative evaluations. In practice, however, the distinction rests with the ways the stakeholders perceive the consequences of the assessment.

For example, it is clear that the evaluation of a program like *Sesame Street* can be considered a policy study. Results have implications for public funding, requirements of television stations regarding time allotments for public broadcasting, and the types of other school-readiness programs that are implemented. In contrast, the decision of a government agency to evaluate "flextime" for its professional staff (allowing personnel to work at times of their own choosing, so long as they put in the required number of hours) may be seen as an administrative evaluation, although it may impact on many persons, including staff of other agencies, clients, and the families of the workers themselves.

Certainly, as evaluations become more generalizable and provide input into decisions that are costly and difficult to reverse (i.e., when the changes they effect impact directly and indirectly on large numbers of persons), they are more likely to be candidates for the "policy evaluation" label. It is important, however, that the extensiveness of policy evaluations not be overemphasized, and that the worth of administrative assessments not be downgraded. In many programs, small and large, evaluations of the implementation of technology, of changes in bureaucratic procedures, and of minor modifications in delivery systems may have important consequences for the effectiveness and efficiency of programs.

We should also stress that the distinction between policy and technical-administrative studies is artificial. In part, it depends on the perspective of the one determining the level of the evaluation. For example, many would view a study of the impact on crime rates of police using marked cars as personal autos as a technical or administrative study. For police administrators, however, matters of cost, insurance liability, police morale, and public acceptance raise major policy issues.

The way a study is viewed also depends on how a program can be and is formulated. There are two national child health programs currently being supported and evaluated. One, conducted at UCLA, consists of developing primary-care ambulatory centers in public schools, staffed by nurse-practitioners (with physicians as backup) who provide services to children of low-income families. If effective and efficient, it could be a model for a federally supported, nationwide program. The nature of the intervention minimizes opportunities for studying individual program components; only the broad intervention question is amenable to full assessment.

The second program, being evaluated by the Rand Corporation, is designed to improve the dental health of schoolchildren. It is an experiment in which a large number of schools and classrooms across the country are assigned to different treatment programs. The most comprehensive treatment consists of dental health education, brushing and flossing of the teeth, fluoridation of teeth, and annual applications of a sealant that suppresses cavities. The design of the experiment includes an opportunity to study the impact and cost-benefits of the program components separately and in all of their combinations. It would be possible, depending on findings, to implement any individual program element. In many ways this could be considered a massive technical study. But it is seen by the staff of the funding foundation and by health planners as a policy-level study because of the impact of dental-health-care costs, including the impact on the work of private dentists, if proven effective and efficient (Robert Wood Johnson Foundation, 1980).

The level of the evaluation, of course, has consequences for its design and implementation in terms of funding support, time for completion, and staffing requirements. To repeat, successful evaluators are those who have made clear to themselves, and to their sponsors and program staffs, how the evaluation is to be used and its level of application. This is necessary whether the evaluation is of an innovative program, a program in need of fine-tuning, or an established program.

WHO CAN DO EVALUATIONS?

Systematic evaluation studies are grounded in social science research techniques that have application in evaluation studies. Hence, most evaluation specialists have had social science training. At first glance, someone unacquainted with evaluation research would un-doubtedly find professional discussions of evaluation difficult to com-prehend. As in any other professional field, evaluators have developed their own vocabulary, shorthand expressions, and rules for doing the work. One of the main purposes of this book is to introduce readers to the special language that evaluators employ. In order to facilitate learn-ing this vocabulary, we provide a glossary of special terms, our key concepts, at the beginning of each chapter.

Some of the complexity of evaluation stems from the inherent tendencies of those in a professional field to develop their own lan-guage, but at least part of the need for special terminology derives from the unique concepts and insights developed in each field. At the most complex level, evaluation activities can be so technically complicated, sophisticated in conception, costly, and of such long duration that they require the dedicated participation of highly trained specialists at ease with the latest in social science theory, research methods, and statistical techniques. Such highly complex evaluations usually are conducted by specialized evaluation staffs. At the other extreme, there are many evaluation tasks that can be understood easily and can be carried out by persons of modest expertise and experience.

It is the purpose of this book to provide an introduction to the field for those whose current positions, academic interests, or natural curios-ity inspire them to want to learn how evaluations are conducted. It is but a start along the pathway to becoming a technical expert in evaluation. Our aim is to provide persons faced with the administration and man-agement of human resource programs with sufficient understanding of evaluation tasks and activities to be able to judge for themselves what kinds of evaluations are appropriate to their programs and projects, and to comprehend the results of completed studies relevant to their organi-zations. We have tried to provide a work that is helpful to those who conduct (or who plan to conduct) evaluations, who contract for them, who oversee evaluation staffs, and who are consumers of evaluation research done by others.

2

Tailoring Evaluations

Every evaluator cannot be a planner and program implementor.
But the links between program and evaluation do require
mutual understanding of the tasks and processes involved on
both sides — thus the need to introduce considerations of
program planning, design, and implementation. Every
evaluation must be tailored to its program. The tasks
undertaken by evaluators differ depending on the stage of
activity at which they are brought in, and the needs and interests
of such stakeholders as policymakers, program managers, and
funding groups.

KEY CONCEPTS

Evaluability Assessment:

A set of procedures for planning evaluations so that stakeholders' interests are taken into account in order to maximize the utility of the evaluation.

Goals:

Statements, usually general and abstract, of desired states in human conditions and social environments.

Impact Model:

The set of guiding hypotheses underlying the planning and implementation of a program.

Objectives:

Specific and operational statements regarding the desired accomplishments of the social intervention programs.

Planning:

The process of converting goals into objectives, formulating specific interventions, and defining relevant target populations.

Management Information System (MIS):

An ongoing data collection and analysis system, usually computerized, that allows timely access to service delivery and outcome information.

---

*E*valuation research is an integral part of broader sets of activities usually described as rational policymaking, scientific decision-making, or program planning and implementation. Still, it must be recognized that the decisions affecting programs almost always emerge from a complex mixture of political considerations, the personal influence of key stakeholders, economic constraints, and the availability of necessary program staff and technology (see Exhibit 2-A). Evaluation research must therefore be seen as just one of the many inputs into the instigation, design, and implementation of programs. To maximize their influence, evaluators must understand the formal and informal organizational arrangements of the environments in which they work. Policymakers and program managers, on the other hand, must see that decision-making, planning, and implementation are conducted in clear, explicit ways if interventions are to benefit from the efforts of evaluators.

Exhibit 2-A: The History of the New Jersey-Pennsylvania Negative Income Tax Experiment

Negative income tax programs as substitutions for welfare have been advocated by such diverse persons as Milton Friedman and more liberal welfare economists.

In 1965, an attempt was made by OEO staff to convince the President's office of the attractiveness of some such program, but without success. Failing to get political approval, the staff sought ways to produce hard evidence on its feasibility.

In 1966 and 1967, a number of plans were submitted to OEO to launch some field tests of various negative income tax plans. The most attractive plan was submitted by Mathematica, a firm in Princeton, New Jersey. While the OEO staff was disposed to accept and fund this proposal, OEO Director Sargent Shriver was unwilling to make so large a grant to a profit-making firm, insisting that the project be carried out with principal responsibility going to the Institute for Research on Poverty at the University of Wisconsin as the prime contractor and Mathematica as the subcontractor.

In the middle of 1967, contracts were signed. Fourteen months were spent in designing the study. It was designed as a randomized controlled experiment in which negative income tax payments were systematically varied in two dimensions, minimum income guarantees and applicable tax rates. From the fall of 1968 through the fall of 1972, payments were given to families in experimental groups and both experimentals and controls were meticulously followed through personal interviews.

Throughout the course of the experiment, several events occurred which illustrate the interaction between political events and the conduct of evaluative activity. The first event was a shift in the welfare policy of the State of New Jersey, shortly after the experiment got under way. New Jersey was picked as a site partially because the then current welfare policy only covered female headed households under AFDC (Aid to Families with Dependent Children). The change made families with unemployed fathers eligible, a shift that made welfare policies in New Jersey competitive with some of the less generous plans.

The same New Jersey policy shift caused other problems. Local welfare officials became concerned with experimental families who were accepting both welfare payments and experimental payments. The director of the project was subpoenaed in the New Jersey courts and ordered to produce experimental records. Although the subpoena was not enforced, Mathematica was required to compensate local welfare departments for overpayments to experimental families.

Later in 1969, as Congress considered welfare reform, pressure was exerted on the research staff to produce results from the experiment that would be relevant to the legislation being considered. Preliminary data were hastily compiled and presented in testimony before the House Ways and Means Committee. Opponents of the legislation, however, saw the experimenters as advocates of the proposed welfare reform and asked the General Accounting Office to conduct a critical analysis of the experiment, including a search of original data and reinterviews with experimental subjects.

SOURCE: Summary, by permission, of D. Kershaw and J. Fair, *The New Jersey Income-Maintenance Experiment*, Vol. 1. New York: Academic Press, 1976, pp. 4-5.

Two cautions should be noted. First, the discussion that follows provides an ideal view of the relations between evaluation activities and program planning, development, and implementation. It presumes there is general agreement between involved parties on the steps of implementation and the order in which they are to be taken. The reader should note that actual task allocation and sequences vary markedly within and between human service areas.

Second, there is wide variation in organizational arrangements. At one extreme, evaluators may do their work almost entirely independently of either planning or program staff. At the other extreme, the same group or person is responsible for program planning, design, implementation, *and* evaluation. It is rare that programs are so well planned, designed, and implemented that the evaluator can concentrate solely on what may narrowly be conceived as technical evaluation tasks. The evaluator's work often includes participating, either fully or partially, in activities that ideally should precede the evaluation effort, or at least be the responsibility of others. Indeed, some evaluators argue that this participation in the broader process is a major contribution of the evaluation effort (Wholey, 1979). A shared commitment to develop and undertake programs in ways that maximize the likelihood of rigorous evaluations is essential. Outlining these activities is the thrust of this chapter.

PLANNING EVALUATIONS OF
INNOVATIVE PROGRAMS

The planning process includes identification of the goals of the organization sponsoring and implementing the intervention, the assessment of the extent to which actual conditions deviate from those goals, and the development of a general framework or strategy for achieving the desired goals by modifying conditions or behavior. The latter, in turn, requires specification of the necessary human and financial resources, designation of individuals responsible for carrying out intervention activities, and creation of a schedule for meeting objectives. Planning is usually predicated on a desire to reduce the gap between the goal and the reality. In some instances, however, the goal may be to maintain the status quo in the face of anticipated deterioration.

The designs of all evaluations have similar generic qualities. Although the ensuing discussion examines these characteristics in relation to innovative programs, many of them will be found applicable to the subsequent sections on evaluations of established programs and fine-tuning.

Setting Goals and Identifying Objectives

Social intervention programs can be developed only in relation to a goal. For evaluation purposes, goal-setting must lead to the operationalization of the desired outcome — a statement that specifies the condition to be dealt with and establishes a criterion of success. We and other evaluation researchers refer to these operationalized statements as *objectives*.

The distinction between goals and operationalized objectives is vital: Many programs, especially those with large target populations or far-reaching effects, initially state their goals in broad and rather vague terms. For example, each year the components of federal executive departments, such as the Department of Health and Human Services, submit "forward plans" or strategy papers to their secretaries with goals reflecting the department's aspirations. Unless these goals are operationalized into specific objectives, it is unlikely that a plan can be implemented to meet them (see Exhibit 2-B).

Achieving an *absolute objective* requires either that an undesirable condition be totally eliminated or that a desirable one be attained for everyone. An absolute objective in the health area might be the immunization of all persons against illnesses like measles or whooping cough. Educators advocate another absolute objective, the elimination of illiteracy. *Relative objectives* establish standards of achievement in terms of some proportionate improvement of the conditions that exist at some point in time. The reduction of gonorrhea by 50 percent would be a relative objective. The relative counterpart of our education example might be reducing the number of persons with less than sixth-grade skills by 75 percent.

Clearly, setting goals and specifying objectives require either assumptions or knowledge about two fundamental aspects of the social situation: values and existing conditions. The immunization goal reflects certain basic values favoring good health and low death rates. The goal to eliminate illiteracy assumes the importance of educational skills to productive participation in our economic system. Both goals, like any goal, are based on an assumption that there is room for improvement — that is, that there is discrepancy between the actual conditions and those specified by the goals.

Although a deficiency in existing conditions may be easy to recognize, refined assessment of the empirical situation is usually required before one can form goals and objectives and plan programs to achieve them. Procedures for diagnosing social problems are discussed in Chapter 3.

Exhibit 2-B: If You Don't Care Where You Get To, Then It Doesn't Matter Which Way You Go

In order to allow a program to be managed to achieve objectives, the program must satisfy three criteria:

a. Measurable objectives have been specified (i.e., those in charge of the program, such as policymakers and program managers, have agreed to measurable objectives for the program, including any necessary measures of program costs, program activities, intended program outcomes, and intended impact on the problem addressed by the program).

b. There exist plausible, testable assumptions linking application of resources to program activities, linking program activities to intended program outcomes, and linking program outcomes to program objectives.

c. Those in charge of the program have the motivation, ability, and authority to manage.

It is recognized that programs may be more or less manageable, according to the extent to which these three criteria are or are not satisfied. Our research reveals that the typical federal social program is unmanageable because it fails to meet one or more of these criteria.

Though every federal program has a number of objectives, the objectives are generally not defined by those in charge (policymakers and program managers) in such a way that progress toward objectives can be measured or important underlying program assumptions tested. The programs are sufficiently well defined to be funded, but are not sufficiently well defined to be managed to achieve specific objectives related to the goals implied in the authorizing legislation. In such programs, whatever activities are carried out tend to become synonymous with objectives; i.e., from a "management" perspective, the intended effect is achieved when the program activities are carried out, regardless of program outcome or subsequent impact on the problem addressed by the program.

SOURCE: From J. N. Nay et al., "If You Don't Care Where You Get To, Then It Doesn't Matter Which Way You Go," in C.C. Abt (ed.) *The Evaluation of Social Programs.* Beverly Hills, CA: Sage Publications, 1976, pp. 97-98.

Once refined estimates of existing conditions have been obtained, goals and objectives may have to be modified. This may be necessary because of external conditions adhering to the target population or problem. For example, the planners of programs may start out with the absolute objective of eliminating all cigarette-smoking, but find that the stubborn persistence of smoking habits necessitates the relative objective of reducing the number of smokers by some specified percentage.

Modification of goals and objectives may also result from conditions within the intervention effort. For instance, it is essential that evaluators, planners, program staff, and sponsors agree on the criteria to be used in assessing whether or not the objectives have been achieved. If a housing program is evaluated partly on the basis of morbidity, specific measures of morbidity (such as the number of days absent from work or school due to illness) have to be agreed upon as indicators of outcome. Failing such agreement, the evaluation may be confronted with rancorous conflict between evaluators and project planners, staff, and policymakers when evaluation results are presented. Sometimes the solution, if adequate resources are available, is to include multiple criteria that reflect the interests of the various parties involved. Another solution is to form objectives in addition to those held by stakeholders, based on current viewpoints and theories in the appropriate substantive field (Chen and Rossi, 1980).

Therefore, an early task for the evaluator is often to work with planners, project managers, and sponsors to transform ambiguous or contradictory objectives into clear, consistent, operational statements. The closer the objectives are to outcomes that can be directly measured, the more likely it is that a competent evaluation will result. Exhibit 2-C presents helpful rules for specifying objectives.

Formal Procedures

There are a number of formal ways to establish objectives, the technical details of which are beyond the scope of this book. A well-known procedure in the evaluation field is the decision theoretic approach (Edwards et al., 1975). This approach permits the formal explication and ranking of the objectives of diverse groups. Each group first defines and ranks its objectives, providing information on those it considers most important. Then, by a set of procedures known as Bayesian statistics, the choices are analyzed and reported back to the groups. On this basis, priorities are reordered. The process of providing information, linking objectives to inferences, and reordering objectives is continued until the groups arrive at a solution that takes into account their diverse views. Such an approach is especially useful when the

Exhibit 2-C: Some Rules for Specifying Objectives

. . . four techniques are particularly helpful for writing useful objectives: (1) using strong verbs, (2) stating only one purpose or aim, (3) specifying a single end-product or result, and (4) specifying the expected time for achievement [Kirschner Associates, Inc., *Programs for Older Americans: Setting and Monitoring; A Reference Manual*, Washington, D.C., 1975, Department of Health, Education and Welfare, Office of Human Development].

A *"strong" verb is an action-oriented verb* that describes an observable or measurable behavior that will occur. For example, *"to increase* the use of health education materials" is an action-oriented statement involving behavior which can be observed. In contrast, *"to promote* greater use of health education materials" is a weaker and less specific statement. The term "promote" is subject to many interpretations. Examples of action-oriented, strong verbs include: "to write," "to meet," "to find," "to increase," and "to sign." Examples of weaker, nonspecific verbs include: "to understand," "to encourage," "to enhance," and "to promote."

A second useful suggestion for writing a clear objective is to state only a *single aim or purpose.* Most programs will, of course, have multiple objectives but *within each* objective only a single purpose should be delineated. An objective that states two or more purposes or desired outcomes may well require different implementation and asssessment strategies, making achievement of the objective difficult to determine. For example, the statement "to begin three prenatal classes for pregnant women and provide outreach transportation services to accommodate twenty-five women per class" creates difficulties. This objective contains two aims — to provide prenatal classes *and* to provide outreach services. If one aim is accomplished but not the other, to what extent has the objective been met? It is better to state a single aim for each objective, such as *"start three prenatal classes* for pregnant women," *"provide outreach services* to twenty-five pregnant women per class."

Specifying a single end-product or result is a third technique contributing to a useful objective. For example, the statement "to begin *three* prenatal classes for pregnant women by *subcontracting* with City Memorial Hospital" contains two results, namely, the three classes and the subcontract. It is better to state these objectives separately, particularly since one is a higher order objective (to begin three prenatal classes) which depends partly on fulfillment of a lower order objective (to establish a subcontract).

A clearly written objective must have *both* a single aim and a single end-product or result. For example, the statement "to establish communication with the Health Systems Agency" indicates the aim but not the desired end-product or result. What contributes evidence of communication — telephone calls, meetings, reports? Failure to specify a clear end-product makes it extremely difficult for assessment to take place.

The reverse is equally true. That is, statements can exist which specify an end-product but no aim or purpose. "To provide all monthly discharge abstracts to the Commission of Professional and Hospital Activities" is an example of a statement with an end-product but no aim or purpose. The implicit aim may be to improve medical staff accountability and management or to improve the quality of medical care, but it is not clear that submitting case abstracts will meet this objective, nor can the objective be assessed in a meaningful way without such a statement of purpose. Those involved in writing and evaluating objectives need to keep two questions in mind. First, would anyone reading the objective, with or without knowledge of the program, find the *same purpose* as the one intended? Second, what visible, measurable, or tangible results are present as evidence that the objective has been met? Purpose or aim describes what will be done; end-product or result describes evidence that will exist when it has been done. This is assurance that you "know one when you see one."

Finally, it is useful to specify the time of *expected achievement* of the objective. The statement "to establish a walk-in clinic as soon as possible" is not a useful objective because of the vagueness of "as soon as possible." It is far more useful to specify a target date, or in cases where considerable doubt exists, a range of target dates — for example, "sometime between March 1 and March 30."

SOURCE: From Stephen M. Shortell and William C. Richardson, *Health Program Evaluation*. St. Louis, Mo., 1978: The C. V. Mosby Co., pp. 26-27. Reprinted by permission.

different stakeholders hold sharply conflicting views and the pool of potential objectives is beyond informal reconciliation. Another formal approach, evaluability assessment, seeks to produce evaluations with maximal potential utility. Although evaluability assessment is applicable to all evaluations, including those of innovative programs, it is most often undertaken in connection with established programs and will therefore be discussed later in this chapter.

Goal-Attainment Scaling

Although most evaluations rely on statements of objectives that involve measuring change in the target group as a whole, goal-attainment scaling makes it possible to tailor goals to individual units within the target population. The results can be summarized to provide a composite estimate of program impact (Kiresuk, 1973). The approach uses relative rather than absolute measures, an idea we have already discussed. For example, an alcohol treatment program may use number of days per three months absent from work as an outcome criterion. In the case of worker A, who is primarily a "weekend drinker," the goal may be to reduce the number of days per quarter from twelve to four. For worker B, who is a "binge drinker," the goal may be to reduce the twelve days to eight. Objectives for the delivery system can also be so developed. For example, the frequency with which therapy appointments are missed can be individualized as in the above example. The evaluator can then calculate difference scores, pooling individual estimates to arrive at a composite result. Goal-attainment expectations can be based on the views of practitioners, those of the targets, those of outside judges, or some combination of the three.

While goal-attainment scaling has utility for evaluations in many areas, such as psychotherapy and special education, it has limitations as well. First, it is time-consuming and expensive for large-scale studies involving many targets. Second, it runs counter to the intervention approaches of the many programs that are concerned with consistent outcome results for the target population. Third, goal-attainment scaling may result in depressed objectives. For example, a weight-reduction clinic might designate a five-pound loss as the objective for a patient who is thirty pounds overweight, thereby equating "success" with minimal impact. Despite those cautions, however, the method remains attractive for some evaluations.

Program Design and Development

In some instances, evaluators take the lead in designing and developing the programs they evaluate. Most commonly, however, this task is primarily the responsibility of program planners and designers or is mandated by program sponsors, such as foundation executives and legislators. Regardless of who does the work, in order to undertake a successful evaluation, both explicit, agreed-upon objectives and a detailed description of how they are to be achieved are required. The absence of a well-specified *impact model* severely limits opportunities to control a program's quality and effectiveness (Freeman and Sherwood, 1970). By analogy, a computer software package is useless if it has not been adequately documented. Even if a program is successful in delivering services and achieving the objectives set for it, without an explicit impact model there is no basis for understanding how and why it worked or for reproducing its effects on a broader scale, in other sites and with other targets. If, when an evaluation is undertaken, there is no impact model (or only an incomplete one), the evaluators must either inspire program staff and sponsors to create one or do the job themselves.

Elements of the Impact Model

An intervention or impact model is an attempt to translate notions regarding the regulation, modification, and control of social behavior or community conditions into hypotheses on which action can be based. Fully explicated models are rare. Too often, the intervention "model" consists of nothing more than the assumptions underlying a program's operation. These assumptions may have been drawn from previous studies — undertaken on small samples or in other locales — or they may have little or no empirical basis, being drawn instead from the untested ways in which practitioners have performed in the past.

The impact model takes the form of a statment about the expected relationships between a program and its goal; it sets forth the strategy for closing the gap between the goal set during the planning process and the existing behavior or condition. It must contain a causal hypothesis, a hypothesis about the intervention, and an action hypothesis.

The Causal Hypothesis. At the heart of any impact model is a hypothesis about the influence of one or more processes or determinants on the behavior or condition that the program seeks to modify. Although there are a number of different ways of thinking about causes, a simple idea of cause suffices in this case. Many social scientists believe, for example, that lack of employment among released felony offenders results in a return to crime (recidivism). A number of investigators (Irwin, 1970) maintain that if released prisoners are unable to find legitimate employment, they will be likely to seek out illegal modes of obtaining income.

The *causal hypothesis* in this case, then, would be that recidivism results from unemployment. But in order to be useful, all hypotheses, including causal ones, have to be stated in a way that permits testing, or measurement. This is the process of operationalization. To operationalize the hypothesis, the evaluator might state that re-arrests for crimes are most likely among released prisoners who either have minimal vocational qualifications or who encounter poor employment markets. It should be noted that this formulation is not the only one that is consistent with the causal hypothesis. Recidivism could be measured by whether or not a person is convicted of a felony; vocational qualifications can mean previous employment history, vocational training while in prison, or scores on various aptitude tests; and community employment markets could be measured by vacancies listed with employment agencies, the measured level of unemployment in the community; and so on.

The important point to grasp is that recidivism, employment qualifications, and employment opportunities have to be measured in the evaluation of any program that is designed to lower recidivism among ex-prisoners. Therefore, part of the task of developing an impact model is to specify the causal variables in operationally measurable terms.

The Intervention Hypothesis. An *intervention hypothesis* is a statement that specifies the relationship between a program, what is going to be done, and the process or determinant specified as associated in the causal hypothesis with the behavior or condition to be ameliorated or changed. The intervention hypothesis in the recidivism control example might be that postrelease employment is related to successfully completing a program of vocational training. Thus, the impact model for reducing recidivism would state as the intervention hypothesis that providing vocational training for released prisoners leads to a reduction in recidivism.

Other intervention hypotheses are also consistent with the causal hypothesis. An intervention hypothesis that directly provided employment opportunities by somehow motivating employers to hire released prisoners (possibly through tax subsidies) would be an alternative to vocational training. So would an intervention hypothesis that emphasized job-search assistance for released prisoners. Indeed, an agency trying to develop an effective program for reducing recidivism might try all three approaches separately and in combination to develop the most effective and efficient intervention program.

The Action Hypothesis. A third type of hypothesis is also required. An *action hypothesis* is necessary in order to assess whether the intervention, even if it results in a desired change in the causal variable, is necessarily linked to the outcome, that is, to the behavior or condition that one is seeking to modify. This third hypothesis is required because although a natural change in existing conditions may cause a desirable chain of events, the introduction of that change by means of an intervention may not result in the behavioral and social processes that occur naturally. An action may be planned and carried out as an intervention, but conditions may necessarily differ from when such actions "ordinarily" occur. Thus, the competencies that result from vocational training may not be the same as those that result from learning that takes place during regular work experiences. Ex-felons who have gone through vocational training courses, for example, may not have — or be viewed as having — the range of qualifications required by employers.

The importance of the action hypothesis can be seen in an interesting piece of research conducted some years ago (Festinger, 1964), on lowering racial discrimination in employment. Causal links were presumed between (1) understanding and knowledge of blacks and (2) prejudice, on the one hand, and between prejudice and (3) discrimination, on the other. A program was developed for employment managers to increase their understanding and knowledge of blacks in order to decrease their prejudice. The odd result of the program was that those employment managers whose attitudes changed the most discriminated more than they had before. Festinger explained this result by arguing that the input of new information led to a polarization of behavior. In other words, in the face of the program, it was impossible for the employment managers to continue behaving as they had before. Therefore, while some of them became less discriminatory, others became more so in their hiring practices. Neither the findings of the study nor Festinger's explanation vitiates the causal links that exist in the normal course of socialization. The point is that even if changes occur in a natural state, we may not be able to induce them. The action hypothesis is, therefore, as important as the other hypotheses in evaluation investigations and needs to be studied empirically.

Sources of Hypotheses. Ideally, the hypotheses embodied in impact models should stem from two sources: experimental studies that permit causal inferences, or well-developed theories, or both. In actuality, causal studies and logically developed theories of social behavior and social processes are scarce. Most impact models are derived either from clinical impressions or from statistical associations between independent (presumably causal) variables and dependent (or outcome) measures. The state of development in a field and knowledge of the results of other action programs are determinants of the sources of hypotheses. Clearly, programs that are successful in both delivery and outcome are most likely when reasonably definitive knowledge is available for impact model development.

Manipulability and Feasibility

Impact models are based on the presumption that the variables associated with the phenomenon to be modified are open to feasible manipulation. First, the intervention model must specify intervention variables that are action-relevant to the target population — that is, interventions that can affect targets directly or indirectly. If an undesirable condition exists because its targets became subject to that condition in a particular manner at a point in time prior to the stage at which the intervention operates, manipulability is precluded. This apparently is partly the case in the area of educational achievement. Much of the variance in students' performance in the high school, for example, evidently is not primarily a function of what happens to them in high school; instead, it is mainly due to the influence of their families and early social environments (Sewell and Hauser, 1975). If poor performance in high school is virtually so determined, any intervention would have to take place when the students are younger, even if children of high school age would be "sacrificed." The focus of a program clearly needs to be on both the variables that are manipulable and the appropriate time to manipulate them.

Second, one must avoid selecting interventions with low feasibility. Low feasibility may be due to program acceptance by sponsors, targets, and other stakeholders, the ideological values and imperatives of community life, or the risk of undesired side effects.

For example, in a program developed to reduce air pollution, certain conditions, such as the amount of fumes given off by automobiles, may be found to be manipulable. Others, such as the reduction of waste from industrial operations, may be found *not* to be manipulable either because of a lack of technical knowledge on reducing industrial fumes or the unwillingness of industry to pay the costs. Ideological and political imperatives can be illustrated by another problem. Social class has been found to be correlated with mental illness, but a revolutionary change in our economic structure is hardly an intervention that would be endorsed by the typical policymaker. Undesirable side effects may result from the use of telephone-tapping to identify certain criminals, such as bookmakers. Since telephone-tapping would of necessity include listening in on the innocent as well as the guilty, its use would be an invasion of privacy, a side effect militating against this kind of intervention.

Evaluators, then, like program sponsors and program staff, need to develop impact models that are sensitive to manipulability. Therefore, they must be concerned with *policy space*. By policy space, we mean the congeniality between intervention actions that are to be undertaken and the feasibility of implementation in terms of the interests, commitments, and outlooks of stakeholders, including targets.

Selecting Target Populations

There is interplay, as should be clear, between selecting the target population and developing the impact model. In some ways the distinction between the two tasks is artificial. The impact model must include a set of hypotheses about the plausibility of one event leading to another. Such hypotheses rest on predictions about the characteristics of the target population in relation to the intervention.

In considering the selection of the target population, the researcher should be aware that it is often desirable to distinguish between the group that will be immediately subjected to intervention (the *direct targets*) and the total population that eventually requires attention (the *indirect targets*). Some impact models imply such distinctions. For example, suppose the problem is to increase the income of the unemployed. Were the government to provide increased welfare payments to the unemployed, the direct and indirect target populations would be the same — those out of work. However, the government might decide to make employers the direct targets, permitting special tax deductions for those who hire workers with a history of unemployment (who are now the indirect targets). To predict the effect of such intervention, the evaluator would have to assess, either from past studies or by collecting new data, the relationship between such tax incentives to employers and increased employment, a task surely as important as predicting the composition of the target population — unemployed workers — from their social and psychological characteristics. (See Chapter 3 for further discussion of direct and indirect targets.)

In addition, because of the relationship between the way programs are organized and their acceptance and utilization by target populations, impact models need to take into account the way a program is organized in terms of *target acceptance*. The health field provides a useful illustration: Correlational studies suggest that lack of prenatal care, particularly during the last months of pregnancy, is related to subsequent health problems for both the mother and the baby — among them, a higher likelihood that the child will be mentally retarded. A major subgroup of the target population is unmarried mothers, particularly in low-income areas. The solution advocated is often simplistic: to increase the available medical facilities in low-income areas that have large populations of young women. It does not necessarily follow, however, that the increase in facilities will lead to the increased use of the medical services by unmarried mothers.

The choice of a target population is a strategic decision. The focus of a program must shift dramatically if it is found that the characteristics of its target population are not what they were originally thought to be. For that reason we shall devote Chapter 3 to a discussion of how targets are estimated.

Delivery System Design

Interventions, no matter how well conceived, cannot be effective and efficient unless there are carefully developed delivery systems. Some delivery systems are comparatively simple, particularly when targets are "semicaptives": Providing health education in classroom settings is a comparatively simple proposition. Other delivery systems are highly complex: Special health care for prospective mothers experiencing "high-risk" pregnancies may require family physicians, obstetrical and pediatric specialists, general hospitals, and centers specializing in infant care.

Elements of the Delivery System

In order to document and assess a program, the elements of the delivery system must be explicated and criteria of performance developed and measured. Among the elements usually monitored, as will be discussed further in Chapter 4, are the following:

- identification of the target problem and population
- procedures and services provided
- qualifications and competencies of staff
- mechanisms for recruiting and obtaining the cooperation of targets
- means of optimizing access to the intervention, including location and physical characteristics of service delivery sites
- referral and follow-up efforts

Each program, of course, has its own set of delivery system elements. An illustration may be useful. A rare but invariably fatal neurological infant disorder is Tay Sacs disease. It is genetically transmitted and confined almost exclusively to Jews of Eastern European background. In one of four pregnancies where both prospective parents carry the recessive defective gene, the child will be affected. (Targets are identified.)

An intervention is therefore designed to prevent such pregnancies: Tay Sacs blood tests are offered to a population of Eastern European background; carriers are counseled about risks with prospective sexual partners who also have the recessive gene; carriers who are pregnant are advised to seek diagnostic evaluation of the *in utero* baby; and in the case of a Tay Sacs fetus, the medical recommendation is to seek a therapeutic abortion (procedures and services).

The program is under the supervision of a genetic counselor; there are nurses to take the blood tests; and a publicity specialist is hired to recruit targets. One of the intervention efforts is carried out on college campuses each semester in a convenient place, such as the student union. Positive cases are referred to the genetic counselor, located at the campus clinic (recruiting, access to sites). Students who are carriers and fail to seek counseling are contacted as frequently and aggressively as possible by their physicians, and once identified they are contacted annually by mail to encourage testing of prospective or current partners (target retention).

In addition to assessing the various elements of the delivery system, provision has to be made for collecting data on costs if an efficiency evaluation is to be undertaken. Salaries, labor, fees, and advertising costs would be relevant in the illustration given above. (See Chapter 4 on monitoring and Chapter 8 on efficiency studies.)

Formative Studies

In the design and development of many programs, it is useful and frequently necessary to undertake evaluative activities *during* the intervention's design.

These evaluation activities may be quite simple or as complex as full-blown evaluations. Sometimes they are directed at specific questions related to developing the delivery system, selecting targets, and structuring the intervention. Other times they are "mini-impact" evaluations conducted in order to gather estimates of the magnitude of impact to be expected with a particular intervention. The need for formative evaluation is a major reason to allow adequate lead time for program planning and development. Many programs fail in the design phase to invest sufficient resources in formative efforts. The consequence can be program impotence. Formative evaluations may include the testing and assessment of a program either at one or a few sites, or with a small sample of targets prior to full-blown implementation.

For example, as part of the planning and design of *Sesame Street,* program staff were concerned about which particular TV characters should·be chosen to be the agents of the messages communicated. Relatively simple experiments were undertaken: The same learning messages were transmitted by different characters and in different sequences. Groups of children viewed the presentations on a television screen and variation in their attention to the screen was estimated. It was on this basis that decisions were made regarding the format of the program (see Exhibit 2-D).

In another example of a formative study, a "typical" portion of the target population is selected to participate in a trial run of the intervention. Such a study was conducted to estimate the number of targets who would utilize a community mental health program requiring attendance at weekly meetings. Careful records were kept of the various means of recruiting targets, the proportion who attended for the full eight-week course, and those who dropped out. Dropouts were interviewed in order to discover their reasons for not completing the program to find better means of retaining targets.

Formative studies vary, of course, in the extent to which they are rigorous and in the sophistication of their data collection and data analysis. In many cases, however, even simple studies provide insight into the problems the intervention may face and ways to overcome them. Further, formative studies also allow opportunities, in many cases, for "pretesting" evaluation procedures and instruments, as well as the intervention itself. Evaluators engaged in formative studies obviously must become involved in the actual design and programming effort, since the emphasis here is on increasing the success of subsequent intervention efforts and their evaluations. Thus, the evaluator becomes an advocate and a partisan participant in the program activities.

Exhibit 2-D: Formative Research for *Sesame Street*

An important part of the formative research that went into the year-and-a-half planning for *Sesame Street* involved measuring the audience appeal of possible programs before they went on the air, since appeal was a vital ingredient if *Sesame Street* was to reach and keep its audience. Small groups of children of the appropriate age and apparent cognitive skills were recruited to come to the Children's Workshop studios to view proposed programs and segments of programs. The program was projected on a monitor set while, on an adjoining wall, slides were projected at an angle to the child. Observers rated the proportion of each 7.5-second schedule that the children viewed the program rather than the projected slide. Producers could then relate the content of the program (or segment of a program) at any one point to the degree of attention that program or segment attained from the test audience of children. From these findings, in addition to accepting or rejecting versions of programs, generalizations were drawn about program features that did or did not attract the attention of economically disadvantaged children. The formative research played a crucial role, producers believed, in reducing the risk that *Sesame Street* would not hold its audience once it reached them.

SOURCE: Summary, by permission, of B. F. Reeves, *The First Year of Sesame Street: The Formative Research.* New York: Children's Television Workshop, 1970.

Program Simulations

Often, time, costs, and other demands preclude the use of formative studies in the design of innovative activities. In such cases, program staff and evaluators may turn to program simulations (see Exhibit 2-E). Simulations can also complement formative efforts.

Some simulations are highly quantitative and formal, incorporating sophisticated computer-based modeling (including ex ante efficiency studies, discussed in Chapter 8). Others apply qualitative approaches, such as scenarios about the consequences of different ways to identify, delimit, and recruit target populations. Likewise, various levels of impact are estimated for programs of various intensities. Finally, evaluators often simulate results from studies of similar programs, so that sponsors, planners, and designers can be confronted with the type and magnitude of outcomes they may achieve.

Much of the simulation work evaluators do during the design phase of the program and throughout its evaluation is similar to what takes place in all research studies. A commonly requested attachment to evaluation designs, for example, is a set of "dummy tables," which show what the results of an evaluation may look like, and into which a range of utilization and impact estimates can be inserted. Dummy tables may alert staff, sponsors, and evaluators to whether or not appropriate

Exhibit 2-E: Involuntary Patient Flow

Following fairly solid experiences of success in aerospace, military, computer science, and business settings, the technique of computer simulation is appearing more and more in social welfare applications. Although in the latter cases the systems being modeled are often less well structured, and outcome variables are frequently less well defined, such simulations are undertaken for reasons typical for the technique: A system of variables exists that is so complexly interrelated that the relationship between input and output is not intuitively obvious and is difficult or impossible to approach analytically. If the system can be adequately represented in a model, then the outputs resulting from particular patterns of input can be estimated, and this information used in whatever decision process is at hand.

In the summer of 1975 data were collected for the period from September 1974 through April 1975 that would allow a description of the numbers of patients following each branch of the decision tree, and the distributions of length of stay for each segment of stay. Subjects were all patients who entered the ward over that period. The primary data source was a computerized data system for a related community mental health center, which at that time also covered all patients entering the psychiatric ward. Additional data were obtained from county records generated by the mental health professionals who performed the initial screening of potential involuntary patients. The data collected included referral source into and disposition out of the ward, dates of admission and discharge, and dates of each hearing and/or change of status while on the ward.

Each patient was then classified as to his or her status for each day on the ward, where the status categories were voluntary admission, converted voluntary (admitted involuntarily, but subsequently agreed to become voluntary), or patients on 72-hour hold, 14-day commitment, or 90-day commitment.

Given this set of patient classifications, computer programs were written that would summarize referral sources and dispositions into and out of the ward, changes in patient status, frequencies and types of legal hearings, distributions of lengths of stay, distributions of numbers and types of admissions, and a day-by-day profile of how many ward beds were occupied by each class of patient.

These outputs were considered useful by the ward psychiatrist, particularly the day-by-day profiles and the information on admissions, hearings, and status changes. A fairly natural reaction to these materials, and in fact the one that occurred, was "What would happen if . . . ?" The two major versions of the question were (a) What would happen if the mix of voluntary/involuntary patients changed? and (b) What would happen if the judges began increasing or decreasing the rate at which they made commitments at the first hearing? These factors are of special interest due to their impact on the mix of voluntary/involuntary patients (since this affects the program), average length of stay, and bed utilization rates. Such issues were of particular salience at the time because the law, which represented a moderately radical change in procedure, was still relatively new, and procedures for responding to it were still settling down. A simulation study seemed an appropriate way to address the questions.

The second, broader purpose of the simulation study was to gain some experience with the technique of simulation in an effort to evaluate its utility for program evaluation and evaluation research functions.

SOURCE: Adapted from Gary B. Cox, "Involuntary Patient Flow: A Computer Simulation of a Psychiatric Ward," *Evaluation Review*, Vol. 4, No. 5, 1980: 571-584.

evaluation questions are being asked, suggest reasonable estimates of impact, and thereby form expectations regarding adoption of the program on a broader basis or its continued support at any level.

Summary of Innovative Evaluation Activities

We must stress that the evaluator, in planning, designing, and testing new programs, must be capable of undertaking a wide range of activities. These will vary, depending on the type of program, when it is implemented, political and resource demands, and the particular skills of program staff and evaluation groups. In most evaluations of innovative programs, the evaluator will participate in at least some of the tasks we have examined in this chapter:

1. identifying and describing of the problem or concern

2. operationalizing objectives for the program

3. developing an intervention model

4. defining a target population

5. designing the delivery system and procedures for monitoring it

6. assessing impact and estimating efficiency

EVALUATING ESTABLISHED PROGRAMS

While the evaluation of innovative programs represents an important activity for the field, by far the greater proportion of program resources, and thus evaluation efforts, go into the assessment of established, ongoing programs. The evaluation efforts related to established programs are less visible than those connected with program innovations. First, more are conducted "in house," by staff connected with operating agencies. Second, part of the evaluation of established programs is associated with the managerial concerns of maintaining and improving program effectiveness and efficiency.

In a sense, the ground rules are different. Established programs are generally a historical response to social concerns. Most have sprung from traditional, long-standing, ameliorative efforts, and rarely are their basic structures open to question. The value of guidance counselors in schools, of vocational programs for the handicapped, of parole supervision for released convicts, and of community health education for the prevention of disease is taken for granted. Not only does the general public expect such programs as a matter of course, but involved advocates and employees, a significant proportion of the national labor force, have an investment in their continuation. Thus, the pressures to maintain them are strong.

At the same time, in many human resource sectors, there is continual and intensifying scrutiny of established programs. Many are rooted in values and intervention models that no longer are relevant; some have even lost their surface rationales and objectives over time. Also, as we noted earlier, there is growing community uneasiness about the proliferation and redundancy of programs. Spiraling costs of programs and increased resource restraints, particularly on public funds, require that we choose what to support, and in what magnitude. Consequently, serious questions are raised about the extent to which programs operate efficiently and follow fiscal, legal, and operational requirements. Finally, constituencies and advocates of different programs are concerned with their impact and costs-to-benefits ratios in comparison to those programs with which they compete for sponsorship and funds. For all these reasons, policymakers responsible for resource allocations, program managers who must defend implementation, and concerned advocacy groups acknowledge the urgent need for evaluation of established programs. Exhibit 2-F describes, for example, the current questioning of alcohol education programs.

The Evaluability Perspective

The idea discussed in this section stems from the experiences of a group at The Urban Institute, whose evaluation activities led to two related conclusions (Wholey et al., 1970; Wholey, 1979). First, they found it difficult, sometimes impossible, to implement evaluations of public programs because managers and other stakeholders resisted, were uncooperative, or failed to grasp the purposes of the studies. Second, they found that too frequently evaluation results were not used to refine and modify programs. This led to the view that a systematic approach, what Wholey termed *evaluability assessment,* should precede any typical evaluation effort. Evaluability assessments, or "preevaluations," are designed to provide a climate for future evaluation work. In addition, as systematic management consultation, such efforts may in and of themselves be utilized by program staff prior to further evaluation activities (Schmidt et al., 1978; Rutman, 1980). Evaluability assessments can also reveal whether implementation corresponds to the program as defined by those who created its policy and operational procedures; if not, any evaluation that is undertaken will probably be useless.

Evaluability assessments require the commitment of program staff and, in many cases, sponsors and relevant policymakers to collaborate in explicating objectives, describing the program, and deciding on evaluation tasks. While it can be argued that program staff should, of their own accord, conduct the activities described as evaluability assessments, evaluators find this is rarely the case. Consequently, such assessments become an evaluator's responsibility, at least in terms of the leadership necessary to get the job done.

Conducting Evaluability Assessments

Evaluability assessment can be considered a series of successive approximations. Evaluability specialists use each encounter with program staff to broaden their knowledge, identify new informants, verify information collected, and test various scenarios of future evaluative activities and alternative program options.

The method is acknowledged to require considerable judgment on the part of the evaluability specialist. Efforts are made in various descrip-

Exhibit 2-F: Does Alcohol Education Prevent Alcohol Problems?

It has been considered a reasonable premise that the prevention of alcohol and drug problems among youth should begin by providing children and adolescents with a factual knowledge of the nature, use, and effects of those often abused substances. However, recent evidence suggesting that drug education programs may actually augment rather than decrease pro-drug attitudes and drug use has produced increasing criticisms of current drug *and* alcohol education efforts and led some to call for a moratorium on educational approaches to primary prevention. With regard to alcohol education, this paper critically examines the evidence for this alleged failure of education as a preventive measure and considers whether an indictment of these methods is warranted at this time. In addition, several necessary characteristics of an adequate test of the effectiveness of alcohol education are discussed. Although this paper is concerned with alcohol education, information from the more abundant drug education literature is included where relevant.

The Ambiguous Effectiveness of Alcohol Education

Although our educational institutions receive hearty endorsement as a primary preventive agent, as evidenced by the fact that virtually all states require instruction about alcohol in the public schools, actual implementation of instructional programs has often been neglected or given only superficial attention. Globetti, citing others, has suggested that the present situation arose when the influence of temperance groups (e.g., the WCTU Department of Scientific Temperance) declined in importance. While the early efforts of these temperance groups had succeeded in making alcohol education a compulsory part of the public school curriculum, their educational materials were often criticized as distorted and based largely on appeals to fear. These criticisms, coupled with the advent and repeal of Prohibition, further damaged the status of the temperance approach and left most states with legal mandates requiring alcohol instruction, but no satisfactory message to replace that of the temperance forces. Faced with this dilemma, educators seem to have responded by avoiding the subject. The result has been an array of programs differing vastly in goals and methods. Materials presently used in public school programs are typically dominated by the topic of alcoholism education and the physiological and behavioral effects of alcohol, with little or no attention devoted to the important topic of adolescent drinking.

A clear statement of measurable objectives is a necessary way to start a program toward meaningful evaluation, yet several authors have pointed out the frequent lack of goals in alcohol education programs. Many programs operate without a clear-cut philosophy and this seems, in part, to be responsible for the absence of well-controlled studies of the effectiveness of such programs. Freeman and Scott reported in 1966 that most alcohol education programs were without specific goals or evidence of impact and that little was being done to remedy the situation. These same problems exist today, more than 10 years later.

SOURCE: Adapted, with permission, from A. Mitch Cooper and Mark B. Sobell, "Does Alcohol Education Prevent Alcohol Problems?: Need for Evaluation," *Journal of Alcohol and Drug Education*, Vol. 25, No. 1, 1979: 54-63.

tions of the method (see Rutman, 1980) to codify procedures in order to render assessments reproducible by other assessors. In general, the following iterative steps are taken:

1. Preparing a Program Description. This description is based on formal documents, such as funding proposals, published brochures, administrative manuals, annual reports, minutes, and completed evaluation studies. It includes statements identifying program objectives and cross-classifying them with program elements or components. In other words, like the impact model discussed for innovative programs, the program description compares how the intervention is supposed to operate with how it actually works.

2. Interviewing Program Personnel. Key people are interviewed to gather descriptions of the program's goals and rationales, as well as to identify actual program operations. From this information, models of both the intentions and the actual operations of the program are developed and subsequently verified with persons interviewed.

3. Scouting the Program. While evaluability assessments do not include formal research in the sense of large-scale data collection, they do generally include site visits to obtain firsthand impressions of how programs actually operate. These impressions are collated with information from documents and interviews.

4. *Developing an Evaluable Program Model.* From the various types of information, the program elements and objectives to be considered for inclusion in evaluation plans are explicated.

5. *Identifying Evaluation Users.* The purposes of evaluation activities and key stakeholders to whom they are to be directed are next identified. In addition, the ways decisions on changes would be made (e.g., administratively or through legislation) are decided.

6. *Achieving Agreement to Proceed.* The final step is to review the evaluation plan with the various stakeholders. The process of information collection during the course of the evaluability assessment typically includes dialogue with key individuals and groups. Thus, at this point most components of the plan have been accepted. It is important before the plan is "signed off" by the various stakeholders, however, to reach explicit agreement on

a. program components to be analyzed, the design of the evaluation, and priorities for undertaking the work;

b. commitment of required resources and agreements on necessary cooperation and collaboration;

c. a plan for utilization of the evaluation results;

d. a plan for efforts required from the program staff to strengthen the evaluability potential of program components not currently amenable to evaluation, and an approach for subsequently building them into the evaluation effort.

In the end, the planning of evaluations of established programs is not qualitatively different from what occurs in innovative interventions. Perhaps the two key distinctions in style are (1) the increased emphasis on inducing a program evaluation model from existing, ongoing program activities, and (2) much more deliberate attention to stakeholders' views, responsibilities, and influence. Exhibit 2-G provides an illustration of an evaluability assessment.

Accountability Studies

Either as a consequence of outside mandates or on the basis of evaluability assessments, accountability studies are directed at providing findings relevant to demands for different types of accountability

Exhibit 2-G: Appalachian Regional Commission

In the Appalachian Regional Commission (ARC), evaluators worked with managers and policymakers to achieve consensus on new program designs more likely to lead to demonstrably effective performance. Evaluability assessment of the Appalachian Regional Commission health and child development program began with collection of data on management's intentions and on program reality. In this evaluability assessment by The Urban Institute, the evaluators

- reviewed commission data on each of the 13 state ARC-funded health and child development programs;

- made one-day site visits to five states to aid in selection of two states to participate in evaluation system design and implementation;

- reviewed approximately 40 pieces of documentation considered essential in understanding congressional, commission, state, and project objectives and activities (including the authorizing legislation, congressional hearings and committee reports, state planning documents, and project grant applications);

- reviewed 50 to 60 other pieces of documentation, including ARC contract reports, local planning documents, project materials, state documentation, and research projects;

- interviewed approximately 75 people on congressional staffs and in commission headquarters, state ARC and other state health and child development staffs, local planning units, and local projects; and

- participated in workshops with approximately 60 additional health and child development practitioners, ARC state personnel, and outside analysts.

Analysis and synthesis of the resulting data yielded a "logic model" that presented program activities, program objectives, and assumed causal links among program activities and objectives. The measurability and plausibility of program objectives were then analyzed, and possible redefinitions of the program design were presented. Here the evaluators moved beyond sterile critiques of program design and suggested how managers and policymakers could establish realistic, measurable objectives and use program performance data to improve performance.

The report presented both an overall ARC program model and series of individual models, each concerned with an identified objective of the program. The report outlined a series of information options, expressed in modeling terms, any one of which could be developed into a specific study or evaluation system. In reviewing the report, then, ARC staff had to choose explicitly among alternative courses of action. The review process used was a series of intensive discussions, with ARC and Urban Institute staff participating, in which we focused on one objective and program model at a time. In each session, we attempted to reach agreement on the validity of the flow models presented in the report, the extent to which the objective was important, and the extent to which any of the information options ought to be pursued.

This evaluability assessment was completed in approximately six months, at a cost of approximately $50,000. Another two months of work with the Appalachian Regional Commission and state and local groups resulted in ARC decisions systematically to monitor the performance of all ARC health and child development projects and to identify and evaluate the effectiveness of "innovative" health and child development projects.

Twelve of the thirteen ARC states have since adopted the performance monitoring system voluntarily. Representatives of those states report that project designs are now much more clearly articulated and that they believe the projects themselves have improved.

SOURCE: Adapted from J. S. Wholey, "Using Evaluation to Improve Program Performance," pp. 92-106 in R. A. Levine et al. (eds.), *Evaluation Research and Practice: Comparative and International Perspectives*. Beverly Hills, CA: Sage Publications, 1981.

concerns. Sponsors, program staff, and a range of community groups may be concerned with all or some of the following issues:

1. Impact Accountability. Program managers are concerned with impact, both for internal operating reasons and in order to justify programs externally.

2. Coverage Accountability. The key questions here relate to the number and characteristics of targets, to the extent of penetration (i.e., what proportion of potential targets are served), to dropout rates, and so on.

3. Service Delivery Accountability. It is usually necessary to assess how the actual operation of a program conforms to program plans. For example, community mental health centers may include in their plans 24-hour emergency treatment; the accountability question is whether or not this is, in fact, provided. Also, many intervention plans specify the qualifications of providers; thus, the extent to which services are delivered by appropriately qualified staff is another accountability issue.

4. Efficiency Accountability. Impact in relation to program costs is obviously important both internally, in terms of judging relative benefits and effectiveness against costs of different program elements, and externally, in competing for resources.

5. Fiscal Accountability. Programs have a clear responsibility to account for use of funds in their fiscal reports. But in addition to what is strictly an accounting responsibility, a range of other cost questions may be pertinent. For example, costs per client and costs per service are data that may not be gleaned from a fiscal report. Incremental and marginal costs are also pertinent, since programs vary in size, different targets are included, and so on. Finally, different costs may be a function of program site, time of year, and the initiation of competing programs.

6. Legal Accountability. All programs, public and private, require commitments in order to meet legal responsibilities. These include informed consent, protection of privacy, community representation on decision-making boards, equity in provision of services, and cost-sharing. In public programs, adequate compliance with legal requirements often is a prerequisite for continued funding.

The scope of a program's accountability activities is determined by both external and internal requirements. For example, many laws, including sunset legislation, require reports of program impact prior to approval of subsequent years' funding. Program managers and the executives to whom they report are concerned with accountability information in order to improve and modify efforts and to administer their interventions efficiently. In many ways, evaluability assessments are seen as a means of developing an accountability strategy that meets current and future needs for information. In developing accountability strategies, there are two important considerations: continuous versus cross-sectional evaluations and internal versus external assessments.

Continuous versus Cross-Sectional Evaluations

Many large programs employ monitoring and information systems, often referred to as management information systems (MIS), that allow them to assess on an ongoing basis the work and results of their programs. These systems record information on each encounter, on the delivery of the service, and on outcome and cost. Continuous systems are often criticized for "overkill," however, and since they do represent a permanent commitment of resources, they need to be justified by constant use.

At the same time, however, individual or cross-sectional studies undertaken from time to time may carry with them expensive start-up costs and be resisted by program staff, since they are not perceived as part of routine operations. Further, they may not be timely and may have less utility for day-to-day administrative decisions.

Again, there is no way to provide rules; rather, a continual monitoring system must be judged in its own cost-to-benefit terms. Many programs use a mix of continual monitoring to assess process and cross-sectional evaluations to estimate at various points their impact and costs to benefits.

Internal versus External Evaluations

Accountability evaluations raise sharply the issue of whether programs should undertake their own evaluations or contract with outsiders to do so. On the one hand, it is clear that in the case of these types of evaluations, the evaluator must know a great deal about program operations, both to design the evaluation and to engage in the consultation, education, and dialogue required to maximize its utility. On the other hand, there is the risk that the evaluator who is part of the program staff will be co-opted, and that sponsors and stakeholders outside the program staff will be suspicious of the authenticity of findings. In large programs, where evaluators can operate as a semiautonomous group, it is probably beneficial and economical for accountability evaluations to be internal. Smaller programs may be better off with outside assessments approximating the methods of fiscal audits. In some cases, a combination of the two, using consultants to provide both technical assistance and oversight, is advantageous.

FINE-TUNING ESTABLISHED PROGRAMS

Often, as we have noted earlier, there is a thin line between what is termed innovative interventions and the implementation of program refinements through *fine-tuning*. Likewise, fine-tuning evaluations often overlap with evaluations of established programs. Program managers, on the basis of ongoing evaluation information, may make day-to-day administrative and technical changes that are quite extensive and are subject to systematic evaluation. The core of fine-tuning, however, is program modification that impacts markedly on intervention efforts. Its essence is captured by the term "initiative," which often is applied to fine-tuning efforts in national and other large-scale interventions.

Program fine-tuning typically occurs because program sponsors and staff are dissatisfied with either the effectiveness or the efficiency of their interventions, or both. The basis for implementing such changes may be the findings of systematic evaluation studies of a monitoring or impact type, the outcome of evaluability assessments, or more impressionistic evidence of dissatisfaction with the way efforts are being conducted.

Some illustrations are useful. In the mental health field, for example, community mental health centers in areas where there are significant Spanish-speaking populations have become aware of the barriers to access that these persons face because of language problems. A variety of different approaches have been taken in order to increase access for persons of Hispanic background. One approach has been to increase the proportion of staff fluent in Spanish, to transmit the bilingual character of the center through dual language signs and mental health educational material in Spanish, and to employ persons of Hispanic background to contact key religious and voluntary groups in the Spanish community. A second approach has been to establish satellite "feeder" programs in heavily Hispanic neighborhoods; here staff, materials, and interpersonal relations reflect the special cultural character of the residents, short-term diagnosis and treatment are available, and patients are referred to the parent center. At issue, of course, is whether these approaches increase access for the target population, and which approach proves most effective.

Another example of fine-tuning concerns the large number of initiatives in connection with neighborhood community health centers, most of which initially exist as "freestanding" organizations. Here, groups external to neighborhood health centers, including the federal government and large foundations, have adopted a variety of programs to link community health centers to hospitals and medical schools. While the basic character of medical care provided in the community health centers is not changed, the initiatives are seen as mechanisms that reduce undesirable overlap of services between hospital facilities and community health centers. Also, such affiliations are said to increase continuity of care for patients, which results in greater client satisfaction. Similar types of efforts to reduce fragmentation of care have taken place: Single-neighborhood centers, for instance, offer welfare recipients and other persons of marginal income a variety of services that were previously available in separate offices at some distance from each other.

Fine-tuning basically requires, on the part of sponsors, program staff, and evaluators, three related sets of activities. We turn to these next.

Reappraising Objectives and Outcomes

Fine-tuning efforts, like innovative programs, are a response to existing conditions. In the case of fine-tuning, however, action focuses on conditions adhering to the program itself, rather than a new and untreated problem. Often, awareness that a program has failed to meet community concerns requires some modification of the program's objectives and outcome criteria. Take our example of community mental health centers and the Hispanic population. The original objective of the centers may have been to provide a range of diagnostic, emergency, and short-term treatment programs to the catchment-area residents. The objective, as originally stated, did not include special consideration for the ethnic and cultural backgrounds of the target population. Fine-tuning in the face of failure to provide access to persons of particular social and cultural backgrounds clearly would require a refinement of objectives. Likewise, the program affiliating community health centers with local hospitals reflects a refinement of objectives; it has redefined and operationalized its objective to include maximum continuity of care.

The need to redefine objectives often becomes apparent after program implementation, particularly as innovative programs stabilize and emerge as established ventures in the human service field. Sometimes, redefinition of objectives stems from the dialogue that almost invariably accompanies administrative and day-to-day working activities. Other times, evaluators undertake special studies, either as independent contractors or as staff members, to obtain data to aid program personnel in revising objectives. In some cases, evaluators and program staff have at their disposal (as we described in discussing established programs) ongoing management and service information systems that provide data on issues surrounding current objectives and the extent to which they are being met. Increasingly, a number of formal approaches are being employed for continual auditing.

Reputability Assessments

We use the term *reputability assessments* to refer to systematic efforts to obtain from relevant stakeholders, particularly targets, opinions and experiential data on which to judge the extent of a program's success in meeting its objectives. Reputability assessments basically consist of obtaining market research data. Some programs provide questionnaires to clients in order to obtain information from them about their satisfaction with programs. This may be done through a special study or as part of an ongoing monitoring effort. The surveys would include questions on various aspects of treatment: waiting time, relations with practitioners, costs and fees, and the like. They may also seek expressions of desired services and unmet needs.

In addition, and particularly for larger programs, evaluators may survey providers of services. While persons rendering services, like clients, have their own biases and stakes in programs, they may nevertheless perceive appropriate gaps and deficiencies that can be corrected through fine-tuning. For example, regular and systematic data may be obtained from classroom teachers about the various types of special services offered by a school, such as counseling on emotional problems and vocational guidance. (More is said in Chapter 4 on monitoring.)

Often reputability assessments will point to fine-tuning efforts that are comparatively simple, such as providing feedback to teachers on what is being done for students, areas in which special programs are needed, and ways to collaborate effectively in order to deal with student problems. Other times, the information may highlight the need for considerable program modification.

Less formal information includes the advocacy pressures exerted by stakeholders and community groups, and probing by persons in the mass media and in political life. When systematic reputability assessments are conducted in advance of these pressures, program management may be able to fine-tune interventions and avoid becoming subject to harassment.

Program Replanning and Redesign

Implementing refinements and fine-tuning, of course, requires a return to the various steps and activities discussed in some detail in our section on evaluating innovative programs. It is necessary that the problem be well identified and described, that objectives be operationalized, that a revised impact model be developed, that the target population be redefined, that the delivery system be redesigned, and that plans be made for whatever revisions are required in monitoring impact and efficiency.

It should be stressed that not only are fine-tuning efforts much more commonplace than innovative interventions in the human service field, but also the consequences of these efforts are extensive. For example, in many high schools, some students are prepared, on an informal basis in such courses as English and mathematics, to take college board examinations. If it can be demonstrated that these students obtain higher college board scores, formal preparatory sessions may be incorporated into the regular high school curriculum — particularly because maximizing students' opportunities for college education and selection of a college of their choice is an objective consistent with one of the general goals of high school education. At the same time, such curriculum modification may increase the gap between students with college aspirations and those without them, require deemphasis of other aspects of the educational program, and interfere with teachers' course plans.

In terms of fine-tuning, then, the evaluator is involved in the following tasks:

1. reappraising objectives

2. using data from previous evaluations, as well as information about program progress gathered as part of the service delivery, in order to seek out ways of modifying programs

3. undertaking and using reputability assessments

4. participating in program replanning and redesign

5. planning and implementing evaluation designs to monitor the program changes and their impact

LINKING EVALUATIONS TO PROGRAMS

In this chapter we have discussed how evaluation fits into the development of innovative interventions, into the conduct of established programs, and into fine-tuning and refining of programs. The primary lesson we would like to convey is that the evaluation must be tailored to the program (see Table 2.1).

In no way, of course, do we wish to downplay the importance of the technical and procedural evaluation activities that follow the conceptualization of studies. Indeed, that is what most of this book is about. Moreover, it is important to recognize that programs and evaluations are "dynamic" in the sense that additional program experience, preliminary evaluation feedback, and shifts in the political, economic, and social contexts in which programs and evaluations occur may require modification and adjustment to evaluation designs. At the same time, unless

TABLE 2.1 Overview of Evaluation Activities

	Innovative Programs	Established Programs	Fine-Tuning
Conceptualizing	1. Problem description	1. Determining evaluability	1. Identifying needed program changes
	2. Operationalizing objectives	2. Developing evaluation model	2. Redefining objectives
	3. Developing intervention model	3. Identifying potential modification opportunities	3. Designing program modifications
	4. Defining extent and distribution of target population	4. Determining accountability requirements	
	5. Specifying delivery system		
Implementing	1. Formative research and development	1. Program monitoring and accountability studies	1. R and D program refinements
	2. Implementation monitoring		2. Monitoring program changes
Assessing	1. Impact studies	1. Impact studies	1. Impact studies
	2. Efficiency analyses	2. Efficiency analyses	2. Efficiency analyses

TAILORING EVALUATIONS • 87

evaluations start strong, and unless they are congruent with program operations and requirements, successful systematic studies are unlikely to follow. While there are limits to how fully the process of tailoring can be "taught" — since it involves not only the orderly formulation and refinement of ideas with data integration, but also dialogue, discussion, and interaction with relevant stakeholders — our message should be clear. The evaluator's understanding and maximal involvement in fitting evaluations to programs is essential to the successful undertaking of systematic evaluations.

3

Diagnostic Procedures

As part of the development of evaluation activities and the application of social research methods to the human service area, systematic and reproducible approaches have been devised to identify problems and conditions that are untreated or insufficiently dealt with by existing programs. These "diagnostic" procedures sometimes constitute the initial step in problem identification; other times they follow stakeholders' impressionistic and judgmental assessments of the need for purposive, organized social action programs. In either case, systematic documentation of program need must be undertaken in order to plan, refine, implement, and evaluate social action efforts.

KEY CONCEPTS

Incidence: The number of new cases of a particular problem or condition that are identified or arise in a specified area during a specified period of time.

Indicators: A measure reflecting a problem or condition and for which time-series information is available.

Need Assessment: Systematic appraisal of type, depth, and scope of problems as perceived by study targets or their advocates.

Population at Need: Units of potential targets that currently manifest a given condition.

Population at Risk: Segment of a population with significant probability of developing a condition.

Prevalence: Number of existing cases with a given condition in a particular area at a specified time.

Rate: Occurrence or existence of a condition expressed as a proportion of units in the population (e.g., deaths per 1,000 adults).

Survey: Systematic collection of information from large study groups, usually by means of interviews or questionnaires administered to a sample of units in the population.

---

*I*f we were close to a utopian world, one where we lived in good health almost forever and where there were no deviance, full social equality, ample opportunities for participation in occupational and social activities, and where existing human service programs effectively and efficiently dealt with individual, interpersonal, and community defects (which, of course, would be minor), few evaluations would be undertaken. Neither new programs nor fine-tuning of existing ones would be needed, and little monitoring of established efforts would be necessary. Evaluation can be seen, then, as a response to efforts to move toward a more perfect world; the myriad of current and anticipated human and social problems, and the extensive pressure to design, implement, and refine programs to mitigate and control them, are the impetus for evaluation.

IMPETUS FOR INTERVENTIONS AND EVALUATIONS

In the overall shape of things, evaluators' contributions to the identification and ranking of human and social deficiencies and to the innovation and refinement of programs to deal with them are modest. Evaluation researchers must be humble about their influence on these matters in light of the actions of political bodies, advocacy groups, investigative reporters, and charismatic personalities. The post-World War II attention to mental illness to a large extent was related to the efforts of a single congressman; federal programs for mental retardation received a large boost during Kennedy's presidency because he had a retarded sibling; improved automobile safety can be credited to a considerable degree to Nader-led advocates; and efforts to control illegal and improper delivery of health and welfare services often come about because of exposés in the mass media and the activities of interest and pressure groups, including the organized efforts of clients themselves.

Nevertheless, evaluators do play a role (admittedly, a partly responsive one) in identifying the parameters of the problems requiring attention and the deficiencies and limitations in current efforts to intervene. What the evaluator adds, by what we here refer to as diagnostic procedures, are systematic and reproducible approaches to the identification of communal problems and the clarification of their scope.

The importance of diagnostic information cannot be overstated. While speculative, impressionistic, and even biased information may spur policymakers, planners, and funding organizations to initiate action, it is essential to have trustworthy information on potential program targets and on the context in which an intervention would operate *before* the program is started. So, too, before fine-tuning an existing initiative or curtailing an ongoing program, the problem's magnitude needs to be estimated. Here are a few examples of what happens when adequate diagnostic procedures are ignored:

- In a social intervention designed to provide rehabilitation treatments to juvenile delinquents in a midwestern suburb, it was discovered — after the program was under way — that there were virtually no juvenile delinquents in the community. The planners assumed that because juvenile delinquency was a general social problem, it would also be one in their particular community as well.

- Planners of many of the urban renewal projects undertaken during the 1960s assumed that persons living in "dilapidated" buildings regarded their housing as defective, would support the demolition of their homes, and would accept relocation in replacement housing. In city after city, residents of urban renewal areas have vigorously opposed the urban renewal projects designed by city planners.

- Media programs designed to encourage people to seek physical examinations in order to detect early signs of cancer had the effect of swamping health centers with more clients than they could handle, since many hypochondriacal persons without any symptoms of cancer were stimulated by the media effort to believe they were experiencing warning signs.

- In an educational television project designed to improve the literacy skills of urban adults in a lesser developed country, it was found after the program had begun that the majority of adults without educational skills did not have access to a television set.

- A birth control project was expanded to reduce the reportedly high rate of abortion in a large urban center. The program failed to attract many additional participants, and it was discovered subsequently that most of the potential clients were already being served. For the most part, potential clients consisted of young women who came to the city from rural areas; a very high proportion of urban residents already practiced contraception.

In all of the examples cited, diagnostic research might have provided information that would have prevented problems of program implementation. It should be noted that these are examples in which the intervention did not fail — it was simply not delivered, because the target population did not exist, did not seek the program provided, was incorrectly identified, or made demands the intervention was incapable of meeting.

ASSESSMENT OF INTERVENTION NEED

A critical step in the design of an innovative program is to verify that a problem either currently ignored or being unsuccessfully treated exists in sufficient degree to warrant a new or additional intervention. Further, justification of ongoing programs and efforts to refine them typically requires evidence of the persistence of unresolved defects in social conditions or in the programs' delivery systems. Verifying and mapping out the extent and location of a problem and its attendant target population is called *need assessment*. Need assessment is essential because both professionals and community members, in their zeal to maintain and expand programs in which they have some self-interest, may often overestimate the size or character of the need. In some cases, although a problem — the prevalence of physical disabilities, for example — may be obviously serious and widespread enough to warrant an intervention, information on its distributional characteristics may be needed. Thus, if physical disabilities are predominantly a problem of older persons, arising from age-related infirmities, the treatment may be different from that for disabilities among younger persons. Need assessments, then, are undertaken to estimate the number and program-relevant characteristics of targets.

What Is a Target?

Targets are often individuals. But they may be groups (families, work teams, firms, establishments, and so on), geographically and politically related areas (such as small communities in a particular region), or physical units (houses, road systems, and the like). Whatever the target, it is imperative at the outset of the diagnostic effort to define the unit of analysis clearly. Definitional criteria vary. In the case of individuals, targets are usually identified in terms of one or more of the following: social and demographic characteristics; location; or targets' problems, difficulties, and conditions. Targets of an educational project in which individuals are pivotal might be specified as male children between ages 10 and 14 who reside in a school district and who are between one and three years below their normal grade in school.

When aggregates (groups and organizations) are targets, they are often defined in terms of the characteristics of the individuals that constitute them — their informal and formal collective properties and shared problems. An organizational target might be elementary schools (K-8) with at least 300 pupils and in which at least 30 percent of the pupils come from households with incomes below the poverty line.

Direct and Indirect Targets

As we noted in Chapter 2, targets may also be regarded as *direct* or *indirect,* depending on whether treatments are delivered to the targets immediately (directly) or eventually (indirectly). Most programs specify direct targets. This is clearly the case in medical interventions, where the person with an affliction directly receives a physician's attention. In some cases, however, either for economic or for feasibility reasons, programs are intended to affect target populations indirectly, by making their immediate targets a population or condition that will eventually impact on those intended to receive benefits. In a rural development project, as an illustration, influential farmers are selected from small communities and provided with intensive training programs. Afterward, they are to return to their own communities and communicate their new knowledge to other farmers. Again, a project that identifies its direct targets as substandard dwelling units may be intended to impact (indirectly) on the occupants of those dwellings.

If targets are defined as indirect, the effectiveness of a program depends to a large extent on the pathways leading from immediate to ultimate targets. The effectiveness of the project that uses influential farmers depends heavily on the abilities and motivation of those farmers to communicate their knowledge to other members of their communities. Similarly, if there is a strong relationship between housing quality and household health, investment in physical improvement of housing may be justified; but if the correlation is low or essentially zero, such investment is likely to be wasteful and ineffective.

Specifying Targets

Specification of the size and distribution of targets may seem simple at first glance. But there are practically no human and social defects that can be estimated easily, by merely counting individuals or other units with a particular problem or condition. Take a single illustration: What is the population of persons with cancer in a given community? First, it depends on whether or not one counts only permanent residents or includes temporary ones as well (which whould be extremely important in Miami Beach). Second, are "recovered" cases counted, or are those without a relapse for, say, five years eliminated from the estimate? Third, the estimate needs to take into account the purpose for which it is being used. If it is to be used in designing a special nursing-home program, persons with skin cancer should not be included, since their condition rarely requires inpatient services.

An illustration of the considerations that go into specifying targets is provided in Exhibit 3-A, which is extracted from a landmark article that

(text continued on p. 97)

Exhibit 3-A: How Poverty Is Measured

Counting the poor is an exercise in the art of the impossible. For deciding who is poor, prayers are more relevant than calculation because poverty, like beauty, lies in the eye of the beholder. Poverty is a value judgment; it is not something one can verify or demonstrate, except by inference and suggestion, even with a measure of error. To say who is poor is to use all sorts of value judgments. The concept has to be limited by the purpose which is to be served by the definition. There is no particular reason to count the poor unless you are going to do something about them. Whatever the possibilities of socioeconomic research in general, when it comes to defining poverty, you can only be more subjective or less so. You cannot be nonsubjective.

Defining the Issue

In the Social Security Administration, poverty was first defined in terms of the public or policy issue: To how many people, and to which ones, did we wish to direct policy concern. Even when we bore this aim in mind, the level of living we used to separate the "haves" from the "have nots" could be as generous or as rigorous as we pleased. The level could be understated so that everyone who was counted in the "have not" group really did not have enough. If we did the reverse, we ran the risk of counting some who should not be there. There is, in short, no one perfect scheme and no value-free scheme.

Since we were attempting to illustrate the level of public concern, we wanted to be sure that every family or consumer unit had its fair chance to be numbered among those who would be considered as needing attention. Indeed, it was precisely to ensure consideration of the needs of large families as well as small, and of young people as well as old, that we refined the initial standard developed by the Council of Economic Advisers. Their standard said that any family of two or more with less than $3,000 annual income, and any single person living alone with less than $1,500, would be considered poor for purposes of antipoverty program planning — but not for program eligibility. This original standard led to the odd result that an elderly couple with $2,900 income for the year would be considered poor, but a family with a husband, wife, and four little children with $3,100 income would not be.

Moreover, when we looked at the poor distributed demographically, by comparison with the total population, we made some unusual discoveries. For example, the percentage of the families classified as poor who had no children was higher than that for the population as a whole; and to make it even more unrealistic, the percentage of the poor families with four children or more was actually less than the representation of such families in the population. We did not think this was correct, so we tried to vary the poverty line — the necessary minimum of resources — with the size and composition of the family. The reason this had not been done by the Council is that no such data were available to them then.

Setting the Benchmark

A concept that can help influence public thinking must be socially and politically credible. We need benchmarks to distinguish the population group that we want to worry about. A benchmark should neither select a group so small, in relation to all the population, that it hardly seems to deserve a general program, nor so large that a solution to the problem appears impossible. For example, in the 1930s, President Roosevelt said, "I see before me one-third of a Nation ill-clothed, ill-housed, and ill-fed." This fraction is now part of our history. No matter how we get our numbers today, if more than a third of the population is called poor, it will lose value as a public reference point.

At the Social Security Administration, we decided that we would develop two measures of need, and state, on the basis of the income sample of the Current Population Survey, how many and what kinds of families these measures delineated. It was not the Social Security Administration that labeled the poverty line. It remained for the Office of Economic Opportunity and the Council of Economic Advisers to select the lower of the two measures and decide they would use it as the working tool. The best you can say for the measure is that at a time when it seemed useful, it was there. It is interesting that few outside the Social Security Administration ever wanted to talk about the higher measure. Everybody wanted only to talk about the lower one, labeled the "poverty line," which yielded roughly the same number of people in poverty as the original $3,000 measure did, except that fewer families with more children were substituted for a larger number of older families without children.

Thresholds of Poverty

We have developed two poverty thresholds, corresponding to what we call the "poor" and "near-poor." These thresholds are set separately for 124 different kinds of families, based on the sex of the head, the number of children under 18, the number of adults, and whether or not the household lives on a farm. The threshold is defined as an attempt to "specify the minimum money income that could support an average family of given composition at the lowest level consistent with the standards of living prevailing in this country. It is based on the amount needed by families of different size and type to purchase a nutritionally adequate diet on the assumption that no more than a third of the family income is used for food." The two thresholds were developed from food consumption surveys that revealed that the average expenditure for food by all families was about one-third of income.

An assumption was made that the poor would have the same flexibility in allocating income as the rest of the population but that, obviously, their margin for choice would be less. The amount allocated to food from the average expenditure was cut to the minimum that the Agriculture Department said could still provide American families with an adequate diet. We used the low cost plan to characterize the near-poor and for the poor an even lower one, the economy food plan.

SOURCE: From M. Orshansky, "Perspectives on Poverty: How Poverty Is Measured." *Monthly Labor Review*, 92 (February 1969): 37-41. Reprinted by permission.

greatly influenced the development of the "poverty line" concept, a definition of poverty that is still employed today.

Target Boundaries

Adequate target specification establishes boundaries, that is, rules of inclusion and exclusion. One risk in specifying target populations is to make the definition too broad or overinclusive. Regarding a criminal as anyone who has violated any law or administrative regulation is useless, since only the most saintly individuals have not in some way or another, at some time or another, violated wittingly or otherwise a law or regulation. Stakeholders committed to alleviating poverty may describe their target population as persons or households whose income cannot support a reasonable standard of living. Clearly, such a definition cannot be the starting point for a useful need assessment or program design. It does not provide criteria specific enough to determine the relevant target group. An overinclusive definition, therefore, may result in overestimating need and thereby causing either uneconomical investment in an intervention whose targets have little to gain from it, or a watering down of the program in order to serve an excessively large target group.

Definitions may also prove too restrictive, or underinclusive — to the point where almost no one falls into the target population. For example, in a program aimed at the rehabilitation of released felons in New York City, it was decided to exclude persons with any history of drug or alcohol abuse. The prevalence of substance abuse was so great among released prisoners that only one of ten was eligible to be included in the target population.

Feasibility

In addition, useful definitions are those that are feasible to apply. A specification that hinges on some characteristic of persons that is difficult to observe — for example, a favorable attitude toward evaluation research — may be virtually impossible to put into practice. Complex definitions requiring much detailed information are just as difficult to apply in selection and should be avoided: The data required to seek out targets defined as farmers who have planted barley for at least two seasons and who have two adolescent sons who are members of a producers' cooperative would be difficult if not impossible to accumulate.

In general, the more criteria a definition has, the smaller the number of units that can qualify for inclusion in the target population. (The farmers satisfying the above criteria would be a small group indeed.) Complex specifications are therefore kin to narrow ones, and carry with them the same risks.

Varying Perspectives on Target Specification

Another issue in the definition of target problems and populations arises from the potentially differing perspectives of professionals, policymakers, and potential recipients of services. What appears as a human or social problem to one group may not be perceived as such by another. Thus, the planners of a program concerned with improving the quality of housing available to poor persons may have a professional understanding of housing quality that stresses criteria different from those of the people who will live in that housing. For example, in the Experimental Housing Allowance Project (Abt Associates, 1977), one of the building standards concerned the ratio of floor area to window area in bedrooms; housing in which the ratio fell below 10 was considered inadequate. The perspectives of homeowners and renters who occupied the buildings were quite different, however; they regarded such housing as quite adequate.

Discrepancies also may exist between the views of policymakers and those of other groups. Congress may plan to alleviate the financial burden on the federal government by reducing special aid to victims of natural disasters. One means of doing so is to encourage states and local governments to invest in such disaster-mitigating measures as flood-plain land use management and building codes that lower risks of damage and injury. States and especially local governments, however, may object strongly to the plan, on the grounds that since floods seldom occur on their flood plains, such measures would burden them unfairly. Indeed, true to their name, 100-year floods occur in any one place only once in every century (on average). However, from the federal perspective, 100-year floods may occur as often as once every few days, since the federal government must be concerned with all the flood plains in the United States (Wright et al., 1979).

While research obviously cannot settle the issue of which perspective is "correct," it can eliminate conflicts that might arise from groups talking past each other. Planning research may involve obtaining need

(text continued on p. 103)

Exhibit 3-B: Assessing Community Mental Health Needs

The consumer model presents the program planner with a method of assessing mental health needs using the consumer as the major source of input. The consumer is defined as any community member who resides within a given geographic area. The model supplies information on the priorities of need for additional services by target problem, age group, and geographic area. Within the model, five consumer groups are surveyed:

1. *Mental Health Agencies* — agencies and individuals that directly or indirectly treat people with mental health problems;

2. *Secondary Related Agencies* — agencies that make referrals to mental health services;

3. *High-Risk Individuals* — individuals who, because of past or present behavior, are using or have used mental health services;

4. *Community and Civic Groups* — groups within the community that are organized around a common goal or for a specific purpose;

5. *Community-at-Large* — a sample of area residents selected at random who may or may not be associated with any of the other four groups.

In order to determine the feasibility of using the model, consumer groups in the Kearny Mesa subregional area of San Diego County were surveyed. Of the 42 subregional areas in the county, Kearny Mesa was chosen because it closely approximated the sociodemographic characteristics of the overall county population.

Questionnaires and Interviews

Mental Health Agencies. Included were a school for the emotionally disturbed, a runaway and family crisis center, a private psychiatric hospital, a family services center, training centers for retardates, outpatient clinics, and a residential treatment facility for children. Of the 13 agencies that received the questionnaire, all 13 (100 percent) returned completed forms.

Secondary Related Agencies. Included were schools, the probation department, the coroner, Juvenile Hall, a general hospital, a convalescent home, a legal services center, a speech and hearing clinic, and an unemployment office. Of the 33 agencies that received a questionnaire, 22 (66.6 percent) returned completed forms.

The questionnaire asked both groups to rank the target problems that required the first, second, and third most immediate attention within three age groups: youth (under 18), adult (18-59), and geriatric (60+). In addition, information was sought regarding the quantity and type of programs already existing in the Kearny Mesa area. Questions were asked about number of persons served, type of problems treated, waiting lists, and age, race, and geographic area served.

Community and Civic Groups. Included were women's auxiliaries of public agencies, a women's social club, a parent-teacher association, men's service organizations, a YMCA, and a boy's club. Of the ten groups mailed a questionnaire, five responded.

The questionnaire required the respondent to check the services that should be made available to a greater number of people in the Kearny Mesa area for the three age groups. In order to ensure a representative sampling across ethnic and socioeconomic groups, each group was asked to state the race, age, income level, and geographic level of members.

Community-at-Large. Questionnaires were mailed to a sample of residents selected at random from the Haines Directory of Locations, which lists all addresses by street and census tract. Two addresses were selected at random from each street. Because of the cost factor, only 594 households, 16 percent of the Kearny Mesa households, were surveyed. Of the 594 households, 53, or 8.9 percent, returned the questionnaire. The 53 households included 176 individuals, or 3.3 per household.

The questionnaire asked respondents to check the services that should be made available to a greater number of people in the Kearny Mesa area. The questionnaire also asked the consumer to indicate the race, age, income, living arrangement, and type of residence of the family members. One open-ended question was included, which asked the consumer to list the person or persons to whom he would go for help if he had a personal problem.

SOURCE: From A. T. Weiss, "The Consumer Model of Assessing Community Health Needs." *Evaluation,* Vol. 2 (1975): 71. Reprinted by permission.

Exhibit 3-C: Need Assessments of Youths

The most recent and comprehensive attempt to develop a methodology and instruments for need assessments of youths is the work by the Behavioral Research and Evaluation Corporation (BREC). The first stage of the recommended strategy is a "social area analysis" which provides information on the social, demographic, and economic characteristics of the community, with special emphasis on youth, and the structure and organization of the community. Here the available census data, police and court records, school data, welfare, unemployment, etc. are gathered and analyzed in order to understand the nature of the community and the extent to which broad categories of problems are present.

The "Youth Needs Assessment" that BREC has developed is intended to survey the needs of all the youth in a population, as opposed to youths who are receiving services. The suggested methodology involves simple random sampling in the schools, or cluster sampling in the schools or homes. Four types of items have been developed for the survey: (1) problems, difficulties, and needs, specifying frequency of their occurrence and perceived seriousness; (2) feelings, attitudes, and behavior regarding four factors: "(a) perceived opportunities for achieving personal goals and desired social roles, (b) perceived negative labeling by parents, teachers, and friends,(c) feelings of alienation and rejection, and (d) self-reported involvement in delinquent behavior"; (3) youths' perceptions and evaluation of available services and agencies; and (4) personal background and socioeconomic data of the respondents. In addition to uncovering needs, these measures also serve as baseline data for subsequent impact assessments.

The perceptions of agency staff regarding youth needs can be measured with the same instrument used for youths, where agency personnel are asked to estimate the percentage of all youths having the problem and to assess the problem's seriousness.

SOURCE: Summary, by permission, of D. C. Elliott et al., *Research Handbook for Community Planning and Feedback Instruments*, Vol. 1 (rev.). Boulder, Colo.: Behavioral Research Institute, 1976.

assessments from the several perspectives. Exhibit 3-B describes a method of assessing community mental health needs by querying five stakeholder groups, each of which contributes its particular perspective. Exhibit 3-C provides an example for youth services, indicating that a variety of sources may be necessary to express the perspectives of agencies, youth, and parents.

Information collected for varying perspectives on needs may lead to reconceptualizing the problem or the prospective intervention, or may indicate the advisability of abandoning the program (especially if the different perspectives turn out to be intensely held and highly contradictory). The consequences of proceeding under the illusion that there is consensus when in fact there is considerable conflict can be seen in the fate of the urban renewal program (Wilson, 1966). This program was predicated on presumed agreement regarding important criteria of housing dilapidation and obsolescence by planners, residents, and institutions. The criteria used by planners often did not correspond with those of residents. Consequently urban renewal projects in city after city created rancorous conflict — so much that in many cases the programs were gradually abandoned.

CONCEPTUALIZING PROGRAM TARGETS

Estimating the nature of a target problem and the size of a target population and its characteristics is a prerequisite to documenting the need for a program, its scope, and the special ways it must be designed to fit in with the characteristics of the target population. As program planning continues, it is necessary to decide on the procedures whereby the target population can be efficiently and economically distinguished from nontarget units during project implementation. There are a number of different concepts that underlie target selection.

Population at Risk

In the specification of targets, the public health concept of *population at risk* is helpful, particularly in projects that are preventive in character. The term refers to that segment of a population that is exclusively or largely subject, with significant probabilities, to developing a condition. Thus, the population at risk in fertility control studies is usually defined as women of childbearing age. Similarly, projects that are designed to mitigate the effects of typhoons and hurricanes may define targets as communities located in the typical paths of tropical storms.

A population at risk can only be defined in probabilistic terms. Thus, women of childbearing age may be the population at risk in a fertility study, but individual women may or may not conceive a child within a given period of time. Hence, specifying a population at risk usually means being overinclusive, that is, citing many persons as targets who may not be in need of treatment.

Need and Demand

A *population at need* is a group of potential targets who *currently* manifest a given condition. For our earlier example of projects directed at alleviating poverty, one may define the target population as families whose income, adjusted for family size, is below a certain minimum. A population at need can usually be defined in absolute terms; that is, one can identify a precise criterion for including a unit among targets (e.g., a screening technique). For instance, there are reliable and valid tests to determine the degree of literacy of any person. These can be used to specify a target population of functionally illiterate persons.

Need must be distinguished from *demand*. As illustrated in Exhibit 3-D, although a fair proportion of new homebuyers need "warranty insurance" to protect them from defective dwellings, neither a mandatory nor a voluntary public program appears feasible because of both costs and homeowner disinterest (i.e., lack of demand).

Exhibit 3-D: Homeowner Warranties: A Study of Need and Demand

The decision to purchase a home often is made without complete information concerning the structural soundness of the dwelling or the condition of its mechanical systems.

This paper presents detailed information on the nature and magnitude of unanticipated home-repair costs on the basis of data obtained from a HUD-sponsored survey of some 1,800 households that purchased existing homes two years prior to the survey. The potential market demand for home inspection and warranty programs is estimated on the basis of data obtained from a second survey of approximately 1,800 recent home purchasers.

It is clear that unanticipated repair expenses pose a serious problem for some purchasers of existing homes, and a government-provided home inspection and warranty program could clearly be of considerable benefit to such purchasers. At the same time, however, many other home purchasers now escape serious unanticipated repair costs, and a mandatory program would result in increased housing expenses for this group without providing them with additional benefits. It also is apparent from the data that at the present time a majority of home purchasers do not consider the benefits of home inspection and warranty services to be worth the cost. Making policy choices in the light of these findings, therefore, becomes a matter of judgment with regard to how appropriately to trade off the costs and benefits to the various individuals who would be affected. Our own judgment is that a mandatory program would not be a desirable policy initiative at the present time, because the benefits of such a program do not, in our judgment, outweigh the substantial administrative costs and the loss of individual choice that a mandatory program would involve.

It is also our belief that a voluntary government-run home inspection and warranty program should not be set up at this time. This judgment is based both on the low projected participation rates for such a program, noted above, and on the fact that a private market for such services seems to be developing.

SOURCE: Adapted, with permission, from J. Alan Brewster, Irving Crespi, Richard Kaluzny, James Ohls, and Cynthia Thomas, *Journal of the American Real Estate and Urban Economics Association*, Volume 8, No. 2, 1980: 207-215.

Actually, some "need assessments" undertaken to estimate the extent of a problem and to serve as the basis for designing programs are "at-risk assessments" or "demand assessments," rather than true need assessments, according to the definitions just offered. This is the case because it is either technically infeasible to measure need or impractical to implement a program that deals only with the at-need population. For example, although only sexually active females require family planning information, the target population for most such programs is *all* fertile women, generally defined by an age span such as 15 to 50 (i.e., those assumed to be at risk). Again, while all nonliterate adults are the at-need group for an evening educational program, only those who are willing or who can be persuaded to participate can be considered the target population (i.e., those at demand). Clearly, the distinctions between populations at risk, at need, and at demand are important for estimating the scope of a problem, anticipating target population size, and subsequently designing, implementing, and evaluating the program.

Incidence and Prevalence

Another useful distinction is the difference between incidence and prevalence. *Incidence* refers to the number of new cases of a particular problem that are identified or arise in a defined geographical area during a specified period of time. *Prevalence* refers to the number of existing cases in a particular geographic area at a specified time.

Again, the concepts are derived from health efforts, where the distinctions between the terms are sharp. For example, the incidence of influenza during a particular month would refer to the number of new cases spotted during the month. The prevalence of flu would refer to the number of people so afflicted at any time in a particular month. In planning projects in the health sector, one is generally interested in incidence when dealing with disorders that are of short duration, such as upper respiratory infections and minor accidents. Prevalence is the important concept for those problems that cannot be eradicated quickly but require long-term management and treatment efforts. These include chronic diseases such as cancer and clinically observable long-term illnesses such as amoebic dysentery and severe malnutrition.

The concepts of incidence and prevalence have been adapted to the area of social problems. Sometimes their uses are clear. For example, in studying the impact of crime on victims, the critical problem is the incidence of victimization — the numbers of new cases that occur per interval of time for a given area. In providing services for alleviating child abuse, new cases of child abuse per month for a city may be the best measure of the need for intervention into that problem.

For other social problems, it is often not clear whether one should define target populations in terms of prevalence or incidence. In dealing with the unemployment problem, it is important to know the numbers or proportions of the total population unemployed at a particular point in time. When the concern is more with the provision of financial support for the unemployed, however, it is not clear whether the definition should refer to persons who *are* unemployed at a particular time or to those who *become* unemployed in a given period. The principle involved centers on the issue of whether one is concerned with detecting and treating cases as they appear, or with detecting existing cases in a population, whatever their time of origin.

Rates

In addition to estimating the size of a problem group, it is also important to know about the *rate* of a particular problem. Many times it is critical to be able to express incidence or prevalence as a rate: The number of new cases of unemployment or underemployment in an area experiencing a recession might be described per 100 or per 1,000 of a population (e.g., 133 per 1,000).

Rates or percentages are especially critical in identifying the characteristics of the target population. For example, in describing the size and characteristics of crime victims, it is important to have estimates by sex and age group. Although almost every age group is subject to victimization in some sort of crime incident, young people are much more likely to be the victims of robbery and assault while older persons are more likely to have experienced burglary and larceny; men are considerably less likely to be the victims of sexual abuse than women; and so on. Being able to estimate targets by various characteristics allows a program to be planned and developed in ways that maximize opportunities to include the most appropriate participants and to tailor the program to the particular characteristics of sizable groups.

Estimates of target populations and their characteristics may be made at several levels of disaggregation. For example, illiteracy rates, calculated by dividing the number of functional illiterates in various age groups by the total number of persons in such age groups, allow one to estimate the target populations that can be reached by tailoring a project to specific age-period cohorts. More powerful statistical techniques may usefully be employed to take into account additional sociodemographic variables simultaneously.

In most cases, it is not only traditional but also useful to specify rates by age and sex. In communities in which there are marked cultural differences, variations in racial, ethnic, and religious background also become important denominators for the disaggregation of characteristics. Other variables useful in identifying characteristics of the target population include socioeconomic status, geographic location, and residential mobility. (See Exhibit 3-E for an example of crime victimization rates disaggregated by age, sex, and race.)

A final set of rates may refer to problems associated with ability to participate in the program and measures related to program implementation. Thus, it may be advantageous in various technical training programs to estimate rates for groups that require 15 minutes, one-half hour, or more that one hour to reach training centers.

Exhibit 3-E: Crime Victimization Rates

Personal Crimes: Victimization Rates for Persons Age 12 and Over, by Race, Sex, and Age of Victims and Type of Crime (rate per 1,000 resident population in each group)

Race, Sex, and Age	Crimes of Violence	Crimes of Theft
White		
Male		
12-15 (14,500)	129	69
16-19 (15,700)	157	133
20-24 (28,100)	139	164
25-34 (29,100)	112	150
35-49 (26,700)	51	93
50-64 (27,700)	54	69
65 and over (19,900)	38	66
Female		
12-15 (13,100)	64	56
16-19 (19,200)	65	187
20-24 (33,400)	73	229
25-34 (31,400)	62	190
35-49 (29,700)	34	131
50-64 (36,500)	31	81
65 and over (34,400)	14	59
Black		
Male		
12-15 (4,200)	71	[1]48
16-19 (3,600)	113	97
20-24 (4,800)	173	160
25-34 (5,900)	59	131
35-49 (5,800)	65	100
50-64 (3,700)	56	81
65 and over (1,800)	154	[1]91
Female		
12-15 (5,000)	47	56
16-19 (4,500)	102	94
20-24 (7,000)	67	82
25-34 (10,100)	64	114
35-49 (8,200)	46	114
50-64 (5,400)	[1]30	123
65 and over (2,200)	0	[1]66

NOTE: Numbers in parentheses refer to population in the group.
[1]Estimate, based on about 10 or fewer sample cases, is statistically unreliable.

SOURCE: From U.S. Department of Justice, *Criminal Victimization Surveys in Boston: A National Crime Survey Report.* Washington, DC: Government Printing Office, 1977, p. 26.

SELECTING PROGRAM TARGETS

Programs are most efficient and effective when the targets reached are restricted entirely to units that need the intervention. That is, in the terms previously used in our section on target boundaries, there is neither over- nor underinclusion.

Overinclusion

Especially in the case of projects for which resources are insufficient to cover all potential targets, selection is generally regarded as most efficient if treatment is given mainly to targets with the highest probability of successful outcome. Such an approach maximizes the likelihood of favorable costs-to-benefits ratios and the probability that positive impact can be demonstrated.

For example, a program designed to strengthen the nutritional content of children's diets by providing school lunches at low cost would be inefficient if it reached a large proportion of children who already had adequate diets. This would be the case even if all children with nutritional deficiencies were also served by the program. Thus, if the program covered all children with nutritional deficiencies but 90 percent of those served did not suffer from that condition, a large proportion of the resources going into the program would be "wasted." Such overinclusion often results in highly uneconomical interventions.

However, the more precise and exacting the selection of targets becomes, the more expensive are the selection procedures involved. A selection procedure for a project to combat functional illiteracy that specified targets by means of screening large numbers of persons through elaborate tests might cost a great deal for each case of illiteracy uncovered, thereby exhausting resources that could be used to provide services.

**Overinclusion and Evaluation
of Program Utility**

The consequences of such inefficiency are often serious for the overall program effort. It is questionable in terms of costs, for example, to expose entire communities to educational, housing, medical, and cultural programs when only a small percentage of the community population is "at risk." Moreover, from the standpoint of estimating program impacts, failure to define the population at risk effectively lessens the chances of detecting positive effects. This is the problem of having too many "false positives" in the target group for an impact evaluation (see Chapter 9). Consider a program aimed at learning disabilities that covers all schoolchildren in a community in which only 5 percent of the children may have learning disabilities. If the program is only effective with the 5 percent, differences in learning from pretest to posttest are unlikely to be revealed (unless the population of schoolchildren is large), since the vast majority of children given treatment would not need it and thus could not be expected to benefit.

Underinclusion

Underinclusion may not only deny opportunities for program participation to targets at need or highly at risk; there is also a tradeoff between selection costs and the resources available for treatment delivery. It may be possible in a preventive health-care program to identify by laboratory tests those persons in a community who have not developed an immunity to polio and to provide only this group with vaccinations. Such a procedure, however, would be foolish, since the necessary resources to undertake the screening are greater than the costs of providing polio vaccinations to all community members. Similarly, a project in which a central water supply is piped to all dwellings in a community, including those that already enjoy potable water, may seem overzealous. However, costs of tailoring the project to skip certain housing units, the possible future contamination of currently potable water, and difficulties of obtaining community acceptance of a selective project present arguments against restricting the target households to those with contaminated wells.

There are also some psychological and political reasons for allowing a looser definition of the target population than necessary solely from a population-at-need or -at-risk standpoint. First, efficient identification of target populations with a condition that may stigmatize them raises serious ethical considerations: Effective screening to locate mildly retarded children for a special project may result in invidious labeling by peers and teachers, with the consequence that any gains from a selective program are far overshadowed by the negative effects of the labeling process. Thus, it might be better to open the project to all children (or at least to those less likely to experience deleterious labeling effects).

Second, when programs include opportunities, goods, and services valued by all community members, and only those with particular characteristics or who live in particular circumstances are admitted, both policymakers and program staff may have to face considerable antagonism and loss of community support. This may explain why projects are underzealous in identifying target populations and selecting those with a definite, high probability of being at need or risk.

PROCEDURES FOR TARGET ESTIMATION

A wide variety of techniques can be employed in order to estimate the scope of problems requiring new and refined intervention efforts, and to estimate the target population in ways that allow for the most effective deployment of available resources and staff. These techniques vary in their complexity and expense. The ones noted here are listed in ascending order of complexity and costs.

Key Informant Approach

The key informant approach is a simple and inexpensive informal survey technique that involves identifying, selecting, and questioning knowledgeable leaders and experts in order to construct estimates of target problems and populations. The technique provides a broad picture of the needs and services perceived as important and the characteristics of the population requiring them. It has the additional advantage of developing the support of community influentials, which may be necessary for project development and continuation.

The major limitation of the key informant approach is that it has the built-in biases of the individuals and the organizations surveyed. It neglects the possibility that the characteristics of targets and the incidence and prevalence of the target problem may be perceived incorrectly by leaders and experts. Moreover, the perspectives of leaders and experts may be colored by their lack of intimate knowledge of all segments of what may be a complex and widespread society, and by their "interests." For example, a landlord's view of housing problems may be very different from that of the tenants.

The key informant approach works best when leaders and experts are asked for specific, concrete information. Thus, one is usually risking a biased perspective by asking leaders to indicate the serious social problems in their communities. In contrast, identifying how many families are located within a block of public transportation lines is usually less subject to upward or downward biases, especially if one consults those familiar with local public transportation services.

When using the key informant approach, it is good strategy to draw up a thorough list of potential interviewees prior to the survey. If the evaluators know the leaders and experts of a small community well, they might draw up a list of some twenty-five key leaders. If they do not know the community, an alternative approach is to start with a smaller number of informants, say five to ten, and then to use a technique referred to as "snowballing." With this technique, the informant is asked at the end of the interview to provide the names of one or two persons who are also knowledgeable about the particular problem sector. Snowballing probably should not be carried beyond fifty interviews.

The two main criteria for the selection of a key informant should be: (1) knowledge of the community, its people, their needs, and the patterns of service already being received; and (2) leadership potential. The first criterion argues for interviewing local professionals and experts (teachers, doctors, nurses, local technical experts, civil servants, and the like) who by virtue of their occupations are brought into contact with a range of persons, households, and conditions in an area. The second criterion is argued from the point of view of possible political benefit to the project. The use of leaders may provide project managers an opportunity to obtain their support, at best, and neutrality, at least. This may prove useful at the project implementation stage if the project meets with some potential opposition among target populations. Other criteria may include accessibility to project managers, whether a potential informant represents a particular subgroup or population, and whether the person is a consumer or a potential consumer of the program.

With this technique, it is useful to construct a data guide in advance — that is, a list of questions that each informant is asked to complete or that is filled in after an informal discussion with the key informant (see Exhibit 3-F for an example). Using a data guide facilitates more rapid collating of the responses of the key informants and helps to standardize information from all informants. Once all the informants have been contacted and interviewed, the information should be summarized and, if possible, put into tabular form. Sometimes it is valuable after the data are tabulated to provide feedback to the key informants, a step that allows checking the information and verifying the collated findings. It also provides a means of keeping the key informants involved in the planning and development of the program.

Community Forum Approach

The community forum approach resembles an open town meeting — a gathering of members of a designated community organization or even an informal group. It is in part a technique to gain citizen involvement, but it is also a way of obtaining estimates from a variety of individuals about the incidence and prevalence of particular problems and about the identifiable characteristics of the targets. The approach also can be used to gather data on how well a delivery system is perceived to be working.

The utility of the community forum approach depends heavily on whether attendance at such open meetings constitutes a balanced

**Exhibit 3-F: Suggested Interview Guide for
Key Informant Approach to Assessing
Community Mental Health Needs**

Possible subjects to discuss with each person interviewed:

I. Community Problems (general)
  • In order of priority of importance.
  • Existing sources of help for each problem.
  • Unmet needs and problems, by groups.
  • Who gets most consistently left out of services?
  • Which problems are not visible?

II. Mental Health Problems
  • A priority listing of seriousness (including prevalence).
  • Existing sources of help for each problem.
  • Community attitudes toward use of public mental health services.
  • Groups that get most mental health services.
  • Groups that are most underserved.

III. Attitudes toward the CMHC
    (community mental health center)
  • Who gets to the CMHC for help?
  • What other mental health resources do people in the community use? Who uses them?
  • Who does not/will not go to the CMHC and why?
  • Which groups in need of mental health services get the least help? (Locate these as possible on a map of community.)

SOURCE: From National Institute of Mental Health, *A Working Manual of Simple Program Evaluation Techniques for Community Mental Health Centers.* Washington, DC: Government Printing Office, 1976, p. 107.

representation of involved community members or targets, and whether participants feel free to express themselves openly. The technique may be superior to the key informant approach for obtaining valid information if the evaluators succeed in bringing together a cross-section of the stakeholders. Often, this can be accomplished by having influential persons or respected organizations sponsor the meeting. Therefore, this technique is sometimes used as a follow-up to the key informant approach.

The forum approach is economical; it allows one to learn the perceptions and diagnoses of a large number of persons at relatively little cost. The limitations are fairly obvious. A forum may restrict the kinds of information persons will reveal. It may also hinder expression of views to those who are most likely to participate, and probably biases against obtaining information and perspectives from individuals who perceive themselves as less powerful in the community. A forum may become an arena in which local political cleavages manifest themselves, and thereby lead to more rancor than data.

The forum technique is most effective when program objectives and delivery system operations can be stated explicitly in ways understandable to the forum group. Otherwise, the information received may prove to be valuable in terms of general need assessment but may not provide estimates of the extent of a particular problem and the characteristics of the targets.

Sometimes, in order to obtain a wider cross-section than one can expect by having a general forum, an effort is made to develop several meetings of the same kind but with varying, carefully defined and selected populations. For example, in communities with several religious groups, separate meetings might be held at the different churches under the sponsorship of local religious leaders.

The strictures on use applying to the key informant approach also apply to the community forum approach. The potential for biased estimates of need, size, and extent of target populations is considerable. This technique should be used only to supplement other methods, to build up supportive consensus for a program, or in the absence of enough resources to employ some of the better methods we describe in the following sections.

Rates under Treatment Approach

The commonly used rates under treatment approach estimates target populations via the services utilized for the same target problem in a similar community. The assumption underlying this approach is that the characteristics of the desired target population and its size will closely parallel the attributes of those who have already received treatment. Sometimes, particularly in communities where there have been no previous interventions, estimates may be derived from one or more geographical areas that resemble the proposed project site. If areas can be found in which the social and cultural properties of the individuals mirror those in the project areas, estimates of target populations in terms of size and characteristics can be derived.

It is almost certain that estimates derived from the rates under treatment approach will be biased downward. Projects rarely attain full coverage of a target population; therefore, any given project's clientele will be a selected subset of a target population. The selection may be forced by the scarcity of funds or by the failure of target populations to make use of the services offered. It may make sense in certain circumstances to regard such estimates as the lower bounds of the estimated size of a target population and to adjust them accordingly.

For example, the Uniform Crime Reports, published by the Department of Justice, are based on crimes reported to the police. The figures are then transmitted to the Federal Bureau of Investigation. The crime rates printed in these reports are, in principle, "rates under treatment" indices, expressing "cases" that have received some treatment (i.e., investigation) by local police departments. When compared with crimes reported in victimization surveys (in which persons are asked about crimes they have experienced as victims), it becomes obvious that the Uniform Crime Reports significantly underestimate (by a factor of about four) the total number of crimes in which a victim is involved. This underestimation occurs in part because some crimes are not reported to the police and in part because the police do not faithfully pass on to the FBI correct figures for all crimes reported to them.

In many ways, the use of service statistics and the opportunities to abstract information from records of treated populations appear to provide an attractive way to estimate target population. Rates under treatment are also used to estimate the extent of coverage of existing programs. For example, if unemployment information provides an estimate of 5,000 unemployed persons between 18 and 25 in a particular community, but statistics reveal only 250 persons of this age currently enrolled in the community's work training programs, it is clear that the programs must be modified.

A number of important cautions must be noted, however. In many interventions, the service records and statistics derived from them are unreliable. It is evident that many agencies regard the maintenance of records as a low-priority activity, particularly when there are strenuous demands for services. Also, since projects receive both economic and political support by demonstrating a large client population, there may be an effort to exaggerate the need for services and the extent of services rendered. Sometimes this is purposeful and other times it is generated more or less unconsciously from the enthusiasm of providers for their particular project.

Indicators Approach

Many federal, state, and community offices maintain relatively good statistical series that may be used as the basis for estimating target populations. Such series include data on trends in fertility, mortality, and the incidence of certain diseases; economic indicators of unemployment and personal and household income; and information on crime, poverty, and juvenile delinquency. In the United States, excellent data are available on the population and housing composition of states, local political jurisdictions (cities, towns, counties), and census tracts within urbanized areas. They can be obtained as published summaries or in the form of computer tapes for public use.

For social problems that are defined in terms for which census data are relevant, the decennial census can provide excellent information for need assessments and for the location of target populations. For instance, it is possible to use the census to locate persons and households by race, age, socioeconomic status, and condition of housing. For standard metropolitan statistical areas (SMSAs, defined as cities and surrounding counties with populations of 50,000 or more), data are available for census tracts — areas that average eight square miles and contain about 4,000 people. Exhibit 3-G describes the use of the 1970 Census to produce estimates of the target population for the Upward Bound and Talent Search projects.

Whether or not one can use census data in either published or unpublished form depends on how quickly the data become obsolete over time and on how relevant the data series is. In areas that have experienced considerable growth and change in population through inmigration, census data can become outdated within a few years, and hence may be useless for target population estimates.

Indicators do have another value, however. They are usually time series. Time-series data derive from observations made at regular intervals so that the trends of incidence and prevalence of particular problems can be assessed (Federal Statistical System, 1976). Sudden and sharp changes in these indicators often signal the emergence of phenomena that require action programs. For example, since there is a known correlation between unemployment and suicide rates, and the time-series data on unemployment point to a sharp rise in the number of unemployed workers, it can be anticipated that, likewise, there will be a marked increase in the number of persons who may want the services of a suicide intervention unit.

Exhibit 3-G: Estimating the Target Population of Upward Bound and Educational Talent Search Programs with Census Data

The purpose of the study was to estimate the size of the UB [Upward Bound] and ETS [Educational Talent Search] target population, and to describe its composition with respect to personal and demographic characteristics. In this study the target population was defined to include all persons from 14 to 24 years old in 1970, whose highest grade attended in school was between grade 6 and grade 12, and whose family income in 1969 was below the poverty cutoff. Persons included in the target population were further classified according to the United States Office of Education (USOE) region and state of their residence, sex, ethnoracial background, and school enrollment status.

Data contained in the 1970 Census of Population records indicated that the UB and ETS target population contained 3,880,000 persons, or 2 percent of the U.S. population in 1970. The target population contained 2.1 million women and 1.8 million men and its ethnoracial composition included 54 percent whites, 36 percent blacks, 10 percent of Spanish descent, and less than 1 percent persons of other ethnoracial backgrounds. In 1970, 2.1 million persons in the target population were enrolled in school between grades 6 and 12, and 1.8 million were not enrolled in school. Geographically, the largest number of persons in the target population were in USOE Region IV, which contained 1,051,200 persons or 27 percent of the total target population, followed by USOE Region VI, with 627,200 or 16 percent of the total target population.

The target population was estimated from a 1-in-100 sample of the 1970 Census of Population basic records, but the aggregate estimates remain valid in terms of this study's objective, even though the size of the national target population declined 13 percent from 1970 to 1974.

SOURCE: Adapted, with permission, from D. H. Stuart and A. M. Cruze, *Estimates of the Target Population for Upward Bound and Talent Search Programs.* Durham, N.C.: Research Triangle Institute, 1976.

Most of the data series of interest to persons dealing with social problems are available but are defined mainly for very large geographic units — the nation as a whole, states, or SMSAs. Social indicator data for areas within cities or counties may have to be constructed by collating data from the agencies that collect such information (e.g., city health departments). Often the collation of such materials and the computation of rates for various periods is time-consuming and costly. Hence, unless time series are readily available in published form, the attempt to construct them for a particular local community may not be efficient or feasible.

Surveys and Censuses

The most direct and usually the most accurate data on target problems and populations can be obtained by conducting special censuses or sample surveys in which the best measurement techniques are used and estimates are derived under the most rigorous conditions. A *census* may be defined as a complete enumeration of a population of units (individuals, households, firms, and so on) in which relevant characteristics of the units are obtained. In contrast, a *sample survey* may be defined as measurements applied to a sample of units in a population, the sample being drawn in a way that minimizes bias in the selection of units. Clearly, there is a close relationship between censuses and sample surveys, since they share measurement problems and strive to provide estimates about populations.

Sample surveys are preferred to censuses for two main reasons: First, they are considerably less expensive; second, when properly conducted they provide estimates of population characteristics to any desired degree of accuracy within calculable limits of sampling error. In addition, surveys usually can be conducted with greater care, minimizing errors of measurement. It should be noted that surveys need not be restricted to the study of individuals. Sample surveys can be conducted with households or larger organized groups as units, or with physical entities, such as dwellings, businesses, agricultural plots, and roads.

The science and art of sample survey research are well explicated (Rossi et al., 1982; Sudman, 1976). Methodologies exist for careful sampling and appropriate interview instrument construction. Surveys use standard measurements to measure the prevalence and incidence of certain problems. For example, a survey schedule might include a checklist measuring the quality of housing; or it may include items and tests to measure functional literacy of family members, the levels of health disability, and the like. These kinds of measures, along with characteristics such as length of residence and family income, allow estimation of target populations with considerable accuracy. Minimum requirements for an adequate sample survey include a sound sampling procedure, a well-prepared and pretested interview schedule or observation guide, and well-trained interviewers or enumerators who are familiar with the area being surveyed and who will not be perceived as intruders.

Exhibit 3-H: National Childcare Consumer Study

The data gathered in this survey represent the most comprehensive examination to date of the current patterns of childcare use in the United States. The data were collected from a stratified national probability sample of approximately 4,600 households with children 13 years of age or younger. Nonwhite and low-income households were oversampled in order to guarantee their inclusion. The survey identifies the following nine modes of care: (1) in-home care by a relative; (2) in-home care by a nonrelative; (3) other home care by a relative; (4) other home care by a nonrelative; (5) nursery and preschool care; (6) daycare centers; (7) cooperative programs; (8) before-and-after-school care programs; and (9) Headstart. A distinction is also made between "market care," for which cash is paid or a government subsidy provided, and nonmarket care, which is provided without a fee or in trade.

Nine out of ten households with children under 14 report using one of the forms of care listed here. It is worth nothing that multiple arrangements for care are quite common. One in three households uses only one method of care, while the remaining two-thirds use at least two methods.

The National Childcare Consumer Study is particularly rich in enumerating the factors that influence a household's selection of its mode of childcare. The importance of various types of services provided by alternative modes — or, put in a demand framework — the characteristics of the good that influence choice — are discussed in some detail. The report is also properly circumspect in pointing out that consumer attitudes often lack concreteness, particularly when some of the questions are interpreted as hypothetical by some or all respondents. Given this caveat together with the fact that the data are not analyzed in a manner that holds other factors constant, it is worth noting that most consumers at least purport to select care for preschoolers for child-oriented reasons rather than their own convenience.

The validity of this result remains questionable, but if confirmed by more vigorous analysis of the data, it — together with the result that most households use a nonmarket mode of care — will give us some insight into how preferences are formed and then exercised in the market for childcare.

SOURCE: Adapted, with permission, from UNCO, Inc., *National Childcare Consumer Study*, 1975.

Surveys can be expensive and technically demanding. Hence, sample surveys should be undertaken only when there is adequate justification for the costs involved and when appropriately trained personnel are available. Most sample surveys, even of small populations, require months of preparation and, in order to provide important and useful predictive information, need to be large-scale. In general, few surveys of less than 1,000 interviews or observations will be useful; larger surveys are often necessary to estimate the incidence or prevalence of relatively rare phenomena.

Exhibit 3-H illustrates the use of a sample survey conducted among families with children under 13 still living in the household. The purpose of the study was to estimate the need for child-care facilities as well as to estimate the usage of various types of child-care arrangements for households of this type in the United States as of 1975. While few evaluation researchers may need to estimate target populations for the United States as a whole, the same principles apply to sample surveys of smaller areas or even within institutions. Exhibit 3-I illustrates the use of sample surveys for smaller areas, in this case Brookline, Massachusetts.

The setting of target characteristics should be based on a combination of knowledge from previous research and practice, experience, and information obtained when determining the size of the population at need, demand, or risk. Often, after deciding on criteria, additional procedures may be undertaken to check on the utility of such target-selection-characteristic decisions. For example, an educational project for literacy training may have as its definition of appropriate targets all community members between 16 and 60 with less than four grades of school. An estimate of 10 percent functional illiteracy of a community of 2,000 adults may have come from a key informant survey. A sample survey would provide data on whether or not using a fourth-grade definition yields one potential target for each ten interviewed.

Exhibit 3-I: A Sample Survey for a Small Area

A sample of low-income families living in Brookline, Massachusetts, during 1964 who had at least one child in the local public or parochial high schools was drawn using health records kept in the schools in question. Preliminary selection of families was made on the basis of information in school records, and a final determination was made after interviews and sometimes credit checks verified the low-income status of the family and the occupation of household head. A sample of 806 households was drawn.

The purpose of the survey was to obtain a group of families that would be likely to use a public dental clinic. Interviews were undertaken with each family to ascertain the current patterns of dental care for members of the family. Dental examinations were made in school of those teen-aged children in the family still attending school to ascertain the dental-care needs of the low-income families, assuming that the children involved reasonably represented the health-care status of the families from which they were drawn.

SOURCE: Summary, by permission, of C. Lambert, Jr. and H. E. Freeman, *The Clinic Habit.* New Haven, Conn.: College and University Press, 1967.

THE IMPORTANCE OF DIAGNOSTIC EVALUATIONS

It is clear that specification and selection of the target population need to be explicit and based on easily detectable and accurately measurable characteristics. From a program management viewpoint, without such specification it is virtually impossible to undertake a successful intervention. Further, unless diagnosis is well accomplished, neither monitoring nor utility evaluations are likely to be of use. As every angler knows, there is little chance of catching fish, indeed of selecting the right bait and tackle, unless one knows what kind of fish are running and the right depth at which to sink the line. So too, the best intentions to better human conditions will do no good unless program staff and/or evaluators can precisely specify the targets and efficiently select them.

4

Program Monitoring and Accountability

The monitoring of programs is directed at two key questions: (1) whether or not the program is reaching the appropriate target population, and (2) whether or not the delivery of services is consistent with program design specifications. There are several reasons monitoring of programs is required. First, monitoring is usually needed for *accountability* purposes; program management and sponsors continually seek information to answer the question, "Who is getting what and how?" Second, monitoring evaluations generally are a necessary adjunct to impact assessments, since the failure of programs often is due to faulty or incomplete implementation of interventions rather than ineffectiveness of the treatments. Third, monitoring information may be either the sole basis for or a supplement to utility assessments; thus they are instrumental in decisions to continue, expand, or terminate ongoing programs.

KEY CONCEPTS

Access Strategy: Plan for reaching and providing services to a target population.

Accountability: The responsibility of program staff to provide evidence to sponsors and superordinate units of conformity to program coverage, treatment, legal, and fiscal requirements.

Bias: The extent to which a program is participated in differentially by subgroups of a target population.

Coverage: The extent to which a program is reaching its intended target population.

Process Studies: A general term referring to evaluation activities related to target identification and assessment of project conformity.

Program Elements: Identifiable and discrete intervention activities.

Service Delivery: Procedures and organizational arrangements actually employed to deliver services to appropriate targets.

---

*A*fter signing a new bill, President Kennedy is reputed to have said to his aides, "Now that this bill is the law of the land, let's hope we can get our government to carry it out." If the President of the United States can express skeptical concern about the implementation of federal law, how much more shaky and uncertain is the carrying out of specific programs? Indeed, whether or not any program is carried out with full attention to the aims of its sponsors and program staff — reaching the population intended to benefit from the program and delivering the services that were mandated — is always problematic.

This chapter takes up the issues involved in monitoring implementation. By *implementation monitoring,* we mean some systematic attempt to measure both *program coverage,* the extent to which a program is reaching its intended target population, and *program process,* the extent to which the service being delivered matches what was intended to be delivered. Together, program coverage and program process are often known as *program outputs,* that is, the products and services that are being delivered to the appropriate beneficiaries. Note that outputs are not to be confused with *outcomes;* the latter refers to the effects of outputs on targets, that is, impact. (For extended discussion of the problems of and research on implementation, see Williams and Elmore, 1976; Williams, 1980; and Pressman and Wildavsky, 1973.)

THE USES OF MONITORING

Monitoring program implementation is an activity that is undertaken at many different points in the development of programs and in the management of enacted programs. Program implementation monitoring is particularly vital to the development process, when programs are tested and refined. Program designers need to know what problems are encountered in implementation so that changes may be made in program design to overcome such obstacles. Unexpected results and unwanted side effects of programs rapidly surface in the course of testing. For example, a medical clinic that is intended to help working mothers and is only open during daylight hours will soon discover that however much demand there may be for clinic services, such hours effectively screen out those who work during the day. A program predicated on the prevalence of severe psychological problems among acting-out children in school may quickly find that most such children do not have deep disorders but superficial ones instead; hence, the program needs to be modified accordingly.

The results of program monitoring are also essential in providing data for program diffusion. In order to be able to reproduce the essential features of an intervention in places other than where it originated, it is necessary to be able to describe the program in operational detail. Critical points in implementation need to be identified, solutions to managerial problems outlined, qualifications of successful program personnel documented, and so on. Good program development includes producing manuals that detail administrative procedures, service delivery, necessary qualifications of personnel, and the like. The results of program monitoring at the development stage can be profitably used in the preparation of such manuals.

For programs that are beyond the development stage and in actual operation, program monitoring serves management needs by providing information on coverage and process, and hence feedback on whether the program is meeting specifications. Fine-tuning of a program may be necessary when monitoring information indicates that targets are not being reached or that outputs cost more than initially projected. Program managers who neglect to monitor a program systematically risk the danger of administering a program that is markedly different from its mandate.

Large-scale programs involving more than just a few sites and expending major amounts of resources may formalize program monitoring by instituting a management information system (MIS). These are systematic, continuing efforts that routinely generate data on what is happening within the program, answering such questions as: How many persons are being reached by the program and what are their characteristics? How many "units of service" are being delivered? How are funds being expended? How long do persons remain in the program? The purpose of a well-designed management information system is to provide program managers and staff with detailed, periodic reports on how well the program is functioning and to alert them to delivery problems as they arise so that corrective action may be taken.

PROGRAM ACCOUNTABILITY

Of course, program-monitoring information is also critical for those who sponsor and fund programs — the levels above day-to-day program management. In these circumstances, the issue is accountability. Are programs' funds being expended properly? Are the designated target populations being reached? How much of the intended service is actually being delivered? Indeed, it appears that for Congress, at least as far as national educational programs are concerned, program-monitoring information is often as important or more important than information on program impact (Raizen and Rossi, 1981).

From a monitoring perspective, accountability takes several of the forms we have already listed in Chapter 2.

- *Coverage Accountability:* Are the persons served those who are designated as targets? Are there beneficiaries who should not be served?

- *Service Delivery Accountability:* Are proper amounts of outputs being delivered? Are the treatments delivered those the program is supposed to be delivering?

- *Fiscal Accountability:* Are funds being used properly? Are expenditures properly documented? Are funds used within the limits set by the budget?

- *Legal Accountability:* Are relevant laws being observed by the program, including those concerning affirmative action, occupational safety and health, and privacy of individual records?

The issues of fiscal and legal accountability are perhaps best left to professionals in these areas. Whether proper accounting procedures are being followed and whether the requirements of state and/or federal laws are being honored are issues requiring the know-how of the accounting and legal professions, and risk inexpert treatment by social-research-trained evaluators working alone. It is therefore coverage and treatment accountability issues that are most relevant to the monitoring of implementation from a social research perspective.

While management-oriented monitoring (including use of information systems), and program accountability studies often are concerned with the same questions, they are differentiated by the purposes to which their evaluation information is to be put. Management information systems typically are designed to detect, on an ongoing basis, faults that need to be corrected by program staffs. Accountability studies primarily provide information that decision makers and sponsors need to judge the appropriateness of program activities and to decide whether or not a program should be continued, expanded, or contracted. Accountability studies usually are conducted in a more critical spirit, while management-oriented monitoring activities are concerned less with making decisive judgments and more with incorporating corrective measures as a regular part of program operations.

Some commentators on evaluation activities (Cronbach et al., 1980) hold that impact results are not so much a product of program management as they are a product of program design, which is usually not in the hands of program managers. Their view, therefore, is that program managers should be held responsible primarily for coverage, treatment, and fiscal integrity.

We agree that program managers should be accountable for delivery of services to the target population. We turn first to procedures for monitoring coverage and then to those that are used in the monitoring process.

TARGET POPULATIONS AND PROGRAM COVERAGE

As stated in the previous chapter, it is essential to define target populations carefully. But doing so is useless unless there also is a procedure for determining the extent to which the *actual participation* of targets takes place. This is particularly essential for the large number of interventions in which program acceptance and participation are voluntary. For example, community mental health centers designed to provide a broad range of services often fail to attract a reasonable number of persons who may benefit from these services. Even many patients recently discharged from mental hospitals, who have been encouraged to make use of the services of community mental health centers after discharge, often fail to contact the centers (Rossi, 1978).

Recruiting Targets

In general, any intervention or treatment that requires participants to learn new procedures, to change existing habits, or to take instruction may encounter difficulties in attracting target groups. Hence, whether or not a program is reaching its target units, those with specified and appropriate characteristics, needs to be verified with monitoring evaluations.

The issue of the extent to which the target population is participating in a project concerns both project managers and program sponsors. Efficient project management requires accurate and timely information on target participation, especially in the many cases where modification of project procedures may be required if target participation is not at the desired level. From the viewpoint of program managers, target participation is a critical measure of the project's vitality and ultimate effectiveness.

Target participation issues are often neglected in the development phase of new programs, when it is assumed that targets are necessarily motivated to participate. This may not be the case: In the Housing Allowance Demand Experiments (Kennedy, 1980; Struyk and Bendick, 1981), less than a third of the eligible families approached participated in one of the treatments, which required families to rent housing that met certain standards. Similarly, a program designed to provide information to prospective homebuyers might find that few persons seek the services offered. Hence, program developers need to be concerned with how best to motivate potential targets to seek out the program and participate in it. In some cases, this may require that outreach efforts be built into the program; in other cases, it might require special geographical placement of program personnel; and so on.

Coverage and Bias

The issues of target population participation consist of problems of coverage and bias. By *coverage* we mean the extent to which a program obtains target population participation, as specified in program design.

Bias is the degree to which subgroups of the designated target population participate differentially. A bias in the coverage of a program simply means that some subgroups are being covered more thoroughly than others. Bias can arise out of self-selection, some subgroups voluntarily participating more frequently than others. It can also derive from program actions: For instance, program personnel may show favor to some clients and tend to reject others. Finally, it may result from such unforeseen influences as the location of a program office, which may encourage greater participation by a target subgroup for which access to program activities is more convenient.

In testing programs, bias usually constitutes a serious threat to the validity of impact assessments. Especially critical is the differential participation of experimental groups receiving the new treatments and untreated control groups who are also observed in order to assess the impact of the intervention. In many impact assessments, control group members drop out more frequently than those receiving treatments in experimental groups. (See Chapter 6, where this issue of coverage in testing programs is discussed in more detail.)

Clearly, coverage and bias are related: A program that reaches all projected participants and no others is obviously not biased in its coverage. But since few social programs ever enjoy total, exact coverage, bias is typically an issue.

It is usually thought desirable that a large proportion of intended targets be served by a program. The exception, of course, is when the resources of a project are too limited to provide the appropriate treatments to all potential target units. In this case, however, the target definition during planning and program development probably was not narrow enough. This problem can be corrected by a sharper definition of the characteristics of the target population and by more effective employment of resources. For example, the establishment of a health center that provides medical services to persons without regular sources of care may result in so overwhelming a demand for services that limited resources and facilities make it impossible for many of those wanting to participate to receive care. Under such circumstances, adding eligibility criteria that consider severity of the health problem, family size, age, and income could reduce the size of the target population to manageable proportions.

The most common coverage problem in social interventions is that full target participation is not achieved, either because there is bias in recruiting participants from the specified group or because potential clients reject the treatment. For example, the Housing Allowance Experiments currently under way have experienced low participation rates: Only 30 to 40 percent of the eligible groups have become involved, despite the apparently obvious advantages of participating in the experiment (Carlson and Heinberg, 1977; Struyk and Bendick, 1981).

However, there are examples of overcoverage: The *Sesame Street* program has consistently captured audiences that have far exceeded the number of originally intended targets, namely, disadvantaged preschoolers. Other audiences, including children who are not disadvantaged and even adults, have been attracted to the program. Fortunately, since these additional audiences are reached at no additional cost, this inappropriate coverage is not a financial drain. However, it also turns out that the advantaged children who view the program benefit more than do the disadvantaged viewers (Cook et al., 1975). Since one of *Sesame Street's* goals was to lessen the gap in learning between advantaged and disadvantaged children, the program's success in reaching a much wider audience than intended has exacerbated one of the problems it sought to remedy.

In other instances, inappropriate coverage can be costly. The bilingual programs sponsored and funded by the Department of Education have been found to include many students whose primary language is English. School systems whose funding from the program depends on numbers of children enrolled in bilingual classes have been known to inflate attendance figures by registering more children than necessary, including inappropriate students (Raizen and Rossi, 1981). In some cases, it has been shown that schools have also used assignment to bilingual instruction as a means of ridding some classes of "problem children," rendering bilingual classes saturated with disciplinary cases.

Measuring Coverage

Program staffs and sponsors need to be concerned with both undercoverage and overcoverage. Undercoverage refers to the proportion of the targets in need of a program that participate in it. Overcoverage, however, is sometimes used to refer to the number of program participants *not* in need compared with the total number *not* in need in a designated population, and sometimes to the number of participants *not* in need compared with the total number in a program. Generally it is the latter figure that is important; efficient use of program resources requires minimizing both the number not served who are in need *and* the number not in need who are served. Efficiency of coverage may be measured by the following formula:

$$
\text{Coverage Efficiency} = 100 \times \left[\frac{\text{Number in need served}}{\text{Total number in need}} \right] - \left[\frac{\text{Number not in need served}}{\text{Total number served}} \right]
$$

The formula yields a positive value of 100 when the actual number served equals the designated target population in need and no inappropriate targets are served. A negative value of 100 occurs if only inappropriate targets are served. Positive and negative values between +100 and −100 indicate the degree of coverage efficiency. For example, if in a particular geographical area it is estimated that 100 targets need a program but in the actual group of 100 served only 70 are appropriate targets, the value obtained by the above formula would be +40. If 100 targets need a program, and only 10 of the 100 in it are appropriate targets, the value obtained would be −80.

The formula provides a means of estimating the tradeoffs in a program including inappropriate as well as appropriate targets. A program manager confronted with a −80 value might impose additional selection criteria eliminating 70 of the 90 inappropriate targets and, by an extensive recruitment campaign, secure 70 appropriate replacements. The coverage efficiency value then would be +60. If the program was inexpensive or it was either politically unwise or too difficult to impose additional selection criteria to eliminate undercoverage, the manager might elect the option of expanding the program to include all appropriate targets. Assuming the same proportion of inappropriate targets are also served, however, the total number participating would be 1,000!

The problem of measuring coverage is almost always the inability to specify the number in need or the magnitude of the target population. The activities described in Chapter 2, if carried out as an integral part of program planning, usually minimize this problem. In addition, three approaches may be used to assess the extent to which the appropriate target population has been served by a particular program.

Use of Records

Almost all programs are required to keep records on targets served. Such information is generally useful in accounting for the time of project staff and resources expended. There is large variation in the quality and extensiveness of records and in the sophistication involved in their storage and maintenance. Moreover, the feasibility of maintaining complete, ongoing record systems for all program participants varies with the nature of the treatment and available resources. Sophisticated computerized management and client information systems, for example, have been developed for medical and mental health systems (Gall and Norwood, 1977). Exhibit 4-A illustrates the use of records to describe participants in a food stamp program. A management information system for a small demonstration project is described in Exhibit 4-B. While this system was initially developed as an aid in describing project activities for the purposes of evaluation, project managers also used the results to retrain service workers so that they could deliver outputs more appropriate to the problems presented by targets.

In measuring target participation, the main concerns are that the data are accurate and reliable. A number of procedures can be undertaken to ensure reliability. Perhaps the most important is to develop a record system that is simple enough not to become burdensome to program staff and yet comprehensive enough to meet evaluation needs. There is often as much risk in developing an overextensive record-keeping system as there is in having one that contains too little information. Failure to think through information requirements may result in a system that is partially ignored because it is cumbersome, tedious, or time-consuming to use.

On the other side of this coin, it is important not only that appropriate forms and other record-keeping instruments are constructed, but also that program staff receive adequate training in the skills and terms associated with their use. For example, if occupation at the time of program admission is an important criterion for defining the target population, then instruction on the recording of detailed occupational information is essential for record-keeping purposes. Moreover, con-

Exhibit 4-A: Description of Food Stamp Program Participants

A national sample (over 10,500) was drawn from homemakers in the U.S. Department of Agriculture (USDA) Extension Service's Expanded Food and Nutrition Education Program (EFNEP). The goals of the program are to improve the nutrition knowledge and diets of poor families and to encourage program families to enroll in USDA food assistance programs.

Homemakers receiving food stamps had better diets, larger families, and higher incomes than those in the food distribution program or those eligible but not participating in a food assistance program.

Approximately 37 percent of EFNEP families participated in USDA food assistance programs in 1969. Twenty-three percent were enrolled in the food distribution program and 14 percent received food stamps. One in four EFNEP families were eligible but did not participate in either program. Twenty-eight percent were ineligible because of high incomes or small family size.

Socioeconomic characteristics were compared for families participating in the food stamp and food distribution programs, eligible nonparticipants, and ineligible nonparticipants during 1969. Families in all groups had low incomes, lived mainly in urban areas, had minority racial and ethnic backgrounds, and relatively low educational levels. About one-third of all families were on welfare. The group with the largest proportions of black families and urban residents were nonparticipating eligibles. Educational levels were lowest (less than eight years of schooling) for food distribution and eligible nonparticipant homemakers. Welfare participation among assistance families was substantially higher than for nonparticipating families.

Average family income was about $200 per month for food stamp participants and $165 for both food distribution and eligible nonparticipating families. Although food stamp participants had larger family food expenditures, food expenditures per person equaled those of eligible nonparticipating families. Nonparticipating eligibles spent more than 40 percent of their income for food — a higher rate than for any of the other groups.

The income of ineligible families exceeded $300 per month. Only 7 percent were on welfare, and average family size was four members. Compared with other families, the ineligibles were more urban, had fewer blacks, and were less often on welfare. The economic advantages of these families were reflected in their higher incomes and food expenditures. Also, they spent a smaller proportion of family income for food and had better food consumption practices.

SOURCE: Summary of J. G. Feaster and G. B. Perkins, *Families in the Expanded Food and Nutrition Education Program: Comparison of Food Stamp and Food Distribution Program Participants and Nonparticipants.* Washington, DC: U.S. Department of Agriculture, 1973.

Exhibit 4-B: A Management Information System for a Small Program

A demonstration program designed to test the feasibility of training paralegal subprofessionals to identify the legal problems of mental health patients within state hospitals who have been deinstitutionalized, and to help patients to obtain their full legal rights, was financed by the National Institute of Mental Health to operate within the Western Massachusetts Mental Health Region. Paralegal workers (mostly college students) are trained to know the relevant portions of state and federal laws and regulations and are sent out to contact mental patients both within hospitals and in community treatment centers. In order to be able to identify the legal problems presented by patients (and hence to adjust training accordingly), a management information system was installed that provides close tabs on encounters between paralegal personnel and patients. After each encounter with a patient, the paralegal worker initiates a case file in which is recorded the complaint of the patient, what actions were taken by the paralegal personnel, dates, times, and cross-references to other files maintained on institutions and contact centers. Thus it was possible to identify areas of legal problems for which too much emphasis had been given in training and those in which too little emphasis had been given. In addition, the information system made it possible to compute the costs of service delivery.

SOURCE: John Hornik et al., *Technical Manual for Management Information System,* Mental Patients' Advocacy Project, Western Massachusetts Legal Services, Northampton, Massachusetts, 1981. Reprinted by permission.

tinual training and retraining, as well as initial instruction, are usually necessary to keep staff apprised of developments affecting record-keeping and to maintain their skills. This may involve checking samples of records against their authoritative sources and noting errors of commission and omission.

Another procedure for ensuring reliability involves quality-control checks on a sampling basis. This may be done by having several project staff members complete records independently and checking the consistency of the information logged. Finally, information obtained from program records may be compared with other available data. For instance, a family planning program may compare its records with those of a local clinic or hospital.

It should be noted that all record systems are subject to greater or lesser degrees of unreliability. Some records will contain incorrect or outdated information and others will be incomplete. The extent to which unreliable records can be used for decision-making purposes depends on the kind and degree of their unreliability and the nature of the decisions in question. Clearly, critical decisions involving outcomes of considerable weight require better records than do trivial decisions. A decision to continue or discontinue a project should not be made on the basis of data derived from partly unreliable records, while a decision to change an administrative procedure may well be taken on data derived from such records. If administrative records are to serve an important role in decision-making on far-reaching issues, it is usually desirable to conduct an audit of those records.

Data from record systems — particularly from management information systems that have been developed by large-scale programs and human service institutions — can be used to estimate both program coverage and program bias. Information on the various screening criteria for a target population may be tabulated to determine if the units served are the ones specified in the program's design. For example, records of participants in a family planning program, whose targets are women under 50 years of age who have been residents of a particular community for at least six months and who have two children under age 10, can be examined to see if the women actually served are within the eligibility limits, and the degree to which participants are under- or overrepresented in particular age or parity groups. Bias in program participation in terms of the eligibility characteristics, observed singularly and together, would be evident from such an analysis. Similarly, coverage and bias can be determined by hospitals, which normally maintain complete counts of persons admitted and patients' diagnoses, insurance coverage, and conditions of discharge. These data are tabulated and then consolidated by the American Hospital Association according to state and region. Many state welfare departments also have excellent management information systems.

Program coverage can also be estimated from record systems used in combination with other available information. A preschool program devised to meet the need for child care would be able to estimate coverage by the formula given above if a previous survey had estimated the number of preschool children in the program's region with both parents working away from home. Such calculations are important when the worth of a program depends partially on whether it provides services at a given level for persons in need (usually designated by area, socioeconomic level, ethnic background, and similar criteria).

When programs are of long duration, as is true of many educational efforts and health interventions, it may be important to update records on a regular basis. Measures such as family size and composition, occupation, income, and place of residence change frequently, and estimates of target population, coverage, and bias must keep up with those changes. In sum, a useful record system must be both reliable and up-to-date.

Surveys of Program Participants

An alternative to using service and management records is to conduct special surveys of program participants. Sample surveys may be desirable when it is not possible to obtain the required data routinely as part of program activities, or when the size of the target group is large and it is more economical and efficient to undertake a sample survey than to obtain the data on all of the participants.

For example, a special educational project conducted primarily by parents in a community may be set up only in a few schools. Children are tested in all schools and referred for additional education to special sites if they do poorly on reading and arithmetic tests. The project may accept all children referred, but the project staff may not have time or training to administer appropriate educational skills tests. Rather, an evaluation group, probably on a sampling basis, could do so in order to estimate the appropriateness of the selection procedures and to assess whether or not the designated target population is being served by the project.

Community Surveys

When projects are not targeted at selected, narrowly defined groups of individuals but at an entire community, the most efficient and sometimes the only way to examine whether the presumed population at need is being reached is to conduct a community sample survey.

The evaluation of *Feeling Good* illustrates the use of surveys to provide data on national audience size and composition. This television program was an experimental production of the Children's Television Workshop, producers of *Sesame Street.* It was designed to motivate adults to engage in preventive health practices: Although the program was accessible to homes of all income levels, its primary purpose was to motivate low-income families to improve their health practices. Gallup conducted four national surveys, each of approximately 1,500 adults, at different times during the weeks *Feeling Good* was televised. The data provide estimates on the viewing audiences as well as the demographic, socioeconomic, and attitudinal characteristics of viewers (Mielke and Swinehart, 1976). The major finding was that the program largely failed to reach the target group.

In addition to educational television, various types of health, educational, recreational, and other human service programs are often communitywide, although their intended target populations may be selected groups, such as delinquent youths, the aged, or women of childbearing age. Surveys are the major means of assessing whether targets have been reached.

To measure coverage of Department of Labor programs, such as training and public employment, the Department started a periodic national sample survey (Westat, Inc., 1976-1980). This large household survey ascertains through personal interviews whether or not each adult member of the sampled households was ever or is currently participating in each of a number of Department of Labor programs. By contrasting program participants with nonparticipants, the survey provides information on the biases in coverages of the programs. In addition, information on the uncovered but eligible target populations is also generated.

Program Utilizers, Eligibles, and Dropouts

Another type of target population assessment is undertaken to detect participation bias by examining differences between individuals who participate in a program and either those who drop out, those who are eligible but do not participate at all, or both groups. In part, the dropout rate or attrition from a project may be an indicator of client dissatisfaction with intervention activities. It also may indicate conditions in the community that prevent persons from full participation. For example, in certain areas lack of adequate transportation may prevent participation of those who are otherwise willing and eligible.

It is important to be able to identify the particular subgroups within the target population who are not initial participants or who do not follow through to full participation. Such information not only is valuable in judging the worth of the effort but also is needed to develop hypotheses about how a project may be modified to attract and retain a larger proportion of the target population. Thus, the qualitative aspects of participation also may be important for subsequent program planning.

As noted previously, information about program dropouts and nonparticipants is essential in order to document and model the nature of self-selection bias. Moreover, and especially problematic for the longitudinal testing of new programs, losses in participation due to attrition or missing data are potentially damaging to the validity of the impact assessment results (Watts et al., 1977).

Data about dropouts may come either from service records or from surveys designed to find nonparticipants. Community surveys usually are the only feasible means of identifying persons who have not participated in a program. The exception, of course, is when there is adequate information about the entire eligible population prior to project implementation (as in the case of data from a census or screening interview). Comparisons with either data gathered for project-planning purposes or community surveys undertaken during and subsequent to the intervention may employ a variety of different analytical approaches, from the purely descriptive to very complex models.

In Chapter 8 we describe methods of analyzing the costs and benefits of programs to arrive at measures of economic efficiency. Clearly, estimates of the size of populations at need or risk, the groups who start a program but drop out, and the ones who participate to completion are important for calculating the costs. Those data have also been the basis for estimating benefits. In addition, they are highly useful in judging the worth of a project for continuation and expansion in either the same community or other locations. Further, such information is essential for staff to meet their managerial and accountability responsibilities. While project participation data are no substitutes for knowledge of impact to judge either efficiency or effectiveness of projects, there is little point in moving ahead with an impact analysis without an adequate description of the extent of participation by the target population.

MONITORING DELIVERY OF SERVICES:
PROCESS STUDIES

Monitoring the delivery of services is important from the standpoint of decisions concerning program continuation and expansion. The extent to which program specifications are actually met in the delivery of the intervention obviously must be fully documented for policymaking. Additionally, research on service delivery is valuable in determining the levels of performance of staff members (see Exhibit 4-C for a report on the impact of a television program on teachers in El Salvador). Before all else, however, evaluators of service delivery seek to determine whether an intervention's actual outputs sufficiently approximate intended ones.

Why Programs Fail

Monitoring the delivery of services to evaluate the actual implementation of a program is undertaken for a number of purposes. A large proportion of programs that fail to show impacts are really failures to deliver the interventions in ways specified. There are three kinds of implementation failures: First, no treatment, or not enough, is delivered; second, the wrong treatment is delivered; and third, the treatment is unstandardized, uncontrolled, or varies across target populations. In each instance, the need to monitor the actual delivery of services and identify faults and deficiencies is essential.

"Nonprograms" and Incomplete Treatment

Consider first the problem of the "nonprogram" (Rossi, 1978). McLaughlin (1975) reviewed the evidence on the implementation of Title I of the Elementary and Secondary Education Act, which allocated billions of dollars yearly to aid local schools in overcoming students' poverty-associated educational deprivations. However, local school authorities were unable to describe their Title I activities in any detail, and few activities could even be identified as educational services delivered to schoolchildren, although the funds had been expended.

Numerous other programs have been documented in the literature as failing to deliver services. Datta (1977) reviews the evaluations on career education programs and finds that the designated targets rarely participated in the planned program activities.

In a recent attempt to evaluate a program designed to motivate disadvantaged high school students toward higher levels of academic achievement, it was discovered that the program consisted mainly of the distribution of buttons or hortatory literature and little else (Murray, 1980). Although the program had received a great deal of publicity, few of the high school students in the participating schools who were supposed to be reached by the program knew of its existence, and even fewer had participated in any of the activities that were supposed to be part of the program.

Exhibit 4-C: Effect of a Program on Classroom Teachers

As part of the Educational Reform in El Salvador, a serious effort was made to retrain all Third Cycle teachers so that they could work effectively with proposed new innovations. Teachers' attitudes toward the Reform therefore became an important aspect of the research and evaluation activities. Briefly, the findings are as follows:

1. Not unlike the student findings, there was a decline from high levels of enthusiasm in 1969 for ITV [instructional television] to less positive attitudes in 1971 and 1972. That is, teachers were more willing to be critical several years after the introduction of ITV and the reform program. Problems other than the presence of instructional television or the basic thrust of the Reform, however, were behind the teachers' negative attitudes.

2. In particular, teachers were not happy with their everyday working conditions because of increases in enrollment and the corresponding increases in teaching loads, with morning and afternoon classes from 7 a.m. to 6 p.m. becoming the norm. Despite this extra work, teachers' salary levels were not adequately improved and remained unattractive. Given these conditions, it was not surprising that two major teachers' strikes occurred within the initial years of the Reform.

3. There was also a general misunderstanding of the part played by the classroom teacher in the new system of student grading and promotion, and a sense of being inadequately prepared to use such a system well. This new system required classroom teachers to be better prepared for their classes and to invest precious out-of-class time in various evaluation activities. At the same time, the new grading system diminished the possibility that a student could be flunked for failure to perform adequately on a single end-of-year exam.

SOURCE: From H. Ingle, "Reconsidering the Use of Television for Educational Reform: The Case of El Salvador," in R. F. Arnove (ed.), *Educational Television: Policy Critique and Guide for Developing Countries*, p. 130. Copyright © 1976, published by Praeger Publishers, reprinted with permission of Holt, Rinehart and Winston.

Instead of not delivering services at all, a delivery system may dilute the treatment so that an insufficient amount reaches the target population. Here the problem may be a lack of commitment on the part of a front-line delivery system, resulting in minimal delivery or "ritual compliance" to the point of nonexistence (Rossi, 1978). Affirmative action laws, for example, have required businesses to advertise job openings to the public. Nevertheless, organizations often place public advertisements when positions have already been filled informally.

Wrong Treatment

The second category of program failures, namely that the wrong treatment is delivered, can occur in two ways. One is that the mode of delivery negates the treatment. For example, a randomized experiment to test the effectiveness of group counseling in prison had to resort to using untrained and sometimes hostile prison guards as group leaders (Kassebaum et al., 1971). In the Performance Contracting Experiment, where private firms were contracted to teach mathematics and reading and were to be paid in proportion to the achievement gains of pupils, the companies faced extensive difficulties in operating the program. In fact, in some sites the school system sabotaged the experiments, and in others the companies faced equipment failures and teacher hostility (Gramlich and Koshel, 1975).

Wrong treatment may also result from an overly sophisticated delivery system. There can be a considerable difference between pilot projects and production runs of sophisticated treatments. Thus, interventions that might work well in the hands of highly motivated and trained deliverers may end up as failures when administered by staff of a mass delivery system whose training and motivation are considerably less. The field of education again provides an illustration: Teaching methods (e.g., computer-assisted learning, individualized instruction) that have worked well within the experimental development centers have not fared as well in ordinary school systems.

The distinction made here between a treatment and its mode of delivery is not always clear-cut. For example, the difference is quite clear in income maintenance programs, in which the "treatment" is the money given to beneficiaries and the delivery modes may vary from automatic deposits in savings or checking accounts to hand delivery of actual cash to recipients. Here the intent of the program is to place money in the hands of recipients; the delivery, whether by electronic transfer or by hand, has little effect on the treatment. In contrast, a counseling program may be handled by retraining existing personnel, hiring counselors, or employing certified psychotherapists. In this case the distinction between mode of delivery and treatment is fuzzy, since it is generally acknowledged that counseling treatments vary by counselor.

Unstandardized Treatment

The final category of program failures is due to unstandardized or uncontrolled treatment implementation, in some cases involving "planned variation" by design. The problem is that discretion on program implementation is often left to the delivery system, with the result that the treatment can vary significantly across sites. Early programs of the Office of Economic Opportunity provide examples. The Community Action Program (CAP) left considerable discretion to local communities to engage in a variety of actions, requiring only "maximum feasible participation" on the part of the poor. Consequently, it is almost impossible to document what CAP programs accomplished (Vanecko and Jacobs, 1970). Similarly, Project Head Start funded local communities to set up preschool teaching projects for underprivileged children. The centers across the country varied by sponsoring agencies, coverage, content, staff qualifications, objectives, and a host of other characteristics (Cicirelli et al., 1969).

Delivery System Concepts

Some programs are simple and straightforward and evaluation of their implementation reqires only minimal resources. Others, however, are exceedingly complex. A combination of evaluation methods usually must be employed to assess their project implementation adequately. Before discussing various methodologies, it may be useful to review a set of concepts that are employed in the assessment of program delivery. During program planning, it is necessary to formulate hypotheses about these features of the delivery system. As part of the planning, testing of decisions on implementation may be advisable.

The delivery system for a program usually consists of a number of separate elements. As a general rule, it is wise to assess all the elements. However, there are instances in which previous experience with certain aspects of the delivery system makes the assessments of some elements unnecessary. The delivery system may be thought of as a combination of pathways and actions undertaken in order to provide an intervention (see Wholey, 1977). Exhibit 4-D lists the elements of a public human service program.

Access

Access refers to the structural and organizational arrangements that provide opportunities for and operate to facilitate program participa-

Exhibit 4-D: A Simple Model of a Human Service System

Elements of the System	Function
Population Served	a group of community members in a specified geographic area receiving services from the system and having their needs and interests represented through governance;
Governance	a group of community members who represent the needs and interests of the population to be served;
Specification	a definition of needs of the population to be served stated in measurable terms;
Needs Audit Mechanism	a means for recording the extent to which the needs of the population to be served have been satisfied by the system;
System Manager	some individual or group who is accountable for the effects and costs of the system;
Client Pathway	a set of system functions through which clients pass from entry to discharge to have their needs met;
System Agent	single point of accountability for client progress through the system;
Information System	a mechanism to provide delivery and management personnel with data to help clients through the pathway and enable corrective action to be taken if clients encounter difficulty.

SOURCE: Adapted from R.M. Bozzo, E.L. Kane, and S. Mittenthal, *Evaluation of the State of Delaware's Human Service Delivery System.* Washington, DC: National Institute for Advanced Studies, 1977, p. 32.

tion. All programs need to have a strategy for providing the services to the appropriate target population. In some instances, access simply may consist of opening an office, and operating under the assumption that the designated participants will "naturally" come and make use of the intervention services provided at the site. In other instances, however, access may include active outreach campaigns to recruit participants, provision of transportation in order to bring persons to the intervention site, and efforts during the intervention to minimize dropouts.

A number of evaluation questions arise in connection with access, some of which relate only to the delivery of services, and some of which are directly relevant to or have implications for previously discussed issues of target participation. First, are the established access operations consistent with program design? Second, do participants remain in the program and terminate as planned? When dropout rates are excessive, not only are the targets minimally reached by the intervention, but costs per potential target may become excessive.

Third, is there access for potential targets to the appropriate services? It has been observed, for example, that community members who originally make use of emergency medical care systems for appropriate purposes may subsequently utilize them for general medical care. Such misuse of emergency services may be overly costly and hamper their availability to other community members (National Center for Health Services Research, 1977). Fourth, does the access strategy foster utilization by targets differentially from various social, cultural, and ethnic groups, or is there access with equity for all potential targets?

Finally, there are projects where it is important as part of access to evaluate participant satisfaction with the program. For example, if a preschool project is viewed with dissatisfaction by the mothers of the children participating, it may fail to draw other children from these families in successive years or from neighboring families influenced by the mothers' reports.

Specification of Services

It is critical to specify in operational terms the actual services that are provided. The first task is to define each kind of service in terms of the activities and actions that take place and/or in terms of the types of participation by various providers. Exhibit 4-E provides guidelines on how to examine an educational program.

Units of services, or *program elements,* may be defined in terms of *time, costs, procedures,* or a *product.* For example, program elements may refer to hours of counseling time provided in a vocational training project; in an effort to foster housing improvement, a unit of service may

Exhibit 4-E: Specifying the Elements of an Educational Program

You can begin describing the program by outlining the elements of the program's *context* — the tangible features of the program and its setting.

- The classrooms, schools, or districts where the program has been installed.

- The program staff — including administrators, teachers, aides, parent volunteers, and secretaries.

- The resources used — including materials constructed or purchased, and equipment, particularly that purchased especially for the program.

- The students — including the particular characteristics that made them eligible for the program, their number, and their level of competency at the beginning of the program.

These context features constitute the *bare bones* of the program and must be included in any summary report. Listing them usually does not require much data gathering on your part, since they are not the sort of data that you expect anyone to challenge or view with skepticism. Unless you have doubts about the delivery of materials, or you think that the wrong staff members or students may be participating, there is little need for backup data to support your description.

In addition to describing context features, however, you will need to devote some time to examining and reporting the *activities* in which program staff and participants took part. Describing important activities demands formulating and answering questions about *how* the program was implemented.

- Were the materials used? Were they used as intended?

- What procedures were prescribed for the teachers to follow in their teaching and other interactions with students? Were these procedures followed?

- In what activities were the students in the program supposed to participate? Did they?

- What activities were prescribed for other participants — aides, parents, tutors? Did they engage in them?

- What administrative arrangements did the program include? What lines of authority were to be used for making important decisions? What changes occurred in these arrangements or lines of authority?

Detailed means the list should include a prescription of the *frequency* or *duration* of activities and of their *form* (who, how, where) that is specific enough to allow you to picture each activity.

SOURCE: Adapted from L. L. Morris and C. T. Fitz-Gibbon, *How to Measure Program Implementation*, Volume 4, in L. L. Morris (ed.), *Program Evaluation Kit*. Beverly Hills, CA: Sage Publications, 1978.

be defined in terms of amounts of building materials provided; in a cottage industry project, a program element may refer to an activity, such as training people to operate sewing machines; and in an educational program, an element may be specific curricular materials used in classrooms. In all these examples, what is important is that there is an explicit definition of what constitutes an element or unit.

There is a tradeoff between specifying a large number of specific, simple program elements and having a few complex ones. For example, if a project providing technical education for preschool dropouts includes literacy training, carpentry skills, and a period of on-the-job apprenticeship work, it is advisable to separate these into three separate sets of service rather than to merge the activities. For purposes of estimating program costs for undertaking cost-benefit analyses, and for fiscal accountability, it is often important to attach monetary values to different program elements or units of services. This clearly is important when the costs of several programs will be compared and where the programs receive reimbursement on the basis of units of services provided.

Simple, specific elements are easier to identify, count, and train persons to record. However, complex elements often correspond more closely to program goals. Hence, the strategic question is how to strike a balance, using program elements that can be identified and counted reliably and at the same time be meaningful as far as the goals of the program are concerned.

The specification of program elements or service units is also an aid in program management. Close monitoring of the actual distribution of service units delivered to participants can help program staff and administration to keep programs more closely aligned with original intents. For example, some types of service units may be more attractive to project personnel than others — simply providing income support payments may be easier than attempting to deliver a variety of supplemental social services — and project personnel may therefore tend consciously or unconsciously to favor the simpler service unit.

A description of project service elements in terms of activities and actions is preferable to a description in terms of the characteristics of the providers. An illustration of program elements is given in Exhibit 4-F. Of course, the scheme reported in this exhibit is very fine-grained, relating to each incident of interaction between teachers and students. Ordinarily, program elements would not be measured with this degree of refinement. The illustration is presented at this point to show the extent to which program element description may go, under appropriate circumstances. It is evident that to the extent concise and detailed description of elements can be offered, it is possible to expand and duplicate programs.

While descriptions of program elements in terms of concrete activities is preferable, in many projects the nature of the intervention allows wide choice in what takes place. In such situations, at least at the outset, it may be possible to describe elements only in terms of the general characteristics of the activities and in terms of the training and skills of the service providers. For example, master craftspersons may be located in a low-income community to instruct community members in various ways of improving their dwelling units. The activities in which the craftspersons engage may vary greatly from one household to another. They may advise one family on how to frame windows and in another case provide instruction on how to shore up the foundation of a house. In such cases, activities can only be described in general terms and by examples. It is possible, however, to describe the characteristics required of the providers. It can be stated that the persons selected for this activity should have a minimum of five years of experience in the construction and repair of homes and that they need to be knowledgeable about carpentry, electrical wiring, foundations, and exterior construction. Of course, during the project it is important to be able to document the actual activities and tasks this adviser undertook.

As a general guideline, monitoring is most successful when programs are kept as simple as possible. Programs that offer many different services and in which there is close tailoring of interventions to indi-

Exhibit 4-F: Measuring What Happens in Classrooms

In an effort to relate what happens in classrooms to the achievement of elementary school pupils, the investigators videotaped a number of individual classroom sessions in reading and math instruction. The videotapes were then coded to show the incidence of certain types of teacher/student interactions that were believed to be important in reading and math achievement. Listed below are a few of the codes developed for "instructional events," all involving actions taken by the teacher in question toward one or more students:

- individual management statements (statements by the teacher addressed to students to direct their behavior; e.g., "Please sit down!")

- individual cognitive statements (statements that contain some instructional materials addressed to a single student)

- whole-class cognitive statements (same sort of statement addressed to the whole class)

The total coding scheme contained literally scores of such categories. Once the videotapes had been coded, it was necessary to summarize the tapes for individual classes and for individual students and relate the resulting summary measures to the amount of learning taking place in the classes as a whole and among individual students.

SOURCE: Cooley, W. W. and Leinhardt, G., "The Instructional Dimensions Study." *Educational Evaluation and Policy Analysis* 2, January, 1980. Copyright © 1980, American Educational Research Association, Washington, D.C. Reprinted by permission.

vidual targets can be difficult to monitor, since it is a problem to unravel the particular intervention modalities that impact favorably in terms of project goals. At the same time, it is evident that many programs offer alternative service elements because of individual target requirements, the contextual conditions under which the program is offered, or competence and expertise of program providers. Monitoring requires that alternatives be identified and specified as much as possible.

The planning phase includes refinement of delivery system concepts, development of operational specifications, and pretesting of the delivery system. During the program implementation, it is advisable for program management to undertake continual or periodic study of the implementation process (see Exhibit 4-G).

Exhibit 4-G: Continuous versus One-Shot Evaluation

If administrators consider evaluation to be one of their central responsibilities, they are apt to believe that evaluation should be a constant and continuous process. In practice, this has led to an emphasis upon input and process evaluation. In social programs the development of statistical systems — often quite sophisticated — and standardized tests are the most notable examples. Statistical systems reflect a desire and a need on the part of managers to know something about the clients being served by their programs and something, in an aggregated way, about what happens to these clients and how staff members spend their time. When such systems are reasonably well developed, they provide fairly detailed information about the demographic characteristics of clients, at least some indication of how clients happen to enter the program (e.g., source of referral), at least a categorical assignment of why the client entered the program (e.g., diagnosis), how staff time is expended among various types of activity (work/time analysis), and often what should be the next steps (disposition). Less often, but still with laudable frequency, such systems also provide information tracking the client through a system or program — services provided, transfers, and so on. Typically, a statistical system provides some of these types of information, depending upon the preferences of managers and the availability of resources, and statistical systems are probably the best developed and most widely used form of continuous evaluation in social programs.

One-shot evaluation is more apt to be a response to a perceived crisis, a particularly difficult policy decision, or possibly the receiving of a grant. Typically, evaluative research is one-shot in nature, because it usually involves a study. For whatever the reason, one-shot evaluation is aimed at answering a specific question about a particular program or program element at one point in time. The sources of crises are legion but usually result in the immediate need for information about a particular aspect of a program. There is a strong tendency, usually out of concern for credibility, to use outside evaluators in crisis situations, although what constitutes "outside" depends upon the organizational level of the crisis. Consultants are often used in just such cases, and management consultant firms have multiplied in large part as a response to the frequency of such crises.

Periodic evaluation is a very useful midpoint between one-shot and continuous evaluation. Although many social phenomena change rapidly (e.g., public opinion and military situations), most do not. The changes wrought by many social programs are often slow in developing, or at least the impact is slow in emerging. This is particularly true for education and prevention programs. In addition, many of the instruments available for measuring change are sensitive only to gross changes. In many instances, particularly those requiring measurement of impact, long-term outcome, or prevention, neither continuous evaluation nor one-shot evaluation is adequate, but some type of periodic monitoring is possible, feasible, and necessary. Periodic evaluation permits some rest to the evaluators while they deal with other problems, and at the same time it does not compromise their or the program's ability to grow.

SOURCE: Adapted, with permission, from J.L. Franklin and J.H. Thrasher, *An Introduction to Program Evaluation.* New York: John Wiley, 1979, pp. 26-29. Copyright © by John Wiley and Sons, Inc.

COLLECTING DATA FOR MONITORING

A wide variety of techniques may be used singly and in combination to gather data on program implementation. The particular approaches used need to take into account resources available and the expertise of the evaluator, as in all aspects of evaluation. There are additional restrictions, however. One concerns issues of privacy and confidentiality. Program services that depend heavily on person-to-person delivery methods, particularly in such areas as mental health, family planning, and vocational education, are not readily amenable to direct observaticn of program activities without violating privacy. In other contexts, self-administered questionnaires may be an economical means of studying program implementation, but functional illiteracy and cultural norms may prohibit their use.

There are four data sources that should be considered in the design of a monitoring evaluation: direct observation by the evaluator, service records, data from program staff who are service providers, and information from program participants or their associates. The actual data collection approach utilized and the analysis procedures overlap from one data source to the next. A comprehensive monitoring evaluation would include data from all four sources.

Observational Data

In many programs, the preferable data collection approach for monitoring purposes is direct observation. Observational methods are feasible whenever the presence of an observer is not obtrusive.

It may be useful in some cases for observers to become, at least for a time, full or partial program participants. Reiss (1971), for example, placed in police patrol cars observers who filled out systematic reports of each encounter between the police and citizens in a sample of duty tours. A similar approach was used in the Kansas City Preventive Patrol Experiment (Kelling et al., 1974). Exhibit 4-H describes the use of observers in that study and some of the problems they encountered.

Investigators wishing to employ participant-observation methods usually find it possible to explain to program personnel and to other participants the purposes served by observation. However, the extent to which the presence of participant-observers may alter the behavior of program personnel, other participants, or the delivery system as a whole is not clear. Impressionistic evidence from the police studies does not indicate that observers affected the delivery system, since police in the patrol cars soon become accustomed to being observed. Nonetheless, participant-observation methods should be sensitive to the problem of observer effects.

An essential part of any observation effort is a plan for the systematic recording of observations made (see Schatzman and Strauss, 1973, and Patton, 1980, for guidance on field research methods). Observers must be trained in how to make observations and how to record them uniformly.

There are three typical ways of making systematic observations. The first approach involves the least imposition of a set scheme for classifying events: The observer is simply asked to record events in as much detail as possible and in the order in which they occur. This is known as the *narrative method*. In its most extreme form, no guides are given to

Exhibit 4-H: The Participant Observer Program in the Kansas City Preventive Patrol Experiment

Trained observers were assigned to ride in patrol cars with officers in the experimental beats. It was felt that such observers would be valuable in observing and recording the unexpected consequences of such an experiment, that they could provide valuable feedback concerning the extent to which there was an experiment, that they could accurately record and provide data concerning those activities performed by officers while on routine preventive patrol (for the expenditure of noncommitted time analysis), and that they could serve as major mechanisms of data collection for the response time and police-citizen encounter portions of the experiment.

The first difficulty stemmed from task force objections to the use of observers. Several members expressed fears that police officers would automatically modify their behavior in the presence of observers, that they would be hostile to close, constant monitoring by nonpolice participants, and that because they would feel responsible for the observers, police officers might jeopardize their own safety in dangerous situations. Discussion eventually moved the task force from hostility to cautious openness and eventually to approval and interest, although the task force did reserve the right to discontinue the use of participant observers should they judge a discontinuance to be in the best interest of the experiment.

One major conflict concerned methods of data collection. The first step in observer data collection involved the gathering of phenomenological accounts (defined as a description sufficiently complete that a well-defined image of the event is generated in the mind of the reader, who is able to infer the moods of the participants from the behavior recorded). Over the course of the experiment this procedure moved toward a more highly structured means of data collection.

A second area of conflict involved the co-optation by the police of most of the participant observers. It should be noted that this problem was never confined to the observers, nor was it premeditated on the part of the police department. Police work has many aspects that are exciting, attractive, and alluring to those not directly engaged in it. As a result, laymen are often easily converted to a police point of view. Some of the observers were overly prepared to defend the police and were convinced that the information being gathered would eventually be used in an unprofessional manner by the police department, the Police Foundation, and individual staff members. Some observers began to insist that they and they alone should decide the degrees of sensitivity involved and, literally as protectors of the police, decide what information should and should not be gathered.

To deal with this problem, a variety of mechanisms were used. First, a police officer from the task force was selected to review regularly the information gathered by the observers and discuss with them the nature and sensitivity of the data. Second, regular meetings with the observers were held to discuss their work, their findings, and problems encountered in the field. And third, the observer portion of the experiment was put under the direct supervision of a full-time staff member to strengthen the administrative function and provide direct, ongoing managerial support.

The observers collected data of great value to the experiment, however, and there is much confidence in the quality of these data. Despite the problems experienced during the initial stages of this program, and the difficulties endemic to ethnomethodological research, there has been, and will be, a high level of return in terms of the data collected and their use.

SOURCE: Adapted, with permission, from G. Kelling et al., *The Kansas City Preventive Patrol Experiment: A Technical Report.* Washington, DC: Police Foundation, 1974, pp. 60-62.

the observer about which events to record and which to ignore. Typically, however, it has been found useful to provide observers with a list of important types of activities to which their attention should be directed.

A second approach is to provide observers with a *data guide* — a set of questions for which answers are required to be given by observers from their observations. A data guide may resemble a survey instrument in which there are blank spaces between questions which observers then fill in. For example, the data guide for observers attending technical training classes may have questions such as, "How did the instructor make use of available training aids? What were they and when were they used?" The use of a recording instrument such as a data guide simplifies analysis considerably. There is also greater likelihood of consistency of information across observers than with narrative reporting. It presumes, however, much more specificity in program design and becomes unwieldly if there are a large number of alternative interventions to be applied to individual participants.

The third approach is to use some form of *structured rating* scheme. Some of the ratings can be solely descriptive, such as a checklist that specifies the proportion of the time devoted to different kinds of activities. Other rating schemes are normative or attitudinal, such as a rating scheme to measure clarity of instructor's presentation or a scale to assess the nature of the encounter between participants and the delivery system.

Although direct observation methods appear to be attractively simple, they are not easily taught to untrained observers, they are highly time-consuming, and they produce data that are difficult to summarize and analyze. These problems are particularly troublesome the less structured the observation method used and the more complex the program services are. Moreover, as noted, observation may change the behavior of program personnel and participants.

In some circumstances, it is possible to reduce observation problems by developing adequate sampling approaches, so that one or a few observers can record project activities in a more economical fashion. Such sampling is sometimes done by randomly selecting for observation a statistically adequate number of time periods. Another approach for projects involving individuals is to sample participants and then to observe them as they interface with project activities.

It is sometimes practical and advisable to combine direct observation with other monitoring approaches, since experience suggests direct observation is difficult to accomplish with a high degree of reliability and is subject to the limitations described above.

Service Record Data

Record data were discussed in the section on measuring coverage. In the same way characteristics of targets can be assessed from records, project service delivery can be monitored from them. (Exhibit 4-I describes the use of a medical chart review to evaluate the delivery of pediatric care.)

Service records vary. They can be the equivalent of narrative reports or highly structured data forms, on which project personnel check whether or not particular services were given, how they were received, and observable results (Cernea and Tepping, 1977). Their level of detail

Exhibit 4-I: Use of Records to Evaluate a Delivery System

The Watts Health Center is a family-oriented neighborhood health center in the predominantly black low-income community in Los Angeles. In operation since October 1967, it offers extensive ambulatory health services to approximately 35,000 people who live within the three-square-mile target area and whose family income is below the federal poverty guidelines.

At patient registration, a permanent file is started for the client and all family members. This registration process, while it facilitates continuity of care, does not commit the registrant to utilize the center.

In December 1970, a 2.5 percent sample (244 families) of the entire registered population of 11,721 families were selected by use of a table of random numbers. With these families, the chart of every patient who was under 17 years of age when registered was studied by a pediatrician, and the information was recorded on a survey form.

"High-quality" pediatric care was presumed to be present when all of the following were recorded in the patient file: at least one comprehensive workup; immunizations appropriate for age according to the recommendations of the American Academy of Pediatrics; attention paid to all abnormal laboratory reports; and appropriate follow-up visits for all significant clinical conditions detected.

One-quarter of the children in these registered families had never been brought in for care at the center. Another 6 percent had been seen only in the dental clinic. Almost half (47 percent) had received medical but not dental attention. The remaining 22 percent had visited both a physician and a dentist.

Of the 339 children who had received at least some medical care at the center, 18 percent had appeared exclusively in the emergency room. Another 58 percent had visited another part of the health center, often in addition to an emergency room visit, but only on an episodic basis. Only 24 percent were adjudged as having received a comprehensive medical evaluation consisting of history, physical examination, and screening laboratory tests (as recommended by the American Academy of Pediatrics).

Thus, only 17 percent of the entire group of children had received all of the selected aspects of both preventive and curative high-quality pediatric care. An additional 11 percent were deficient only in immunizations, as recorded in the chart. The largest group, 58 percent, were receiving episodic care but all laboratory and clinical abnormalities had been noted and followed up. With the remaining 23 percent at least one instance of inadequate follow-up had occurred whether or not the evaluation and immunizations had been complete.

SOURCE: Adapted, with permission, from H. M. Lieberman, "Evaluating the Quality of Ambulatory Pediatric Care at a Neighborhood Health Center: Creative Use of a Chart Review." *Clinical Pediatrics*, 13 (January 1974): 52-55.

is related to the complexity of the project and to the number of alternatives that can be specified in advance. (See Exhibit 4-J for a simple procedure in a nutrition evaluation.) Service records also vary in sophistication with respect to storage and access; in clinical contexts, for example, computerized information systems have been devised based on management science principles.

Many times, service record systems are simply too complex to be used properly for monitoring purposes (a problem, as we noted earlier, that plagues records on target populations). This occurs because they are designed primarily to serve the administrative and management needs of program staff. In such cases, record forms are often either not filled in completely or the parts that are believed to be irrelevant by project staff are completed haphazardly. On the one hand, there is a risk that adding monitoring components will prove overly burdensome to program personnel, will limit staff cooperation, and will therefore render the resulting data incomplete and unreliable for monitoring purposes. On the other hand, record information is inexpensive and efficient. Clearly, its use depends on adequate training of program staff to maximize reliability, on providing motivation to staff, and on quality-control checks to ensure timely and appropriate completion.

As with records on target populations, a few items of data gathered consistently and reliably are generally much better for monitoring purposes than a more comprehensive set of information of doubtful reliability and inconsistent collection.

A second rule is that, whenever possible, it is useful to structure record forms as checklists so that program staff can check off various

Exhibit 4-J: Program Implementation in a Nutritional Experiment

An example of a project in which there is precise measurement of the program variable is the Institute for Nutrition of Central America and Panama's (INCAP) evaluation of the impact of a high-calorie, high-protein supplement on physical growth and development and cognitive functioning of preschool children. In two villages the calorie supplement is provided twice a day at the same time periods to all villagers who receive it. The feeding spot is near the village school. In two other "control villages" a less fortified but still beneficial supplement is provided.

All persons entering have their names checked off from available census lists of village members. Each person receives the supplement in a standard cup and when they have drunk as much as they wish, the cup is returned to the project staff person, who can then measure the amount ingested, subtracting the total from the amount remaining in the cup. Since villagers are permitted as many cups as they desire, there is no reason for them to switch cups with one another, although they are carefully observed.

These daily logs are then brought back to INCAP and through a computerized system become part of the individual record for each mother and child who participates in the study.

SOURCE: Summary, by permission, of H.E. Freeman et al., "Relations Between Nutrition and Cognition in Rural Guatemala." *American Journal of Public Health* 67 (March 1977).

items rather than provide narrative information. Such a procedure not only minimizes the time required of project staff, but is most convenient for subsequent analysis.

The third rule is that it is important to review completed records for consistency and accuracy as carefully and as soon as possible. Timely editing and quality-control procedures can catch omissions and inconsistencies.

Again, it is important to emphasize that there are risks in using service records as the only data source. Program staff, intentionally or unintentionally, may exaggerate the extent to which different program elements are being delivered to targets. Sometimes this is the result of an overzealous concern with maintaining appearances of efficiency and responsibility. At other times it may be because program staff are disenchanted with procedures for providing certain project services, although there is a formal requirement that they adhere to them. Finally, there are occasions on which project staff's interpretation of a particular intervention service differs from that of either the program designers or the evaluators.

Service Provider Data

Rather than relying on information recorded in administrative and service records, program managers can require staff to provide special information for monitoring purposes. (Exhibit 4-K illustrates the use of staff to generate monitoring data for a Choctaw family education program.) Sometimes, narrative reports are required of project staff in the form of diaries. Sometimes staff may be required to code or complete rating forms for the evaluator from diary information. Diaries are generally used only for backup information.

A compromise between a highly structured interview or questionnaire and a complete narrative is some form of semidirected interview or semistructured questionnaire. This approach is analogous to the data guide discussed under observational methods. It allows for some depth of information but at the same time cuts down on the time and effort of program staff.

The most efficient approach is the use of a highly structured survey instrument that can be completed by interview or by the staff person alone. Structured instruments lend themselves readily to tabulation. As in the case of observation efforts, it is often wise to sample either time periods or target encounters in order to minimize work for staff. In doing so, it is important that a representative sample be employed, leaving a choice of time periods or particular targets as the subjects of inquiry may otherwise encourage project staff intentionally or unintentionally to bias accounts of project implementation.

Program Participant Data

The final approach to collecting monitoring information is to obtain data on program delivery from participants themselves. Such information is valuable not only because of the different perspective from which it is offered, but because, among other reasons, it may be the only way to find out what was actually delivered. Participant data may be neces-

Exhibit 4-K: Home Visitors as Providers of Monitoring Information for a Family Information Project

The Choctaw Home-Centered Family Education Project demonstrates a workable early childhood model for a rural, reservation group. Specifically, one objective was to use the Choctaw home visitor to work with the mother or her surrogates in establishing an environment to stimulate the cognitive development of the Choctaw child from birth to 4 years of age.

The instructional home visit was the principal component used to maintain contact with the client families. In this approach, the interaction between mother and child was the central focus. The home visitor demonstrated the instructional techniques. Her behavior served as a model for those attitudes and practices being communicated to the mothers. The home visitor and mothers were encouraged to adapt the instruction to the household materials and individual style of the mother. The proposed cognitive stimulation occurred as a part of a program designed for the whole child: language, motor, sense, perception, social, and intellectual. The home visitors were given training in the stages and sequence for all these developmental areas in addition to community dynamics, early childhood instruction, behavior management, and learning. The home visitors planned, implemented, and evaluated the intervention for each family. Home visits were planned on a weekly basis at a time convenient for the mothers.

In addition to the functions and roles of the home visitor, the Choctaw home visitors were required to perform program evaluation functions. They were required to rate the home situation for its stimulation potential, to test the children, and to collect any additional information required by the evaluators to document or assess the project.

SOURCE: Adapted, with permission, from P. Quigley, L. Morris and G. Hammett, *The Choctaw Home-Centered Family Education Demonstration Project.* Tucson, AZ: Behavior Associates, 1976, p. 8.

sary for providers to know what is important to clients, including their satisfaction with and understanding of the intervention.

There may be disparities in many programs between services and interventions provided and those actually received or utilized, as the family planning literature has shown. For example, as part of a technical education program, participants may receive study guides, exercises, manuals, and equipment for additional extraclassroom use. While project staff may believe that these are employed as planned, it may well be that this is not the case. For such projects it may be critical to query participants to find out whether certain services were used or even were received. Such participant data may also be generated by measures that indirectly test whether services were received, such as extraclassroom assignments consisting of calculating distances and converting them to standard values. In that case, not only could participants be interviewed regarding whether or not they used the services in the manner intended, but they could also be tested on whether they can perform reasonably on tasks whose learning was supposed to be enhanced by the services in question.

The previous discussion on access pointed out that there are times when participant satisfaction with a program is a key indicator in monitoring program implementation. Clearly, here the participant is the appropriate and sole information source. (See Exhibit 4-L for an example of a study of client satisfaction with medical services.) In Exhibit 4-M we show the use of a community survey in the Kansas City Experiment to examine the effect of the experiment on the larger community.

Finally, Nicholson and Wright (1977) have shown that in interventions involving complex treatments, it is important to ascertain participants' understanding of such treatments, the program operating rules, and so on. In short, it is necessary not only to establish that designated services have been delivered, but also that they were received, utilized, and understood as intended.

Information from participants must necessarily be obtained by self-administered questionnaires or interviews. Participants may be sampled in some systematic way, or an entire census may be conducted.

ANALYSIS OF MONITORING DATA

In general, the analysis of monitoring data addresses the following three issues: description of the project, comparison between sites, and program conformity.

Exhibit 4-L: Consumer Satisfaction with Prepaid Group Practice

Client's satisfaction with the delivery of medical services in a prepaid group practice plan, and comparative data from an alternative Blue Cross insurance plan, were obtained by means of household surveys. The results (showing the items asked) are summarized as follows:

Measures of Satisfaction	Blue Cross (N = 354) %	Prepaid Practice (N = 356) %
Proportion of respondents receiving services in past year	73	70
Percentage very satisfied among respondents receiving services in past year		
With amount of privacy in doctor's office	92	86
With the amount of time the doctor spends with you	82	74
With the doctor's concern about your health	85	70
With the doctor's warmth and personal interest in you	83	67
With the amount of information given to you about your health	81	64
With doctor's training and technical competence	93	78
With the doctor's friendliness	89	79
With friendliness of nurses, receptionists, etc.	84	81
With quality of medical care received	88	77
With adequacy of office facilities and equipment	93	84
With the doctor's willingness to listen when you tell him about your health	86	78

SOURCE: From R. Tessler and D. Mechanic, "Consumer Satisfaction with Prepaid Group Practice: A Comparative Study." *Journal of Health and Social Behavior*, 16 (March 1975): 99. Reprinted by permission.

Exhibit 4-M: Kansas City Community Survey to Determine the Effect of an Intervention

A random survey of households was designed to examine six general aspects of the experiment's possible effects on the community:

1. citizens' perceptions of the likelihood of being victimized (by robbery, rape, assault, burglary, auto theft), violent crime, and general neighborhood safety;

2. the degree to which citizens protected themselves and their property along with the kinds of protective measures taken;

3. citizens' perceived need for police officers, random police patrol, and aggressive police patrol;

4. citizens' perceptions of police officers' reputations, police effectiveness, and citizens' respect for officers;

5. citizens' perceptions of police officers' behavior, fairness, and treatment of citizens; and

6. citizens' perceptions and satisfaction with police service.

SOURCE: From G. Kelling et al., *The Kansas City Preventive Patrol Experiment: A Technical Report.* Washington, DC: Police Foundation, 1974, pp. 240-241. Reprinted by permission.

Description of the Project

An important question is the extent to which the program as implemented resembles in crucial details the program as designed. A description of the actual project derived from monitoring data would cover the following topics: estimates of coverage and bias in participation; types of services delivered and intensity of services given to participants of significant kinds; and reactions of participants to services delivered. Descriptive statements might take the form of narrative accounts, especially when monitoring data are derived from more qualitative sources. But of greater utility are quantitative analyses. Increasingly, sophisticated analytic methods and measures are being developed (see Miley et al., 1978; Heumann, 1979).

Comparison Between Sites

When a program includes more than one site, a second question concerns differences in program implementation between sites. Comparison permits an understanding of the sources of project diversity, such as staff, administrative, target differences, or differences in the contextual environment of the program, and can also facilitate efforts to achieve standardization. In addition, between-site differences may provide clues to why projects at some sites may be more effective than those at other sites.

Program Conformity

The third issue, of course, is the one with which we began: the degree of conformity and convergence between program design and program implementation. Discrepancies between the two may lead to respecification of project design or to efforts to move project implementation closer to design. Such analysis also provides an opportunity to judge the appropriateness of an impact evaluation and, if necessary, opt for a more formative evaluation in order to develop the necessary convergence.

FEEDBACK FROM MONITORING

As we have noted, monitoring data have a number of uses, depending on who has sponsored the monitoring and the state of program development. When conducted as part of a more comprehensive evaluation, monitoring data provide guidance on congruence between program design and program implementation. Often it is recommended that they be collected prior to a firm commitment to undertake an impact analysis, although it may also be necessary that they be carried out parallel with an impact analysis, since a monitoring study undertaken in advance may not provide valid evidence of design conformity once the project is under way.

Monitoring evaluations undertaken for project managerial and accountability purposes are often fed back to project managers and staff on a continual basis. For an established project for which there is a continual set of evaluations undertaken, fluctuation and changes over time may allow one either to redesign or to fine-tune the programs and reassess the extent to which the pool of targets and project implementation need modification. Evaluators cannot assume, however, that merely providing information assures its use. Thus, as we discuss in Chapter 9, there is a need to be concerned with maximizing dissemination and utilization of monitoring — matters that in themselves call for evaluation.

5

Strategies for Impact Assessment

Impact assessment is directed at establishing, with as much certainty as possible, whether or not an intervention is producing its intended effects. Given the nature of all scientific activity, such estimates cannot be made with certainty, but only within limits of error and with varying degrees of plausibility. To reduce the size of such errors and to raise the plausibility of effectiveness estimates, impact evaluation needs to be undertaken as systematically and as rigorously as possible. Only in this way can the evaluator identify the effects of an intervention.

The outcomes of social programs are assessed by comparing information about participants and nonparticipants, before and after an intervention, or by other, less powerful, research designs. But the essential considerations involve the systematic rejection of alternative, competing explanations for the observed outcomes other than the intervention.

KEY CONCEPTS

Confounding Factors:	Extraneous variables resulting in outcome effects that obscure or exaggerate the "true" effects of an intervention.
Gross Outcome Effects:	Measured overall impact found by an evaluation, only part of which might be caused by the intervention.
Net Outcome Effects:	Impact of an intervention, after confounding effects have been removed.
Proxy Measure:	A variable that is used to "stand in" for one that is hard to measure directly.
Reliability:	The extent to which scores are reproducible in repeated administrations, assuming all relevant factors are the same.
Stochastic Effects:	Measurement fluctuations attributable to chance.
Valid Measure:	A measure for which there is evidence or presumption that it reflects the concept it is intended to measure.

---

*T*he obstacles to impact assessments arise from several sources: First, the social world is complex, and most social phenomena have many roots and causes. With so many "moving parts," the severity of a social problem may be influenced by a number of circumstances in addition to those introduced by a program. Second, theories and empirical generalizations of social science are weak and incomplete. It is difficult to develop models of social phenomena that can serve adequately as the framework within which impact assessments are to be undertaken. Third, social programs cannot be expected to have more than relatively small impacts on the social world. A welfare program cannot be expected to eradicate poverty, nor can a criminal rehabilitation program be completely successful in every case. More often than not, we can expect effects to be small and difficult to detect. Finally, some social programs are especially hard to assess because they have been in operation for a long term. Ongoing programs covering vast target populations can only be assessed by making heroic assumptions that often tax credibility.

There are two points in the total evaluation process at which impact assessment is especially important. The first (and perhaps the most appropriate) is in the testing of new, proposed programs or proposed changes in existing programs. Coverage in these programs is often partial, and thus it is often possible to conduct experiments that will provide relatively definitive estimates of program effects.

The second point is in the review of existing, ongoing programs. Even when an established program appears to be either working well or at least not obviously failing, stakeholders or program staff often want plausible estimates of *how* well the program is fulfilling its designated purposes. Besides, things are often not as they appear to be: Systematic, objective observations often contradict general impressions. Policymakers may need impact evaluation results to justify expansion of what may already be widespread resource commitments in the face of persistent competition for funds and the political pressures of various interest groups. Program managers need impact results to learn how to fine-tune their programs and increase their efficacy and efficiency.

As we outlined in Chapter 2, the prerequisites for assessing the impact of an intervention are as follows: First, either the project should have its objectives sufficiently well articulated to make it possible to identify measures of goal achievement, or the evaluator must establish the objectives. Second, the intervention should have been sufficiently well implemented for there to be no question that its critical elements have been delivered to appropriate targets. It is obvious that it would be a waste of time, effort, and resources to estimate the impact of a program that lacks measurable goals and has not been properly implemented.

The task of eliciting objectives or reaching consensus on them can be handled by one or several of the techniques described in Chapter 2. Discerning a set of objectives for a given program is not an impossible task, even when stakeholders are in disagreement over goals or when they deny that there are any goals. All programs do something, if only providing some income to their staffs. Often, as Chen and Rossi suggest (1980), the perceptive social scientist, drawing on his or her general knowledge of the workings of our society and of its organizations, can make rather reasonable inferences about what effects a program can be expected to have, given the working assumptions of the program and the relevant body of social science knowledge. The main point we make here, however, is that such goals must be specified *before* impact assessment can be undertaken.

We cannot overstress the difficulty of undertaking impact evaluations. While the fundamental rules for conducting them are well established, the evaluator must constantly cultivate the cooperation of program staff and target participants, and meet the pressure to produce timely and unambiguous findings.

LINKING INTERVENTIONS TO OUTCOMES

The problem of discerning the effectiveness of a program is identical to the problem of establishing that the program is the "cause" of some specified effect. Hence, establishing impact essentially amounts to establishing causality. There are many deep and thorny issues surrounding the concept of causality, and we cannot concern ourselves with them here. Rather, we shall accept the view that the world is orderly and lawful and that "A is the cause of B" can be a valid statement.

In the social sciences, causal relationships are ordinarily stated probabilistically: Thus, the statement "A is the cause of B" usually means that if we introduce A, B is *more likely* to result than if we do not do so. The statement does not imply that B always results if A is introduced, nor does it mean that B only occurs after A has been introduced. The phrase "is more likely to occur" means that the probability of B, given A, is higher than the probability of B, absent A.

Consider this example: The introduction of voluntary employment training projects for adults *may* reduce the amount of unemployment among the unskilled, at least in the short term. That is, it is more likely that unemployment will decline in the presence of such a program than in its absence. But no training program, no matter how well designed, will completely eradicate unemployment. Some adults will simply refuse to take advantage of the opportunity offered; others will be unable to benefit (because of infirmity, disability, or other obligations), even though they are willing. Furthermore, unemployment levels are influenced strongly by job vacancies. Obviously, if there are no jobs, the unemployed cannot be absorbed into the labor force, no matter how well trained.

A training program is also not the only way in which the unemployment of unskilled workers can be reduced. On-the-job training opportunities can be made available, special "sheltered" jobs can be created to enable workers to gain experience while learning, and so on. Hence, the assessment of whether or not a specific employment training project can increase employment is complicated by the fact that employment trends are responsive to many factors, among which a specific training program is only one.

The critical issue in impact evaluation is, therefore, whether or not a program produces more of an effect, or outcome, than would have occurred either without the intervention or with an alternative intervention.

GROSS VERSUS NET OUTCOME

The starting point for impact assessment is the identification of one or more *outcome measures* that represent the objectives of the program. Thus, in studying a program designed to increase adult literacy, the objectives of the program may be represented as increasing reading-level scores on a standard educational skills test. The program may be considered successful if, after the program, participants' scores are higher than what would be expected absent program participation. (Ways of measuring outcomes are discussed later in this chapter.)

A distinction must be made between gross outcomes and net outcomes. *Gross outcomes* are changes in an outcome measure that are observed after a program has been operating. The gross outcome measure in our adult literacy program is the increase in the participants' reading-level scores that results from the program and any number of other influences (e.g., the simultaneous introduction of educational television into the community in question). *Net outcomes,* on the other hand, are those results attributable to the intervention, free and clear of the effects of other causes in the program's context.

In symbolic terms, the relationship between gross and net outcomes can be expressed as follows:

$$\text{Gross Outcome} = \begin{bmatrix} \text{Effects of} \\ \text{intervention} \\ \text{(net outcome)} \end{bmatrix} + \begin{bmatrix} \text{Effects of} \\ \text{confounding} \\ \text{factors} \end{bmatrix}$$

Thus, an observed upward gain in literacy measured in before-and-after observations of a group of persons who participated in an adult literacy program (gross outcome) is composed of two parts: first, the effects of the program (net outcomes) and, second, the effects of other events, experiences, and so on, that influenced literacy during the period in question (confounding factors).

CONSTRAINTS ON ASSESSING NET OUTCOME

Given that gross outcome reflects not only the effects of an intervention but also those of other processes occurring at the same time, impact assessments must arrive at estimates of *net* intervention effects. To accomplish this, the evaluator must "purify" gross outcome effects by purging them of contaminating elements, known as confounding factors. These are the extraneous "causes" that compete with intervention efforts to explain changes in the target problem or population after the program has been put into operation.

Extraneous Confounding Factors

Confounding factors vary according to the social phenomenon in question. Thus, we would expect that an intervention designed to improve the nutritional habits of families would compete with processes quite different from those affecting a program to improve the occupational skills of young people. Despite the idiosyncratic features of each program and the special characteristics of the particular target population it is designed to reach, certain processes are general enough to be identified as potential competitors with any intervention (Campbell and Stanley, 1966; Cook and Campbell, 1979). Some of the most important of these are outlined below.

Endogenous Change

Social programs operate in environments in which ordinary or "natural" sequences of events influence outcomes. For example, most persons who recover from acute conditions do so "naturally," an endogenous change that medical researchers term "spontaneous remission." Thus, medical experiments testing a treatment for some pathological condition (say, influenza) must distinguish its effectiveness from the fact that many patients spontaneously recover without treatment.

Similarly, in testing for the effects of a social intervention, one must take into account that the condition for which the intervention is seen as a remedy may change of its own accord. Thus, a program for training young people in particular occupational skills must contend with the fact that some people will obtain the same skills in ways that do not involve the program. Likewise, a program to reduce poverty has to consider that some families and individuals will become economically better off without help from the project.

Secular Drift

Relatively long-term trends in the community or country in question may produce changes that enhance or mask the effects of a program. Thus, in a period when a community's birthrate is declining generally, a program to reduce fertility in that community may appear to be effective because fertility trends are generally downward. Again, a program to upgrade housing quality may appear to be effective mainly because the national trends in real income enable everyone to put more resources into their housing. Such secular trends may also mask program effects: A project to increase crop yields may appear to fail because weather conditions lead to poor growing conditions during the program period. Similarly, a program to provide employment opportunities to released prisoners may appear to have no effects because it coincides with a depressed period in the labor market.

Interfering Events

Like long-term secular trends, short-term events may produce enhancing or masking changes. An earth tremor that disrupts communications and makes the delivery of food supplements difficult may interfere with a nutritional program. The threat of war with another nation may make it appear that a program to enhance local community cooperation has been effective, when it is actually the potential crisis that is bringing community members together.

Maturational Trends

Programs that are directed toward changing persons in infancy, childhood, or adolescence (indeed, in any age-determined target population) have to cope with the fact that over time there may be considerable change in individuals' lives. Thus, evaluation of an educational program designed to increase the language-handling capacities of small children has to compensate for the fact that such capacities increase with age. Similarly, the effectiveness of a campaign to increase interest in sports among young adults may be masked by a decline in such interest that occurs when young adults enter the labor force. Maturational trends can affect adults also: A program to improve preventive health practices may seem ineffective because health declines with age.

Self-Selection

Perhaps the most serious obstruction to the assessment of the intervention's impact is the fact that the portions of a target population easiest to reach are usually also those most likely to change in the desired direction because of targets' differential potential to change. Clearly, projects based on the voluntary cooperation of individuals, households, or other units are most likely to be affected by self-selection processes. Thus, a project designed to enhance vocational abilities appears most attractive to persons who are interested in enhancing their occupational skills. Such persons are likely to manage to improve their skills whether or not they enroll in a project.

In some voluntary programs, self-selection may occur involuntarily from the viewpoint of participants, as a result of political or administrative actions. Consider a community that, through its municipal government, "volunteers" for a program to improve sewage disposal by installing an appropriate technical infrastructure. Although individual community members do not volunteer participation, all persons living in the area are subject to the "treatment" and hence can benefit from the program. Similarly, in the adoption of a new (and presumably improved) textbook for elementary schoolchildren, individual pupils do not volunteer to use the textbook. The "volunteering" in this case is done by the school system.

There are similar processes at work, but in the opposite direction, that lead to differential attrition. It is seldom the case that participation in a treatment is carried through to the end either by or for all participants. Dropout rates vary from project to project but are almost always disturbingly significant. Subjects that leave a program may be different in quite understandable ways from those who remain throughout. For one thing, those who are clearly benefiting from the intervention are likely to remain or be encouraged to do so, while those who find the project unrewarding or difficult are likely to drop out or be discouraged from remaining in the program.

Although several evaluators have identified additional extraneous confounding factors (see especially Campbell and Stanley, 1966, and Cook and Campbell, 1979), these are either primarily applicable to laboratory conditions or are encountered rarely. The extraneous confounding factors listed above are those to which an evaluator must be particularly alert in designing impact assessment research.

Measurement Error

The confounding factors we have just discussed are neither equally nor uniformly distributed across all impact evaluations. They are present or absent depending on the substantive area involved. Thus, one may not have to be much concerned about maturational effects in a study of the potential work disincentives of unemployment benefits, since they are usually given to adults in the prime of their working lives and for relatively short periods of time. Maturational effects are undoubtedly much more important for the study of intellectual development impacts of programs directed at preschool children.

Measurement errors, on the other hand, are always present. Fortunately, our knowledge about these "method effects" is more complete than our understanding of other confounding factors. Hence, it is possible to estimate and sometimes compensate for such errors, while the extent of extraneous confounding effects is always problematic. In the following discussion, our emphasis is on the two most prevalent measurement errors: stochastic effects and unreliability.

Stochastic Effects

In any measurement effort, chance or random fluctuations, termed *stochastic processes,* may make it difficult to judge whether a given outcome is large enough to warrant attention. These variations result from the fact that each set of observations is a sample from a target population or from all possible trials of that project. Sampling theory, applied appropriately, describes how much variation one can expect and how often one can expect a variation of a particular size, given a large number of samples drawn with probability methods (Kish, 1965; Sudman, 1976). Applying the results of appropriate statistical tests, one can judge how often a given result would occur by chance alone, even though the true outcome is zero. Thus, a given effect, say a 5 percent difference in a crop yield for farmers who have adopted a new fertilizer, may turn out to be a highly unlikely outcome for a program in which the "true" effect is zero. The statistical significance of a particular outcome is estimated by comparing it with what would be expected by chance when sampling from a hypothetical set of trials in which the "true" effect is zero.

Unreliability

Data collection procedures are always subject to a certain degree of unreliability. The reliability of a measure is defined as the degree to which identical scores or values would be obtained on a measure in repeated data collection efforts with the same subjects. A major source of unreliability is the measurement instrument itself. For example, many attitudinal measures reveal low reliability when applied to the same or similar subjects. The testing or measuring situation, observer or inter- viewer reliability, and even subjects' mood swings also contribute to unreliability. There are no hard and fast rules about acceptable levels of reliability. Measures generally lose their utility, however, when their reproducibility falls below 75 to 80 percent. (See Blalock and Blalock, 1968, for ways to estimate unreliability.) Note that stochastic variation and unreliability are separate and distinct design effects.

Employing unreliable measures of outcome obscures whatever real effects a project may have. The more unreliable a measure, the larger the actual, real differences must be to indicate a significant result. Because reliability is constantly at issue in outcome measurement, we shall discuss it in fuller detail at the end of this chapter.

A Formula for Impact Assessment

A gross outcome is derived from *all* the elements discussed above *plus* the "pure" or net effects of the project; gross outcome is always a function of net program effects and confounding elements. In order to obtain unbiased and precise estimates of the net effects of projects, it is necessary to take into account the confounding or contaminating ele- ments.

Another way of summarizing the items discussed in this section is through the following formula:

$$\text{Net Effects} = [\text{Gross Outcome}] - \begin{bmatrix} \text{Endogenous Change} \\ \text{Secular Drift} \\ \text{Interfering Events} \\ \text{Maturational Trends} \\ \text{Self-Selection} \\ \text{Unreliability Effects} \end{bmatrix} + \begin{bmatrix} \text{Stochastic} \\ \text{Effects} \end{bmatrix}$$

The task of impact assessment is delineated by this formula; it is necessary to purify gross output measures by developing estimates of the magnitude and direction of possibly confounding processes. In fact, each of the confounding effects can be either positive or negative numerically. Fortunately, it is not always necessary to estimate the magnitude of each of the seven major confounding factors separately. Rather, through the use of appropriate research designs, it is possible to develop fairly adequate estimates of the combined impact of obscuring effects.

Intervention-Related Obscuring Factors

In this addendum to our discussion of impact assessment constraints, we consider some of the obscuring effects that might arise out of the evaluation effort and the measurement of impact themselves. Especially in evaluations that require that special measurements be undertaken beyond what might be generated ordinarily, there is the risk that these additional obscuring factors may be a concern. It should be noted, however, that such effects have rarely been shown to be very large.

Hawthorne Effect

In a famous experiment — an attempt to determine the effects of varying light intensity on the productivity of women assembling small electronic parts (Roethlisberger and Dickson, 1939) — it was discovered that any change in the intensity of illumination, positive or negative, brought about a rise in worker productivity. The Hawthorne Effect (named after the site where the experiment was conducted) was interpreted by the experimenters as the result of experimenting, which included continuous observations of work-group members. Roethlisberger and Dixon reasoned that the workers took the fact that they had been singled out as an experimental group and given a lot of attention by the experimenters as a sign that the firm was interested in their personal welfare. Their response was to develop a high level of work-group morale and to increase their productivity. The measured outcome of the experiment was a combination of the intervention (increased illumination), the delivery of that intervention (apparent concern on the part of the management and the presence of experimenters in the workplace), and the constant observation.

The Hawthorne Effect is not specific to social experiments. It may also be present in any circumstance in which there are human subjects. For example, in medical experiments, especially those involving pharmacological treatments, the Hawthorne Effect is known as the "placebo effect." Subjects may be as much affected by the knowledge that they are receiving treatment as by the treatment itself. Thus, the evaluation of the effectivness of a new analgesic (painkiller) usually involves either a placebo control, consisting of a group of patients who are given essentially neutral medication (sugar pills), or a control given the "standard" pill commonly prescribed. The effectiveness of the analgesic is measured by how much more relief from the new drug is reported in comparison to that reported by those who received either the placebo or the standard pill.

A recent reanalysis of the Hawthorne experiment (Franke and Kaul, 1978) casts considerable doubt on whether the work actually demonstrated any Hawthorne Effect at all, a finding that underscores the fact that the effect is rare.

Delivery System Contaminants

Another obscuring factor is that treatment is rarely delivered in a "pure" form. Thus, counseling therapy for juveniles who have been delinquents usually involves not only the therapist but also other personnel (the intake clerks, for example), a setting in which the therapy is conducted, the reactions of those of the juveniles' peers who know of the therapy, and so on. The intervention delivery system, then, including the physical plant, personnel, rules and regulations, and the labeling of targets, affects the outcome of a planned intervention — indeed, so much so that monitoring the delivery of interventions almost always is a necessary adjunct to impact assessments.

It should be emphasized that the obscuring effects of intervention and measurement are of most concern when the program is a weak one. A powerful intervention that produces strong results will tend to override those that come from delivery and measurement effects. Thus, when an intervention is weak, one particularly needs to worry about whether the effects or lack of them are the result of stochastic, realiability, or other measurement errors.

DESIGN OPTIONS FOR IMPACT ASSESSMENTS

Again, the strategic issue in impact assessment is how to obtain estimates of what would be the difference between two conditions: one in which the intervention is present and one in which it is absent. Ideally, the absent condition should be identical in all respects to the present condition, save for the intervention. There are several alternative approaches that vary in effectiveness; all involve the establishment of "controls." These approaches are sketched below, and will be discussed in detail in this and the following two chapters:

- *Randomized Controls:* Targets are randomly divided into an experimental group, to whom the intervention is administered, and "randomized controls," from whom the intervention is withheld.

- *Constructed Controls:* Targets to whom the intervention is given are matched with an "equivalent" group, constructed controls, from whom the intervention is withheld.

- *Statistical Controls:* Participant and nonparticipant targets are compared, holding constant statistically differences between participants and nonparticipants.

- *Reflexive Controls:* Targets who receive the intervention are compared to themselves, as measured before the intervention.

- *Generic Controls:* Intervention effects among targets are compared with established norms about typical changes occurring in the target population.

- *Shadow Controls:* Targets who receive the intervention are compared to the judgments of experts, program administrators, and/or participants on what changes are "ordinarily to be expected" for the target population.

Note that the alternatives listed above are not mutually exclusive. Randomized controls may be compared with experimental groups, and statistical controls may be used as well; constructed controls and statistical controls, at the margins, are difficult to distinguish from each other in practice.

The alternatives are also not listed in strict order of preference. While using randomized controls may be the best possible procedure to follow, reflexive controls are sometimes better than constructed controls, and using statistical controls may be inferior to employing generic controls. The nuances of such judgments are described in greater detail in the next two chapters.

Full versus Partial Coverage

The most severe restriction on strategy choice is whether or not the intervention in question is being delivered to *all* (or virtually all) members of a target population. For programs with total coverage (as in the case of long-standing, ongoing, fully funded programs), it is usually not possible to identify a group that is not receiving the intervention and that is in essential senses comparable to the subjects who are beneficiaries. In short, it is not possible to define a control group. In such circumstances, the main strategy available is the use of reflexive controls and before-and-after comparisons. In contrast, interventions that are to be tested on a demonstration basis ordinarily will not be delivered to all of the target population. Hence, in the start-up phase, new programs are, almost by definition, programs with partial coverage.

In all likelihood, no program has ever achieved total coverage of its intended target population. Even in the best of programs, there are some persons who refuse to participate, others who are not aware that they can participate, and still others who are declared ineligible on technicalities. Nevertheless, many programs achieve almost full coverage. The Social Security Administration's retirement payments, for example, reach more than 85 percent of the eligible portions of the population.

As a rule of thumb, when programs reach as many as four of five eligible units (80 percent coverage), a program has "full coverage" for the purposes of the present discussion. The smaller the proportion who are not reached, the greater the differences are likely to be between those who are covered and those who are not: For all practical intents, almost all children between the ages of six and fourteen attend school; those who do not, suffer from temporary or permanent disabilities, receive tutoring at home from parents or private tutors, or accompany migratory families as they move from site to site. Hence, those children who at any point in time are not enrolled in school are likely to be so different from those who attend that no amount of matching of use of statistical controls will produce comparability of the sort needed for the designs using randomized, constructed, or statistical controls.

Fortunately for our purposes, there are enough programs with full coverage that are not uniform over time or over localities. Policies change and programs change with them. An intervention's administrators may also institute modifications in order to meet some new condition or to make administration easier. Thus, from time to time, social security benefits have been increased to take into account new conditions or to add new services (e.g., Medicare). Similarly, sufficient local autonomy may be given to states and local governments so that a program (e.g., Aid to Families with Dependent Children) may vary somewhat from place to place. With proper precautions, such "natural variation" may provide a leverage point for the estimation of program effects.

For partial-coverage programs, a variety of strategies are available. If the program is under the control of the evaluator (as may be the case in new or prospective programs), the ideal solution is the use of randomized controls: A set of potential target subjects are selected in some way and randomly sorted into an experimental group and a control group. This process of randomization assures *probabilistic equivalence* of the beneficiaries receiving the intervention to others who are not. When an evaluator cannot employ randomization in the formation of experimental and control groups or conditions, adequate constructed control groups often may be formed by uncovered target subjects, if proper precautions are taken.

A Typology of Impact Assessment Designs

The crossing of intervention features and data collection strategies produces the schematic classification shown in Table 5.1. Each of the boxes shown in the table will be discussed separately below:

Randomized "True" Experiments

"True" experiments are applicable only to partial-coverage programs. The essential feature of true experiments is the random assignment of treatments to targets and the random withholding of treatment from targets, constituting respectively an experimental and a control group.

Randomized true experiments may vary greatly in complexity, as the following examples illustrate. (See also Boruch et al., 1978, for a relatively complete list of randomized social experiments.)

- To gauge the effectiveness of educational techniques of training films used in World War II, alternative versions of training films were shown to randomly selected troops whose understanding of the lessons was measured before and after viewing. The versions were then compared (Hovland et al., 1949).

- To test whether provision of limited amounts of financial aid would help prisoners released from state prisons to adjust to civilian life, 400 prisoners released from the Maryland prisons were divided randomly into three experimental groups, one that received eligibility for 13 weeks of unemployment benefits, one that received 13 weeks of benefits and job placement help, and one that received job placement help only. A fourth group received neither benefits nor placements. The 400 persons were interviewed periodically, over the year following release (Rossi et al., 1980).

- To assess whether reducing mothers' anxiety about minor surgery for their children resulted in better posthospital sequelae for their children, mothers were first randomized into experimental and control groups. The former received counseling and reassurance when their children were admitted; the controls received "usual" care (Skipper and Leonard, 1968).

- To test how best to handle cases of spouse abuse, a Minneapolis police precinct agreed to participate in a randomized experiment in which cases of spouse abuse reported to the police were handled randomly in one of three ways: The abusing spouse was arrested and kept in jail overnight; the abusing spouse was asked to leave the home and not to return for 16 hours; or the police attempted to conciliate the dispute between the spouses (Sherman, 1980).

- In the Experimental Housing Allowance Demand Experiment, a random sample of poor households in Pittsburgh and Phoenix were randomly placed either in one of twenty-three experimental groups or in a control group. The experimental groups were offered one of a variety of plans subsidizing the costs of housing. The plans varied in generosity and in the conditions under which payments would be made. Each of the participating families was followed for four years with periodic interviews and housing inspections (Kennedy, 1980).

Corresponding to complexity, the costs of the experiments described above varied widely, the most expensive being the Housing Allowance Demand Experiment and the least being the small-scale experiments conducted with World War II soldiers.

TABLE 5.1   Strategies for Impact Assessment Research Designs

Intervention Features		*Data Collection Features*		
Coverage of Target Population	Assignment of Intervention to Targets	Multiple Measures Before and After	Only Pre- and Postintervention Measures	Only Postintervention (cross-sectional) Measures
Partial Coverage	Randomized or unbiased assignment	← "TRUE" EXPERIMENTS →		
	Nonrandom assignment	CONSTRUCTED CONTROL GROUPS AND /OR STATISTICAL CONTROLS		STATISTICAL CONTROLS
Full Coverage	Nonrandom variations over time or places	REFLEXIVE CONTROLS: Time-Series Analyses	Before-and-After Studies	
	Constant intervention			GENERIC AND SHADOW CONTROLS

Data Collection Points

Evaluation designs that may be applied to impact assessment also vary in the data collection plans that are employed. These fall into two categories: *Longitudinal designs* are those in which at least two observations are made, one before and one after the intervention has been put into place. Ideally, additional observation data points also are used. *After-only designs* are those in which only one observation is made after the intervention is in place.

The most elaborate true experiments, as well as other designs (to be discussed in the following section), consist of observations of experimental and control groups taken at many points over time. Most of the large-scale field experiments undertaken over the past two decades to test proposed programs have been longitudinal randomized experiments. For example, the several negative income tax experiments have all employed the same basic longitudinal design, varying one from the other in the kinds of treatments tested and in the length of time over which the intervention treatments were given. The New Jersey Income Maintenance Experiment (Kershaw and Fair, 1976; Rossi and Lyall, 1976) was designed with eight experimental groups, each of which was offered a slightly different income maintenance plan, and one control group. Eligible families were randomly assigned to one of the nine groups. Each participating family was studied over a three-year period, during which the experimental group families were offered benefits.

Most randomized experiments are designed with pre- and post-measurements of outcome. The main reason for doing so is to hold constant the initial starting points of targets in subsequent analyses of experimental effects. (The statistical reason for doing so is explained more fully in Chapter 6.) However, there are often circumstances in which preintervention measures are simply undefinable. For example, prisoner rehabilitation experiments that are designed to affect recidivism can only be based on postintervention measures, since recidivism cannot be defined before release from prison. Similarly, intervention efforts designed to reduce the incidence of disease or accidents have undefined preintervention outcome measures. Several examples of post-only experiments are given in Chapter 6.

Nonrandomized Experiments with Constructed and/or Statistical Controls

A large class of impact assessment designs consists of nonrandomized approaches, all of which have in common comparisons between experimental groups, created out of targets who have elected (in some fashion) to participate in a program (or have been selected administratively as participants), and "constructed controls," groups of nonparticipants who are in some critical ways comparable to participants. Such comparisons may be made through the construction of groups of nonparticipant targets (hence, the term "constructed controls").

Closely related to constructed controls are controls defined through statistical analysis. Both are efforts to approximate the ideal of randomized controls. Persons who have not participated in a program are compared to those who have, using statistical techniques that hold constant known differences between participants and nonparticipants. Of course, statistical controls can be used by themselves, with post-only measures, in which case the design is really that of a cross-sectional survey. But statistical controls can also be used with pre- and post-measures of outcomes in connection with constructed control groups. In short, the line between nonrandomized experiments with constructed controls and one-shot surveys is often obscure. The important point, however, is that the reasoning involved in both is much the same: Both attempt to estimate net effects by creating control groups that presumably represent potential targets who were unexposed to the intervention. Several examples of constructed controls follow:

- In order to estimate the effect of housing allowances on the supply of dwellings offered by builders and landlords, demonstration housing allowance programs were run in Green Bay, Wisconsin, and South Bend, Indiana. After several years of the demonstration, the prices of housing in those two cities were to be compared with prices in comparable cities in the Midwest (Struyk and Bendick, 1981).

- Students attending public high schools in a random sample of such schools were compared with students attending denominational or secular, private schools, holding constant socioeconomic factors. The comparison was made to see whether the type of school attended had any effects on average levels of achievement in critical subject areas (Coleman et al., 1981).

- Families who were selected for admission to public housing in Baltimore were matched with families who had applied but were not admitted to the units. Both the public housing families and the constructed controls were repeatedly interviewed over a five-year period (Wilner et al., 1962).

Some of these designs involve many measurements of outcomes made both before and after the interventions. For example, a recent study compared monthly crime rates in Boston, before and after the enactment of new gun-control legislation, with trends in comparable jurisdictions in nearby states and in the entire New England region (Pierce and Bowers, 1979).

Cross-Sectional Surveys

The column on the righthand side of Table 5.1 defines cross-sectional surveys, which are one-time sample surveys of target populations, some of whom have not received treatment (or who have received a variation of the treatment). Targets who receive the treatment are compared with those who do not on postintervention outcome measures, using statistical techniques to hold constant differences between the two groups. Although cross-sectional designs are among the less expensive ways to estimate impact, they are also among the more difficult to carry out rigorously. Therefore they should be employed with all the cautions that will be discussed in the next chapter.

When cross-sectional surveys are used with partial-coverage programs, they are to be considered a variant of constructed controls. However, their use to gauge the effectiveness of full-coverage programs that vary from place to place constitutes a unique application. Thus, there are several studies that attempt to gauge the effectiveness of gun-control legislation by contrasting levels of restrictions on licensing and gun usage in different states (Krug, 1967; Geisel et al., 1969; Seitz, 1972). In this case, the states constitute the units, with the observations being rates for various sorts of crime in a particular year. Note that such impact assessments lead to estimates of how much of a net effect one variation in the treatment has compared to others. Hence, we may be able to assess whether or not Medicaid plans of varying levels of generosity affect medical-care usage, but we will not be able to tell whether Medicaid per se has any effect on medical-care consumption.

Constructed controls used with after-only measures are also quite frequent. A controversial evaluation of Head Start (Cicerelli et al., 1969) was based on a comparison of children in the first grade who had participated in Head Start at nursery school age with first-graders of comparable background in the same or nearby schools who had not participated. An evaluation of the effects of federally supported family planning clinics (Cutright and Jaffe, 1977) followed the same plan, contrasting the birthrates in counties that had very active clinics with those of counties with less active clinics.

The issues involved in the proper design and analysis of one-shot surveys of existing, full-coverage programs with treatment that varies by site are complicated, and more will be said about them in Chapter 6.

Time-Series Analyses

Full-coverage programs present especially difficult problems in impact assessment because they lack an uncovered target population that might serve as a control or yield control observations. However, if extensive, over-time, before-program-enactment observations on out-come measures exist, it is possible to use the quite powerful techniques of time-series analyses. Thus, it may be possible to study the effect of the enactment of a gun-control law in a particular jurisdiction, but only if the evaluator has access to a sufficiently long time series consisting of crime statistics that track long-term trends in gun-related offenses. Of course, for many ongoing interventions such long-term measures do not exist; for example, there are no long-term, detailed time series on the inci-dence of certain acute diseases, making it difficult to assess the impact of Medicare or Medicaid on them.

Although the technical procedures of time-series analyses are quite complicated, the ideas underlying them are quite simple. The trend before the treatment is analyzed in order to obtain a projection of what would have happened without the intervention. The trend after the intervention is then compared to the resulting projections and statistical tests are used to determine whether or not the observed postintervention trend is sufficiently different from the projection to infer that the treatment had an effect. For example, the effects of changing pricing policies on household water consumption can be studied by time-series analysis by analyzing the consumption trends before the pricing policy changes, projecting water consumption trends on that basis, and com-paring actual consumption with the projections (Berk et al., 1981).

Some of the limitations of time-series analyses are detailed in Chap-ter 7. Perhaps the most serious limitation is that many preintervention observations are needed in order to model accurate preintervention time trends (more than 30 points in time are recommended). For this reason, time-series analyses are usually restricted to outcome concerns for which governmental or other groups routinely collect and publish statistics.

Before-and-After Studies of
Full Coverage

For many full-coverage programs, long time series before and after program enactment may not be available; instead, only a single, before-enactment measure may exist. With the addition of a measure taken after the intervention has been in place (and appropriate caution), impact assessments can still be made. For example, if state government officials anticipate a legislative limitation on state real-estate taxes, they may undertake a survey of state residents' appraisals of local services, which are bound to be affected by lowered real-estate tax revenues. After the amendment has been in place long enough to influence local and state service expenditures, a second survey might be undertaken to measure changes in residents' satisfaction levels.

There are many difficulties with before-and-after designs, as will be indicated in detail in subsequent chapters. The main problems are obvious and stem from the possibility of confounding factors obscuring the impact of the program in question.

Generic and Shadow Controls

Finally, in the lower righthand corner of Table 5.1 are designs in which only generic and shadow controls can be used to develop estimates of what would happen without intervention. Because no preintervention measures exist, no reflexive controls can be used; since everyone is covered by the program and the program is uniform over places and time, neither randomized nor constructed controls can be used.

Generic controls consist of estimates based on studies of what ordinarily happens over time. For example, we do know that the average age at first marriage in the United States is approximately 22 for males. A program that is designed to change the antinuptial incentives of income tax laws can be evaluated by observing how much change occurs in the average age at marriage for males after the laws have been changed. Most constructors of psychological tests publish "norms" indicating how much change one might "normally" expect in, say, reading achievement from year to year as children progress through the elementary grades. Similarly, one might look to the Current Population Survey of the U.S. Bureau of the Census for data on the average earnings of persons in particular jobs in order to estimate what those attending a vocational training program might have earned without participating in the program.

The use of generic controls is fraught with danger. Some of the norms published by test manufacturers are not based on very carefully conducted research. Published census reports may not offer information sufficient to pinpoint individuals who would be comparable to targets experiencing an intervention.

Shadow controls may also be used. These controls consist of the judgments of experts, program administrators, or participants, and may yield even more fragile estimations of whether outcomes can be interpreted as net effects. While expert judgments may be sufficient in some fields, precise knowledge of the sort needed is ordinarily not available for most social programs, even to the most experienced of experts. Thus, while it may make some sense to rely on an engineer's appraisal of the safety of a bridge design, it may make very little sense to rely on an engineer's appraisal of the safety of a bridge design, it may make very little sense to ask a criminologist to judge the effectiveness of a particular prisoner rehabilitation program.

Generic and shadow controls are the only controls available for full-coverage, uniform programs for which no preintervention measures exist. This class of programs includes most of the long-standing, established programs (e.g., old-age pensions under the Social Security Administration or compulsory elementary education). Therefore, estimates of what would be the effects of abolishing such programs must be treated with caution, since they are largely speculative.

Still, because generic and shadow control estimates are relatively inexpensive and take little time, it is tempting to use them. This can be done with relatively little risk in some impact assessments: Generic controls might be used to judge whether or not an educational program is successful, comparing participants' after-program reading scores with the national norms for children of the same grade that are published by the test constructor. Likewise, the efficacy of a vocational training program for adults might be assessed by calling on experts. Nevertheless, generic or shadow controls are recommended only as a last resort. The reasons for this recommendation are given in Chapter 7.

TYPES OF DATA USEFUL FOR IMPACT ASSESSMENT

The previous section's discussion of research designs has been almost exclusively in terms of quantitative studies. Whether the data collected should be qualitative or quantitative is a separate issue. Quantitative data can be defined as observations that readily lend themselves to numerical representations: answers to structured questionnaires, pay records compiled by personnel offices, counts of speech interactions among co-workers, and the like. In contrast, qualitative data, such as protocols of unstructured interviews and notes from observations, tend to be less easily summarized in numerical form. These distinctions are obviously not hard and fast; the dividing line between the two types of data is fuzzy. Furthermore, qualitative data may be transformed into quantitative data by content analysis, while quantitative data may be treated as qualitative data by disregarding the numerical values (say, those given to responses to structured interviews, treating each interview schedule as a unit instead).

The relative advantages and disadvantages of the two types of data have been debated *ad nauseam* in the social science literature (Cook and Reichardt, 1979). Critics of quantitative data decry the dehumanizing tendencies of numerical representation, claiming that a better understanding of causal processes can be obtained from intimate acquaintance with people and their problems and the resulting qualitative observations. In response, the quantitative advocates reply that qualitative data are expensive to gather on an extensive basis, are highly subject to misinterpretation, and usually contain information that is not uniformly collected across all cases and all situations.

We cannot resolve here the debate surrounding data preferences. As we have indicated in previous chapters, qualitative observations have extremely important roles to play in certain types of evaluative activities, particularly in the monitoring of ongoing programs. However, it is true that qualitative procedures are difficult and expensive to use in many of the designs described in Table 5.1. It would be virtually impossible to meld a long-range randomized experiment with qualitative observations at any reasonable cost. Similarly, large-scale surveys or time series are not ordinarily built of such qualitative observations.

In short, while impact assessments of the structured variety shown in Table 5.1 could be conducted qualitatively in principle, considerations of cost and human capital usually rule out such approaches. Assessing impact in ways that are scientifically plausible and that yield relatively precise estimates of net effects requires data that are quantifiable and systematically and uniformly collected.

TECHNICAL NOTES ON OUTCOME MEASURES

Accuracy in measurement is traditionally viewed as two separate issues, reliability and validity (Bohrnstedt, 1970). In order to have any worth, an impact assessment must meet the requirements of both.

Choosing Valid Outcome Measures

The issue of *validity* is difficult to deal with. A measure is valid to the extent that it measures what it is intended and presumed to measure. While the concept of validity is easy to comprehend, it is difficult to test whether a particular instrument is valid, since for many social and behavioral variables, no agreed-upon testing standards exist. For example, the validity of a measure of willingness to take business risks, if formulated as an attitude scale, would require as a validity test some behavioral measure of the extent to which an individual is willing to take actions that might be profitable but also involve a good deal of risk.

In practice, there are a number of ways such attitudes can be measured; that is, there are many different questions that could be asked that would be related, at least conceptually, to the idea of risk-taking. If there were one way or a small number of ways that everyone could accept as the "best" methods of measuring risk-taking, then potential measures could be compared to the "best" measure. However, in the absence of a best measure, the question of whether a particular measure or set of measures is valid is usually a matter of case-by-case argument.

Clearly, a valid measure must also be reliable, a concept that will be considered at the end of this section. However, reliability, although necessary, is an insufficient criterion of validity. A valid measure must demonstrate what is often termed in the evaluation literature *construct validity* (Campbell and Stanley, 1966; Cook and Campbell, 1979). In addition to reliability, this includes the following criteria:

1. Consistency with Usage. A valid measure of a concept must be consistent with past work that has used that concept. Hence, a measure of "adoption of innovation" must not contradict the usual ways the term "adoption" has been used in previous studies of innovation.

2. Consistency with Alternative Measures. A valid measure must be consistent with alternative measures that have been used effectively by other evaluators. It must produce roughly the same results as other measures that have been proposed, or, if different, have sound conceptual reasons for being different.

3. Internal Consistency. A valid measure must be internally consistent. That is, if several questions are used to measure a concept, the answers to those questions should be related to each other as if they were alternative measures of the same thing.

Deciding on Measures

How to choose valid measures of outcomes is quite critical and often not easy to decide (Blalock and Blalock, 1968; Bohrnstedt, 1970.) For example, a family planning program might consider the following alternatives for measuring outcomes, each of which fulfills the three criteria outlined above:

- proportion adopting effective contraceptive practices
- average desired number of children
- average number of children born to completed households
- attitudes toward large families

These four possibilities do not exhaust all of the measures that can be reasonably viewed as relevant to the goal of reducing fertility.

Furthermore, they vary in terms of ease of measurement and data collection costs. Thus, although a reduction in the average number of children born to "completed" families (i.e., those past childbearing) may be the best expression of the eventual goal of a fertility program, the use of that measure to define outcome implies a long-term evaluation of considerable complexity and cost. In contrast, it may be easy to measure attitudes toward large families, proceeding on the assumption that an effective fertility-reduction program is reflected in low approval of large families.

Alternative measures of outcome can be viewed as more or less direct expressions of program goals. Given what is known about the often small and erratic magnitude of the relationship between attitudes and behavior, a downward shift in the average desirability of large families is likely to be a remote measure of the goals of a fertility-reduction program. Changes in such attitudes often may occur without a corresponding shift in fertility practices.

In other words, a good outcome measure is one that is feasible to employ, given the constraints of time and budget, and one that is more or less directly related to the goals of the program and hence valid. Of the four alternatives listed for measuring reductions, shifts in contraceptive practices may be, on balance, the best choice as a measure. They can be studied over relatively short periods of time; there are ample precedents for adequate measurements in previous research; and, in terms of what is known about fertility behavior, shifts in contraceptive practices are directly related to fertility. (See Exhibit 5-A for discussion of how a variety of outcome measures have been established for a program designed to improve the use of public health clinics in preventive children's health practices.

Proxy Measures

An outcome measure that is used as a stand-in for a goal that is not measured directly is called a *proxy measure*. The selection of a proxy measure is clearly a critical decision. Ideally, a proxy measure should be closely related to the "direct" measure of the project goal but should also be much easier to obtain. In practice, it is often necessary to accept proxy measures that are less than ideal. While there are no firm rules for the selection of appropriate proxy measures, there are some guidelines.

First, for goals and objectives that are measurable in principle but too costly to measure, previous research may include studies that test the worth of alternatives. For example, one may be concerned with whether jobs obtained by persons completing training programs are better than those trainees might have found otherwise. In principle, the

Exhibit 5-A: Program Outcome Measures

In a program to increase the use of a public health clinic by young persons for preventive health care rather than episodic care for emergency conditions, the outcome was measured in a variety of ways:

A. Measures of the success of the clinic's immunization program.

    1. Average age at which patient received each of seven different immunizations.

    2. The percentage of patients receiving their first polio immunization before 3 months of age.

    3. Percentage of patients receiving all of their immunizations before the age of 30 months.

B. Measures of the clinic's success in reducing accidents and illnesses.

    1. Percentage decrease (or increase) in acute episodes of accidents and illnesses from the first to second year of enrollment in clinic.

C. Measures of continuity of health care.

    1. Rate of broken appointments with clinic.

    2. On-time arrival rate.

    3. Rate of return of patients for follow-up visits after initial treatment.

SOURCE: Summary, by permission, of M. S. Augustin, E. Stevens and D. Hicks, "An Evaluation of the Effectiveness of a Children and Youth Project." *Health Services Report*, 88 (December 1973): 942-946.

quality of jobs may be measured by some weighted combination of earnings, wage rates, steadiness of employment, working conditions, or other measurable job attributes. Several reasonable proxy measures can be employed instead of such a long and expensive procedure: Earnings and wage rates are good proxies, since previous research has shown that such job attributes are highly correlated (i.e., better-paying jobs tend to have better working conditions, more employment security, and so on).

Second, goals and objectives that are expected to be reached in the far future can be represented by proxy measures that are intermediate steps toward those goals. For example, while the objective of a project on family fertility is to reduce average family size, that goal can only be measured definitively after the women in those families have passed through their childbearing years. Proxy measures that center on the adoption of practices that will reduce completed fertility are reasonable surrogates (e.g., adoption of contraceptive practices and changes in expressed desired family size).

The selection of proxy variables in the first instance should be guided by the validity criteria above. In addition, proxy variables and other measurements should also be reliable, a topic to which we now turn.

Reliability of Outcome Measures

A measure is *reliable* to the extent that the application of the measure to a given situation produces the same results repeatedly, given that the situation in question does not change between measurements. Thus, the measurement of height and weight in adults through the use of standard devices is regarded as more reliable than the measurement of intelligence. That is, the use of measuring devices for height and weight in the hands of reasonably competent persons will produce less variability in measurement from one administration to another than will the repeated application of various intelligence tests.

The effect of unreliability in measures is to dilute and obscure real differences when they exist. A truly effective intervention whose outcome is measured unreliably will appear to be less effective than it actually is. To detect such effectiveness requires a larger sample than would be the case were a more reliable measure used.

The effect of unreliability is shown in Table 5.2, where two measures of differing reliability are compared in a hypothetical example of an educational intervention designed to raise levels of cognitive achievement among children from a disadvantaged background. The "true" outcome of the hypothetical program is shown in Panel I. In the participating group, 40 out of 50 (80 percent) reached high achievement levels at the end of the program, but only 25 out of 50 (50 percent) of the nonparticipating or control individuals reached those levels. These "true" results would be observed if we had a *perfectly reliable* measure of cognitive achievement.

The reliability of two measures, A and B, is compared in Panel II: Measure A is less reliable than Measure B. Note that when a child is "truly" a high achiever, Measure A shows that individual to be correctly classified 60 percent of the time; when a child is truly a low achiever,

TABLE 5.2 A Hypothetical Example of Attenuation Effects of Measurement Unreliability on Intervention Outcomes

I. True outcome without measurement error:

	Participants	Nonparticipants
High Achiever	40 (80%)	25 (50%)
Low Achiever	10 (20%)	25 (50%)
	True Program Effect = 30%	

II. Comparison of percentages correctly classified on measures of achievement that vary in reliability:

	Observed Measurement for Measure A		Observed Measurement for Measure B	
	High	Low	High	Low
High Achiever	60%	40%	90%	10%
Low Achiever	40%	60%	10%	90%

III. Measured outcomes using Measure A and Measure B

	Measure A		Measure B	
	Participants	Nonpar-ticipants	Participants	Nonpar-ticipants
High Achiever	28 (56%)	25 (50%)	37 (74%)	25 (50%)
Low Achiever	22 (44%)	25 (50%)	13 (26%)	25 (50%)
Measured Effect =	6%		24%	

Measure A shows that individual as a low achiever only 60 percent of the time. In contrast, the corresponding figure for Measure B, the more reliable measure, is 90 percent. In short, Measure A makes mistakes in classification 40 percent of the time, while Measure B makes such mistakes only 10 percent of the time.

The different effects of the application of the two unreliable measures to the outcome of the hypothetical intervention are shown in the bottom panel of Table 5.2. On Measure A, we find twenty-eight high achievers, or 56 percent of the participating group: (60 percent of 40 = 24) + (40 percent of 10 = 4) or 28. With Measure B, we would obtain thirty-seven high achievers, or 74 percent of the experimental group: (90 percent of 40 = 36) + (10 percent of 10 = 1) or 37. Using Measure A, we get a contrast between the participating and control groups of only 6 percent more high achievers in the participating group, while for Measure B the contrast is 24 percent. Clearly, Measure B, because it is more reliable, comes closer to showing the extent to which the program was effective.

Note that neither Measure A nor Measure B provides an accurate estimate of the hypothetical program's effects, both *under*estimating the true effects considerably. The problem is known as *attenuation due to unreliability* and is well documented (Bohrnstedt, 1982; Nunnally and Durham, 1975). In most cases, it is not possible completely to eradicate measurement error, although it is possible to make adjustments in results that take such errors into account, if the degree of unreliability is known. The point of the example shown in Table 5.2 is to emphasize the importance of care in both the construction and the application of measurement devices.

THE "RIGHT" IMPACT ASSESSMENT STRATEGY

Although the thrust of this chapter has been to emphasize that randomized experiments provide the best estimates of net program effects, we wish to stress here that the approach to be preferred in a particular circumstance depends on a variety of contextual factors. For some types of programs, randomized experiments are simply inapplicable. In other circumstances, time, funds, and skills may preclude an experimental approach. With proper care, the other designs described in this chapter can be used with considerable confidence. In the next two chapters we present examples of all these approaches, detailing their advantages and limitations.

6

Comparative Designs for Impact Assessment

Although the randomized controlled experiment is presented in this chapter as the best research design for assessing net impacts of interventions, we also recognize that constructed and statistical controls are often the practical designs of choice and that they can also yield useful estimates — if the evaluator is careful to recognize their limitations. This chapter contains many examples of the uses of the three comparative approaches, specifies circumstances under which each is most applicable, and identifies some of the risks associated with each. Special attention is paid to the use of statistical controls, a method that is especially appropriate for the assessment of ongoing programs and one that is recommended in combination with evaluations using either randomized or constructed controls.

KEY CONCEPTS

Control Group:	A group of untreated potential targets that is compared to experimental groups on outcome measures in impact evaluations.
Constructed Controls:	A group of untreated targets selected by nonrandom methods as comparable in crucial respects to targets in intervention groups.
Cross-Sectional Studies:	Studies in which data are collected at one time point.
Experimental Group:	A group of potential targets to whom an intervention is delivered and whose outcome measures are compared with those of control groups.
Matching:	The construction of control groups by finding individuals who are identical in relevant respects to persons in experimental groups.
Partial and Full Coverage:	Degrees to which a program reaches some or all of its intended targets.
Randomization:	Chance selection in the assignment of potential targets to experimental and control groups.
Statistical Controls:	Using statistical techniques to hold constant differences between treatment and control groups.

---

*T*he purpose of this and the next chapter is to provide a more detailed description of the impact assessment designs introduced in Chapter 5 and to illustrate their use in actual impact assessments. Since the evaluator is always operating within the constraints of time, budget, the contexts within which programs are undertaken, and technical limitations, the actual solutions reached in particular situations are nearly always compromises between the ideal and the feasible.

Hard and fast rules about when and how to compromise cannot be written, although some very general guidelines may be stated: First, the more important a program is considered to be, the better should be the research design. Indeed, it may not make any sense at all to evaluate with any care programs that are anticipated to have minor impacts or few costs attached to them (Cronbach et al., 1980; Rossi, 1979). In contrast, programs expected to be very costly or potentially harmful to targets or others should be evaluated for impact with as much precision as possible.

In the past, some commentators, including one of the authors (Rossi, 1979), have stated that impact assessments ought not to be made if the information that would result is not likely to be used in subsequent decision-making or program management. Thus, if a given program has such widespread support among decision makers that it is highly unlikely that impact assessment findings would change the amount or direction of support, an impact evaluation is not justified, if only in the interest of conserving resources. While currently we do not fully subscribe to this position, the rationale of conserving resources is quite persuasive. Be that as it may, the evaluator must recognize that the uses to which an impact assessment may be put condition the care and resources that should be devoted to it.

At the outset, a note on units of analysis is important. The language of this chapter might lead the reader to believe that impact assessments are conducted only with persons as the intended intervention targets. We do not wish to convey such an impression, as the reader should be aware from earlier chapters. It is easier to write as if only individuals were targets, but, as we pointed out in Chapter 3, interventions may also be directed at households and families, neighborhoods and communities, business firms and other organizations, counties and states, and even nations. The logic of impact assessment in general is not changed as one moves from one kind of unit to another, although the difficulties of conducting field research may increase with the size and complexity of units. For instance, the confounding factors that affect individual students also influence classes; hence, the same formal designs may be necessary to remove confounding influences from gross outcomes. However, while sample sizes in the two cases are respectively composed of students and classes, gathering data on a sample of 200 students is usually easier and considerably less costly than accumulating similar data on 200 classes.

The choice of units of analysis is not arbitrary but determined by the nature of the intervention involved. Thus, a program designed to affect communities, say through block grants to local municipalities, requires that the units studied be municipalities. An impact assessment of block grants conducted by contrasting two municipalities has a sample size of two — completely inadequate for many purposes, even though observations may be made on very large samples within each of the two communities.

The evaluator attempting to design an impact assessment is advised to start by identifying the units designated as the targets of the intervention in question and hence to be specified as units of analysis. In some cases defining the units of analysis presents no ambiguity; in other cases the decision may require careful appraisal of the intentions of program designers. In still other cases, interventions may be addressed to several types of targets: A housing subsidy program may be designed to upgrade both the dwellings of individual poor families and the housing stocks of local communities. Here the evaluator may wish to design an impact assessment that consists of samples of individual households within samples of local communities.

ASSESSING IMPACT OF PARTIAL-COVERAGE PROGRAMS

By *partial-coverage programs* we mean those that are to be tested on a trial basis or are not reaching (for whatever reasons) all or virtually all of the members of the population intended to benefit. It is mainly under these circumstances that it is possible to construct comparisons between groups of persons who are receiving the intervention's services and those who are not.

The Concept of Control and Experimental Groups

One may conceptualize net outcomes as the difference between persons who have participated in a project and *exactly* comparable targets who have not participated. Since the same confounding effects would be present in both groups, both would be subject to endogenous change, secular drift, and the other confounding factors listed in Chapter 5. The only difference between the two groups would be caused by the intervention *and* by stochastic effects. Commonly, the contrasting group is called the *control group,* while those participating in the intervention are designated the *experimental group.*

On the basis of the formula developed in the last chapter, estimating a project's net effects in terms of control and experimental groups can be shown as follows:

$$\text{Net Effects} = \begin{bmatrix} \text{Gross outcome for an} \\ \text{experimental group} \end{bmatrix}$$
$$- \begin{bmatrix} \text{Gross outcome for a} \\ \text{control group} \end{bmatrix}$$
$$\pm \begin{bmatrix} \text{Stochastic effects} \end{bmatrix}$$

Since the effects of stochastic processes can be estimated through the use of appropriate statistical tests, using control groups along with estimates of stochastic effects provides close approximations to a project's net effects.

A critical element in estimating net outcome is the identification and selection of *comparable* experimental and control groups. Comparability between experimental and control groups means, in ideal terms, that the experimental and control groups should be identical except for their participation or nonparticipation in the program under evaluation. In more specific terms, comparability requires:

- *Identical composition:* Experimental and control groups contain similar mixes of persons or other units.

- *Identical experiences:* Experimental and control groups should experience over the time of observation the same time-related processes: maturation, changes or "drifts" over time, and so on.

- *Identical predispositions:* Experimental and control groups should be equally disposed toward the project; i.e., self-selection tendencies should be identical in both groups.

Implementing Control
Group Evaluations

While ideally, comparability of the most precise sort could be achieved by matching each target in an experimental group with an identical target in a control group, this is clearly impossible. There are no two individuals, families, or other units that are exactly comparable in all respects.

Fortunately, exact one-to-one comparability is not necessary. It is only necessary that experimental and control groups be identical in aggregate terms and in respects that are relevant to the intended effects of the program being tested. Thus, it may not matter at all to an impact evaluation that experimental and control group members differ in place of birth or vary slightly in age — as long as such differences are neither statistically nor substantively significant. One of the important implications of this statement is that impact assessments require more than just a few cases. The larger the number of units studied (given the methods of selection discussed below), the more likely are experimental and control groups to be statistically equivalent. In short, *studies in which only one or a few units are in experimental or control groups rarely, if ever, suffice for impact assessments.*

While the discussion above has pictured control or comparison groups as consisting of targets who receive "no treatment," this is not generally the case. More often, targets in control groups are receiving existing treatment programs or alternative treatments. For example, an evaluation testing the effectiveness of a nutrition program may have a control or comparison group consisting of persons who are following a variety of nutritional practices, some of their own devising and others directed by their doctors. All this means is that the effectiveness of the program under evaluation is estimated relative to whatever treatment or mix of treatments is being experienced by the controls or comparison targets. Another variation on the design consists of comparing in a more systematic way two or more programs. There may be several experimental groups, each of which is following a particular nutritional regimen, with the net effects of each estimated relative to the others being tested.

A note to the reader: While a useful distinction between control and comparison groups is made above, in most of the following discussion this distinction is not very relevant. Hence, we will use the term "control" group to refer to both control and comparison groups, excepting discussions in which the distinction is important.

There are several commonly used approaches to constructing or identifying comparable control and experimental groups. They vary in feasibility, cost, and resultant clarity and validity of findings. Unfortunately, those that are best from the point of view of scientific criteria can be the most difficult to implement in practice.

Broadly speaking, these approaches follow one of four strategies or research designs: First, there are experimental designs in which targets are randomly assigned either to experimental groups who then receive the intervention or to control groups from whom the intervention is withheld — the randomized experiment method (Mendenhall, 1968; Namboodiri et al., 1975; Riecken and Boruch, 1974; Winer, 1971). Second, participants in programs may be contrasted with nonparticipants selected for comparability in important respects — the nonrandomized comparison group method. Third, participants may be compared to nonparticipants by controlling statistically for known differences between participants and nonparticipants — the statistical controls method. Finally, one may pursue a mixed strategy in which randomized or nonrandomized controls and statistical controls are used together.

In the next few sections, we discuss evaluation designs in which there is *only one intervention* being tested for impact. As indicated earlier, this restriction is not inherent in the designs; it simply makes for convenience in exposition. The designs can be easily extended to involve the testing of several alternative interventions (or combinations of interventions) simultaneously. Indeed, there is much to be gained in the way of useful information for policymakers and project managers if evaluations of interventions are undertaken comparatively, so that a given intervention is compared not only to the condition in which no intervention is made but also to alternative interventions. Multiple-intervention impact assessments provide more information on such issues as how best to modify treatments, alone or in combination, to maximize effects at a given level of funding; they are discussed in some detail in a later section.

RANDOMIZATION TO ESTABLISH COMPARABILITY

Comparability between experimental and control groups is best accomplished by randomly allocating members of a target population to the groups. Whether a person (or other unit) is offered a treatment or is left untreated is decided by chance, that is, randomly. It is important to note that "random" does *not* mean haphazard or capricious. On the contrary, random allocation of persons to experimental and control groups requires that extreme care be taken to ensure that every unit in a target population has the same chance as any other unit to be selected for either the experimental or the control group (Fisher, 1935; Rieken and Boruch, 1974).

Because the resulting experimental and control groups only differ from one another by chance, *whatever processes may be competing with a treatment to produce outcomes are present in the experimental and control groups to the same extent, except for chance fluctuations.* For example, persons who would be more likely to seek out the treatment if it were offered to them on a free-choice basis would be equally likely to be in the experimental as in the control group. Hence, the confounding factor of self-selection tends to be present just as frequently in one group as in the other, and cannot affect whatever outcome differences are observed between experimental and control groups.

Randomization is therefore the surest way of obtaining comparability between experimental and control groups. Of course, even though persons are allocated randomly, experimental and control groups will never be exactly comparable in any single instance. For example, chance fluctuations may place more women in the control group than in the experimental group. But if the random allocation were made over and over again, these fluctuations would average out to zero. In addition, the expected proportion of times that a difference of any given size will be found in a long series of randomizations can be calculated from appropriate statistical models. Any given difference in outcome among randomized experimental and control groups can be compared to what is expected on the basis of chance (i.e., generated only by the randomization process). A judgment can thus be made on whether a specific difference is due simply to chance or whether it might represent the effect of the treatment. Since the treatment in a well-run experiment is the only difference other than chance between experimental and control groups, such judgments can become the basis for discerning the existence of a *net effect.* The statistical procedures for making such calculations are quite straightforward and may be found in any text dealing with statistical inference (e.g., Namboodiri et al., 1975; Hanushek and Jackson, 1977). They will also be discussed in relation to reflexive, generic, and shadow controls in the next chapter.

The Meaning of Randomization

It is important not to confuse randomization, as used in the sense above, with random sampling. *Randomization* means taking a set of units and *allocating* each unit to an experimental or control group, using some randomizing procedure. *Random sampling* consists of *selecting* units in an unbiased manner to form a sample from a population (Sudman, 1976; Kish, 1965). One may use random sampling to select a study group from a target population and *then,* by randomization, allocate each member of the resulting sample to experimental or control conditions on a random basis. Although the use of random samples to form a set of targets that is then randomized to form experimental and control groups is a highly recommended procedure, many randomized experiments are conducted using sets of targets that are not the result of random sampling (i.e., that do not necessarily represent a given population).

Randomization Procedures

Randomization is technically easy to accomplish. Tables of random numbers are included in most elementary statistics or sampling textbooks. Many computer statistical packages can generate random numbers easily. Even some of the better hand calculators have random number generators built into them. Flipping coins or rolling dice that are unbiased can also be used as randomizing devices. (See Riecken and Boruch, 1974, for a discussion of how to implement randomization; for alternative randomization procedures, see Conner, 1977; Goldman, 1977; Roos et al., 1977.)

A typical randomized experimental design can be represented by the following modification of our basic impact assessment formula:

$$\text{Net Effects} = \begin{bmatrix} \text{Scores on outcome measures after} \\ \text{intervention for randomized} \\ \text{experimental group} \\ \\ - \quad \text{Scores on outcome measures after} \\ \text{intervention for randomized control} \\ \text{(unexposed) group} \\ \\ \pm \quad \text{Stochastic effects} \end{bmatrix}$$

Note that the formula assumes only after measurement on outcome measures. Later in this chapter we will consider what is to be gained or lost by employing after-only measures or by having multiple measures before and after an intervention.

Table 6.1 presents a schematic diagram of a simple before-and-after randomized controlled experiment, indicating the logic behind the estimates of net effects that can be computed. Of course, the differences

TABLE 6.1 Schematic Representation of a Randomized Experiment

	Outcome Measures		
	Before Program	After Program	Difference
Experimental Group	E_1	E_2	$E = E_2 - E_1$
Control Group	C_1	C_2	$C = C_2 - C_1$
	Net Effects of Program $= E - C$		

Where:
E_1, C_1	= measures of intervention goal *before* the program is instituted, for experimental and control groups, respectively
E_2, C_2	= measures of intervention goal *after* program is completed, for experimental and control groups, respectively
E, C	= gross outcome measures for experimental and control groups, respectively

NOTE: The stochastic component that represents randomization is always present and may introduce differences between experimental and control groups: i.e., $E - C$ may be nonzero, on the basis of chance. Statistical significance tests assess whether $E - C$ is too large to be generated by chance when the true value of $E - C$ is zero.

between the experimental and control groups, $E - C$ (E minus C), necessarily contain the stochastic effects described in Chapter 5. Hence, it would be necessary to apply tests of statistical inference in order to judge whether in any particular case, $E - C$ can be viewed as so large that it is not likely to be stochastic error, i.e., whether $E - C$ is larger than one can expect in chance fluctuations when the true value of $E - C$ is really zero. Conventional statistical tests for before-and-after experiments include analysis of variance and t tests. (See, for example, Namboodiri et al., 1975; Hanushek and Jackson, 1977; and Winer, 1971 for details on computation and interpretation of standard statistical tests.)

Note that the schematic presentation in Table 6.1 defines effects as differences between pre- and postmeasures of outcome. While most experiments in the social sciences are designed in this fashion, obtaining both pre- and postmeasures is not essential. For some types of outcomes, a "preintervention" is not possible to define, as we have discussed earlier. There are some statistical advantages to having pre- and postmeasures; greater precision in effect estimates can be made when premeasures are used to hold constant each individual target's starting point before the intervention. The critical measurements, of course, are the postintervention outcome measures for both experimentals and controls.

Stochastically generated differences between experimental and control groups depend almost entirely on the number of observations (i.e., targets) in the two groups and on the variability in outcome among the units involved. This means that the larger is the number of units in the experiment, the smaller are the stochastic effects and the more likely any true impact of the intervention will be detected. It also means that the more effects are uniform among all targets, the more likely it is that such effects will be detected. Hence, for interventions that are likely to have small effects, both experimental and control groups must be quite large. For example, in the TARP experiments testing the impact of unemployment insurance eligibility on recidivism among ex-felons, experimental groups contained close to 1,500 and control groups nearly 2,500 ex-felons (Rossi et al., 1980). (See standard statistical texts for details on how to plan appropriate sizes of experimental and control groups: e.g., Namboodiri et al., 1975; Hanushek and Jackson, 1977.)

Exhibit 6-A provides a detailed description of a randomized experiment to test the effectiveness of a televised educational program for Mexican preschool children. The reader's attention is directed to several of the experiment's features. First, note that a number of output measures were employed, covering the multiple objectives of the educational project. Second, observe the care taken to ensure that control group children were not exposed to the television program. Third, statistical tests were used to aid in judging whether net outcome, in this case the experimental group's observed superiority in learning, was not simply a chance difference. Note also that outcome measures were taken in the course of the experiment as well as before and after.

(text continued on p. 207)

Exhibit 6-A: A Randomized Controlled Experiment of the Effect of a Preschool Television Program in Mexico

In Mexico in 1971, a completely new production of *Sesame Street,* called *Plaza Sésamo,* especially adapted to Latin American culture, was developed. Educators, psychologists, psychiatrists, and other specialists cooperated in planning and conducting evaluative studies of a formative nature to assist the producers of *Plaza Sésamo* in developing the program.

These experiments were carried out with preschool children in daycare centers in Mexico City. A total of 221 children (3-, 4-, and 5-year-olds) from three different lower-class daycare centers were equally divided by age and sex and were randomly assigned to experimental and control groups. Children in the experimental groups watched *Plaza Sésamo* programs for fifty-minute periods, five days a week, until the entire series of 130 programs had been broadcast — a total of six months of continuous viewing. At the same time, children in the control group were viewing cartoons and other non-educational television programs on a different broadcast channel in a separate room.

Since *Plaza Sésamo* was a relatively new program, none of the control children had ever seen it before. Strenuous efforts were made to prevent the control children from viewing *Plaza Sésamo* on another channel when it was broadcast each evening from 6:00 to 7:00 p.m. Further investigations toward the end of the experiment revealed that only a handful of control children viewed any *Plaza Sésamo* broadcasts when they were absent due to sickness. In no case did it appear that the experimental design had been compromised in any way.

The impact of *Plaza Sésamo* on the children who viewed it was evaluated by a series of individually administered tests given in both the experimental and control groups at three points in time: (1) pretest — immediately prior to the exposure to *Plaza Sésamo* or the control films; (2) during treatment — seven weeks after beginning the experiment; and (3) post-test — at the end of the experiment.

Dropouts were relatively few. Of 221 children in the initial sample, 173 completed the experiment. No discernible bias due to dropouts could be discovered.

Nine individual tests were employed to measure the amount of learning for each child over the six-month period. Three of these tests — General Knowledge, Numbers, and Letters and Words — are criterion measures of skills specifically taught in the *Plaza Sésamo* programs. Five other tests — Relations, Parts of the Whole, Ability to Sort, Classification Skills, and Embedded Figures — are indirectly related to *Plaza Sésamo* but are not specifically criterion measures. The ninth test, Oral Comprehension, has no relation to the stated goals of *Plaza Sésamo,* although it measures an important cognitive ability related to school readiness among preschool children.

Statistical tests were carried out to see whether or not the *Plaza Sésamo* viewers did significantly better than the children who watched only cartoons. In general, children in the experimental group showed greater gains in test performance over the six-month period than did those in the control group.

The main results can be summarized as follows:

1. Regardless of age-group, the children who watched *Plaza Sésamo* for six months did significantly better on at least four of the nine criterion tests than did the control children who only watched cartoons during this period.

2. The greatest increases for *Plaza Sésamo* viewers occurred on the three tests most closely related to the stated goals of *Plaza Sésamo* — General Knowledge, Numbers, and Letters and Words.

3. Oral Comprehension, the test unrelated to *Plaza Sésamo,* also revealed significantly greater gains for the *Plaza Sésamo* viewers than for the control children in all three age groups.

4. The 4- and 5-year-olds showed the greatest gains from watching *Plaza Sésamo*, while the 3-year-old experimental children failed to differ significantly from the control children on five of the nine tests. Test-retest correlations across the six months showed satisfactory stability (.41-.59) for four of the tests — General Knowledge, Numbers, Embedded Figures, and Oral Comprehension — but showed instability for the remaining five tests (correlations of .08 to .25). In spite of weaknesses in these five tests, positive results favoring the *Plaza Sésamo* viewers were obtained for them just as they were obtained for the more reliable tests.

5. Although the most rapid gains of the experimental children over the control groups occurred in the first seven weeks of viewing *Plaza Sésamo*, the gap between the experimental and control groups continued to grow throughout the six months.

6. Within the combined experimental group, the degree of attention to *Plaza Sésamo* correlated positively (as high as .49) in six of the nine post-test measures, indicating that children who regularly pay attention to the *Plaza Sésamo* program gain more than children whose attention wanders.

7. Experimental children with a large number of absences did less well on the post-treatment test battery than did children who attended regularly.

SOURCE: Adapted, with permission, from "Plaza Sésamo in Mexico: An Evaluation," by R. Diaz-Guerrero, Isabel Reyes-Lagunes, Donald B. Witzke, and Wayne H. Holtzman, in the *Journal of Communication*, Vol. 26, No. 2, pp. 145-154. Copyright © 1976 by The Annenberg School of Communications.

Exhibit 6-B contains a description of another randomized controlled experiment testing the effectiveness of group counseling as a rehabilitative measure in California prisons. Taking advantage of a prison that was about to open and be filled within a short period of time, the experimenters randomly assigned entering prisoners to one of two programs or to a control group. The prison's architectural features facilitated the experiment; there were four relatively self-contained units, communications among which could be carefully controlled. Hence, prisoners in each quadrangle could not communicate to those in the other quads the treatment they received.

Note that in the example the subjects of the experiment were recruited within an institution — prison — and a high degree of control

---

Exhibit 6-B: A Randomized Control Experiment Evaluating the Impact on Parole Success of a Group Counseling Intervention in a California Prison

In the 1960s the California Adult Authority (the agency in charge of prisons) had installed in most state prisons a voluntary group counseling program that attempted to help prisoners develop an understanding of their motivations for criminal activity through participating in weekly group counseling. Presumably the understanding gained would reduce adherence to peer-group norms within prison and enhance the ability to adjust successfully to civilian life and thereby succeed on parole.

Taking advantage of a new prison that was to be constructed, the authors received permission and encouragement from the California prison agency to run a randomized controlled experiment in the new prison. The prison in question was built in more or less isolated "quads." Two of the quads were designated to receive varying forms of counseling — small and large group counseling — a third quad was designated as a control to which no counseling would be given, and the fourth quad was reserved for special behavior-problem prisoners. As new prisoners were assigned to the prison when it was opened, random assignments among the first three quads were made of prisoners who were not assigned by the prison, for behavioral reasons, to the fourth quad.

When prisoners in both the control and the experimental groups were released on parole, their parole records for a period of two years beyond release were examined for evidence of adjustment to civilian life. No differences were found among the experimental and control groups. The group counseling interventions were judged to have failed.

SOURCE: Summary, by permission, of G. Kassebaum, D. Ward and D. Wilner, *Prison Treatment and Parole Survival.* New York: Wiley, 1971.

over them could be exercised. Field experiments with noninstitutionalized populations as targets are more difficult to run, since they require voluntary cooperation and maintenance of experimental integrity over time; in addition, they are more subject to interference by outside events.

Exhibit 6-C describes an experiment to determine the work disincentive effect of providing income support payments to poor, intact (i.e., two-spouse) families. The study was the first of a series of five, each varying slightly from the others, run by the Office of Economic Opportunity and the Department of Health, Education and Welfare to test various forms of guaranteed income and their effects on the work efforts of poor and near-poor persons. All of the experiments were run over relatively long periods, the longest involving more than five years; all had difficulties maintaining the cooperation of the initial groups of families involved; and all found the income payments to create a slight work disincentive, especially for teenagers and mothers with young children — those in the secondary labor force (Rossi and Lyall, 1976).

Despite their power in allowing valid conclusions about the net outcome of interventions, randomized experiments still account for a relatively small proportion of impact assessments. Political and ethical

Exhibit 6-C: The New Jersey-Pennsylvania Income Maintenance Experiment

In the late 1960s, when federal officials concerned with poverty began to consider shifting welfare policy to provide some sort of guaranteed annual income for all families, the Office of Economic Opportunity (OEO) launched a large-scale field experiment to test one of the crucial issues in such a program. Economic theory predicted that the provision of such supplementary income payments to poor families would be a work disincentive (i.e., they would reduce the amount of work).

Started in 1968, the experiment was carried on for three years, administered by Mathematica, Inc., a research firm in Princeton, New Jersey, and the Institute for Research on Poverty of the University of Wisconsin. The experiment was aimed at a target population of intact families below 150 percent of the poverty level, whose male heads were between 18 and 58. The eight treatments consisted of various combinations of guarantees, pegged to what was then the current "poverty level," and the rates at which payments were taxed or adjusted to earnings received by the families. For example, for a family in one of the treatments with a guaranteed income of 125 percent of the then-current poverty level, if no one in the family had any earnings, the family would receive that guaranteed amount. However, if their plan had a tax rate of 50 percent, and someone in the family received earned income, payments would be reduced at the rate of $.50 for each dollar earned, until payments were reduced to zero. Other treatments consisted of tax rates that ranged from 30 percent to 70 percent, and guarantee levels that varied from 50 percent to 125 percent of the poverty line. A control group consisted of families who did not receive any payments.

The experiment was conducted in four New Jersey communities and one Pennsylvania community. A large household survey was undertaken to identify families who were eligible. Families identified were invited to participate; after agreement had been achieved, families were randomly allocated to one of the experimental groups or the control group. Families who were in the experimental group reported their earnings each month. If their earnings statement indicated eligibility for transfer payments, a check was mailed to the family.

Families were interviewed in great detail prior to enrollment in the program and at the end of each quarter over the three years of the experiment. These interviews generated data (among others) on employment, earnings, consumption, health, and various social-psychological measures. The data were then analyzed along with the monthly earnings reports to determine whether those receiving payments in any way diminished their work efforts (as measured in hours of work) in relation to the comparable families in the control groups.

Although about 1,300 families were initially recruited, by the end of the experiment 22 percent had discontinued their cooperation. Others had missed one or more interviews or had dropped out of the experiment for varying periods. Less than 700 remained for analysis of the continuous participants.

SOURCE: Summary, by permission, of D. Kershaw and J. Fair, *The New Jersey Income-Maintenance Experiment*, Vol. 1. New York: Academic, 1976.

considerations may impede randomization, particularly when interventions simply cannot be withheld (although the idea of experimentation does not preclude delivering some alternative treatment to a control group). Despite the many serious obstacles to randomized evaluation design, there is a clear consensus on their desirability (Cook and Campbell, 1979), a growing literature on how to enhance the chances of success (Bennett and Lumsdaine, 1975; Riecken and Boruch, 1974), and increasing documentation of their feasibility (Boruch, 1975; Campbell and Boruch, 1975; Boruch et al., 1978).

Some of the conditions that facilitate or impede the utilization of randomized experiments to assess impact will be discussed in a later section of this chapter.

Surrogates for Randomized Selection

Although randomization is the surest way of selecting equivalent experimental and control groups, there are other methods that also may satisfy the criterion of equivalence. *Unbiased selection* (not to be confused with bias as discussed in Chapter 4) requires the probability that any individual selected for either experimental or control group membership is identical for all targets in the study. Correspondingly, *biased selection* occurs when some individuals have a higher and some a lower probability of being selected for different groups.

Systematic assignment from serialized lists can often accomplish the same end as randomization, provided that the lists are not ordered in some way that results in a bias. For example, in allocating high school students to experimental and control groups, it might be sensible to place all those with odd ID numbers into the experimental group and all those with even ID numbers into a control group. As long as the numbers were not originally assigned to differentiate "odd" from "even" students, the result will be the same (statistically) as random assignment. However, if for some reason the school in question gave only odd ID numbers to female students, reserving the even numbers for males, this systematic bias would result in the experimental and control groups differing in sex composition. Hence, before using such systematic selection procedures, it is necessary to understand how the agency that generated the list accomplished serialization.

Often, ordered lists of targets may have subtle biases that are difficult to detect. For example, an alphabetized list might tempt one to select, say, all persons whose last names begin with "D" as experimentals and those whose last names begin with an "H" as controls. In an eastern city, this would result in an ethnically biased selection: Many French names begin with "D" (e.g., DeFleur) while virtually no Hispanic names begin with "H." Numbered lists often reveal age biases: Since the federal government assigns Social Security numbers sequentially, those with low numbers are older than those whose numbers are higher. (See Sudman, 1976, for further precautions to be taken in systematic selection strategies.)

Occasionally, randomization occurs "naturally" for some unplanned interventions. Such situations can be regarded as equivalent to a randomized experiment. An example from a proposed study of flood effects illustrates a fairly valid "natural" randomized experiment: Hydrologic engineers have marked off the flood plains of most American rivers into regions characterized by the expected return times of floods. Thus, the "ten-year flood plain" marks off those regions in a river basin in which floods are expected, on the average, to occur every ten years. Although each year the areas within the ten-year flood plain have a one-in-ten chance of experiencing a flood, whether or not a flood occurs in a particular year in a particular spot can be regarded as a random event. Neighborhoods built on flood plains can be divided into "experimentals" — those in which floods actually occurred during, say, a two-year period — and "controls" — those in which no floods occurred. Growth trends in the two groups are then compared to discover the impact of floods on the growth of housing and population stocks.

Of course, floods are events that can be understood as outcomes of particular natural processes. But since those processes do not "select" particular flood plains more than others, floods may be regarded for our purposes as random events. The validity of this approach depends heavily on whether or not the hydrologists correctly marked out the ten-year flood plain. Such maps are made partly on the basis of historical trends and partly on the basis of knowledge about how rivers behave in given terrains. The flood plain contours are still subject to some error.

Whether or not natural or unplanned events in fact provide adequate substitutes for randomized controls must be judged with close scrutiny of the circumstances of those events. If there is any reason to suspect that the events in question were likely to affect some units (persons, communities, and the like) more than others, then the conditions for a "natural experiment" do not exist. For example, communities that have fluoridated their water supplies cannot be regarded as an experimental group to be contrasted with those who have not, since the act of adoption cannot be regarded as a random event in the sense used here. Similarly, households that have purchased townhouses cannot be regarded as appropriate controls for those who have purchased freestanding homes, since the very act of making such purchases is an indicator of other potential differences between the two groups.

Data Collection Strategies for
Randomized Experiments

Although under some conditions after-only measures of outcomes are necessary (see Exhibit 6-B), it is ordinarily the case that more frequent measures of outcomes, taken both before and after an intervention is put into place, are better. They increase the reliability of measurement and provide more information on which to build estimates of net outcomes. Measures taken before an intervention begins provide estimates of the preexperimental states of the experiment's subjects, which are useful for adjusting experimental and control groups and for measuring how much of a gain the intervention effected.

For example, preintervention measures of earnings for experimentals and controls in a vocational retraining project provide better estimates of how much earnings will improve as a result of training and at the same time offer a variable to hold constant in the analysis of outcomes.

Periodic measurements taken during the course of an intervention are also useful; such series allow evaluators to see how the intervention works. For instance, if a vocational retraining program produces most of its effects during the first four weeks of the six-week project, shortening the training period would cut costs without seriously curtailing the project's effectiveness. Likewise, multiple, periodic measurements can lead to a fuller understanding of how targets react to treatments. Some reactions may be slow-starting and later accelerate; others may be strong initially but soon trail off to preintervention levels. For example, the response to the 55-miles-per-hour speed limit is reputed to have consisted of an initial slowing down of average vehicular speed, followed by a gradual return to higher speed averages. Being able to plot reactions to interventions allows evaluators to fine-tune treatments for fuller effectiveness.

For some types of interventions, only postintervention measures may be available (as, for example, in the California prison counseling experiment described in Exhibit 6-B). Likewise, a program designed to help impoverished high school students go on to college can only be judged definitively by whether experimentals go on to college more frequently than controls, a measure that can only be taken after the intervention. However, such cases aside, the general rule that can be drawn is that the more measurements made before and after the intervention, the better measured the estimates of net effects will be.

Thus, there are two compelling reasons for taking many measures before, during, and after an intervention: First, the more measures taken, the lower will be unreliability of composite measures. Second, interventions can be expected to have their effects over time; hence, longitudinal series (see Chapters 5 and 7) can allow the evaluators to reconstruct the way the intervention works.

Complex Randomized Experiments

Several of the examples given above (see Exhibits 6-B and 6-C) are tests of several treatments considered simultaneously, a strategy that considerably enhances the value of findings. In the New Jersey-Pennsylvania Income Maintenance Experiment, eight treatments were tested, each differing from the other in the amount of income guaranteed and in tax penalties on family members' earnings. The variation from treatment to treatment was included in the experiment in order to test the sensitivity of work effort to varying degrees of disincentive resulting from the different payments. A related evaluation question was whether or not the work response to payment would vary with the amount of payment offered and the extent to which earnings reduced the payments offered. Similarly, in the Housing Allowance Demand Experiment (Kennedy, 1980), 23 experimental groups were used. Each group was offered a different subsidy. Some subsidies required the families to obtain housing that met certain standards; some simply were a rent rebate of up to 25 percent of family income; and others were rent rebates conditional on payment of rents at current market values or higher.

Complex experiments along these lines are especially appropriate for testing new policies, since it may not be clear what exact form the new policy should take. Here, testing variations can offer information to guide program construction toward effectiveness and economic efficiency. For example, it was shown in the Housing Allowance Demand Experiment that tying the allowances to occupancy of rental housing meeting certain building standards reduced participation greatly; consequently, only about a third of eligible families actually received payments. Also, simple rent rebates (payments equal to some percentage of the rent paid) unfairly penalized those families who were careful or lucky housing shoppers and occupied "bargain" dwellings.

Under some circumstances, one might be concerned that the methods considered for administering a new program may seriously compromise the treatment being tested. For example, in the California group-therapy prison experiment (Exhibit 6-B), an evaluator might have anticipated that the use of prison guards as group-therapy leaders would seriously undermine the intervention's worth. This possibility might have been tested by an experimental treatment employing trained therapists from outside the prison system. Indeed, had the design contained this component, the later criticism that the experiment did not address the issue of therapy effectiveness could have been avoided.

Similarly, the negative income tax experiments were criticized (Rossi and Lyall, 1976) for requiring monthly income reports from each of the participating families. Since the welfare system ordinarily does not require frequent income reports from families receiving payments, the experiment's stipulation appeared to critics as a stricter "means test" than that required by ordinary welfare regulations, and hence as potentially demeaning. Again, had the evaluators provided for an experimental group operating under the ordinary income-reporting rules, the criticisms would have been undercut.

Of course, one cannot endlessly proliferate experimental treatments to test every conceivable variation on a proposed program; a degree of restraint is required. Some evaluators have proposed the concept of "policy space" (Kershaw and Fair, 1976) as a rule for determining those program variations that should be subject to testing. Policy space, as we noted earlier, includes program alternatives that are likely to be politically acceptable, if the proposal is found to be effective and is then considered by policymakers or administrators for broad implementation.

Experiments should concentrate primarily on program variations that are clearly within the policy space defined by policymakers and administrators, perhaps extending a bit beyond but not too far. In the income maintenance experiment, eligibility requirements ruled out families of full-time students on the grounds that Congress would be very unlikely to make that group eligible, even though their income levels may have been well below the poverty line. Nor did it seem likely to the Housing Demand experimenters that homeowners would be made eligible for housing allowances.

Limitations on the Use of Randomized Controls

Despite the attractiveness of the technical features of randomized experiments, there are limitations to their use in the evaluation of social programs. Randomized designs were initially formulated for use in laboratory or field agricultural research and can be adapted to social programs only with some difficulty.

First, randomized experiments are not fruitful in the very early stages of program development. Under such circumstances it is often necessary to change features of a program for the sake of perfecting the treatment or its delivery. Although a randomized experiment can adapt to such changes, some degree of precision is lost, making it difficult in the final analysis to discern which of the several treatments or combinations thereof produced the effects observed. For example, in a program that starts out with group therapy and ends up with individual counseling, it is difficult to tell whether one style of treatment or the other produced the observed effects. Hence, expensive, longitudinal field experiments are best reserved for tests of firmly designed treatments. A series of small-scale randomized experiments might be more suited to the development stage of a social program, as in the exemplary efforts of Fairweather and Tornatzky (1977) with respect to the development of halfway homes for discharged mental hospital patients.

Second, some persons have ethical qualms about randomization, seeing it as arbitrarily and capriciously depriving control groups of positive benefits. Often the reasoning of such critics runs as follows: If it is worth experimenting with a program (i.e., if the project is likely to help targets), it is a positive harm to withhold services from some units. To do so would be unethical. The counterargument is obvious: Ordinarily, it is not known whether a treatment is effective; indeed, that is the reason one wishes to experiment.

Sometimes an intervention may present some possibility of positive harm, and decision makers may be reluctant to authorize randomization on those grounds alone. In some of the utilities pricing experiments, for instance, there was a good chance that household utility bills would increase in some of the experimental groups. Experiment designers countered this argument by promising experimental households that any such overages would be reimbursed by the evaluators after the study was over. (Of course, this reimbursement changes the character of the treatment, possibly fostering irresponsible usage of utilities.)

Third, many of the major, large-scale field experiments used money payments (e.g., the negative income tax experiments and the housing allowance experiments). With such standardized and easily delivered treatments, one can be relatively certain that the experimental intervention will be similar to that of a fully implemented program, since there are only a limited number of ways that checks can be delivered. However, for more labor-intensive, high-skill interventions (job placement services, counseling, teaching, and the like), the treatments delivered in a field experiment are likely to be delivered with greater fidelity to designer intentions than when implemented as a program. Indeed, the very real danger of treatment deterioration in implementation is one of the reasons for monitoring programs, as advanced in Chapter 4. In addition, such possibilities argue for at least two rounds of experiments: a first round, in which treatments are tested in their purest form, and a second round, in which effective methods of service delivery through public agencies are tested and compared.

Fourth, randomized experiments are costly and time-consuming. Ordinarily, they should not be undertaken to test programs that will never be considered and that lie outside any conceivable policy space. Nor are experiments to be undertaken when information is needed in a hurry. To underscore this last point, it should be noted that the New Jersey-Pennsylvania Income Maintenance Experiment cost $34 million and took more than seven years from design to published findings (Kershaw and Fair, 1976).

In sum, large-scale, randomized field experiments are best reserved to test services that can be standardized and easily transferred to operating agencies.

NONRANDOMIZED STUDIES: CONSTRUCTED CONTROLS

When randomized or true experimental designs cannot be executed, the evaluator must choose one or some combination of procedures for approximating the equivalence of control and experimental groups achieved through randomization. These alternatives are referred to generically as *quasi-experiments* (Campbell and Stanley, 1966; Cook and Campbell, 1979).

The term does not imply that the procedures described are considerably inferior to the randomized controlled experiment and hence are inappropriate for impact evaluations. It is true that without randomization, equivalence, as described previously, cannot be established with as much certainty. The possibility always remains that the outcome of a program is really due to a variable or process that has not been explicitly considered in the design or analysis. However, quasi-experiments, properly conducted, can provide information on impact that is free of most, if not all, of the confounding processes listed in Chapter 5. Indeed, the findings from a properly executed quasi-experimental design can be more valid than those from a poorly executed randomized experiment. Moreover, quasi-experiments may be the only feasible approach under many circumstances.

The Concept of Constructed Controls

In *constructed control* selection approaches, the evaluator attempts to identify and select a group of potential targets comparable in essential respects to those exposed to treatment. Several examples illustrate the use of such constructed control or comparison groups:

- In an attempt to assess the effects of nutritional supplements on intellectual functioning of children, nutritional supplements were given to all children in some villages while observations were also made on children in other villages to whom nutritional supplements were not given (Freeman et al., 1977).

- To assess the impact of manpower training for the unemployed, subsequent work histories of program participants were compared to those of relatives and neighbors of the participants who were also unemployed. The rationale for the use of unemployed friends of participants was that such friends were likely to share the same age, residential location, attitudes, and perhaps motivations of their participant friends and, hence, be similar to the participants in most aspects relevant to the manpower program (Main, 1968).

- In a study of the effects of attending church-related and -supported schools, Catholics who had attended such schools were compared with a control group of Catholics who had attended government-supported schools (Greeley and Rossi, 1966).

The basic formula for impact assessment, shown below, looks superficially very similar to that shown earlier for randomized experiments, but this superficial resemblance masks important differences:

$$\text{Net Outcome} = [\text{Outcome for program group}]$$
$$- [\text{Outcome for constructed control group}]$$
$$\pm [\text{Stochastic error}]$$

Whether or not this formula holds depends largely on how closely the constructed control group resembles the intervention group in all essential respects.

A constructed control group of agricultural districts designed to match a set of districts participating in a program of increasing fertilizer usage may differ from the program districts in a variety of ways that are difficult to detect. Although the constructed control group of districts may match with respect to average rainfall, average size of farm holdings, crops planted, and average amount of capital equipment per holding, there may be still other (perhaps unknown) differences that might be related strongly to crop yield. Some districts that participate in the project may be more "progressive" in relation to innovations (or perhaps simply have a greater propensity to take risks). To the extent that project groups volunteer (or are volunteered by officials) to be in the project intervention group, self-selection processes may be at work that would tend to mask or enhance the effects of the project as computed through the above formula. As Cain (1975) argues, it is essential that self-selection processes be investigated and incorporated into the analysis model to ascertain program effects (see also Heckman, 1980).

Self-selection is not the only possible contaminating difference between the intervention group and the constructed controls. Administrators in charge of the project may be exercising the selection choice and maximizing the chance of showing positive project effects by choosing districts that they know from their own experience are more likely to adopt the new agricultural practices enthusiastically. In such cases the effects, as computed through the formula shown above, would overestimate the potential crop yield benefits of the program to increase the use of fertilizer.

Devising an appropriate constructed control group is not a mechanical task (see Cook and Reichardt, 1976). The basis for such construction is prior knowledge and theoretical understanding of the social processes in question. It is such knowledge that instructs the evaluator in which specific ways a constructed control group should resemble the experimental group. For example, we would draw on prior knowledge about the factors that affect crop yields to select agricultural districts for a constructed control group in a study of a project that is designed to affect such yields. Likewise, if we were interested in studying the effects of a program to increase the mathematics competence of secondary school students, our prior knowledge concerning the characteristics of individuals and settings that affect learning would be used in constructing appropriate control groups (e.g., measures of intelligence, parental background, sex, age, and school organization).

The prior knowledge necessary for constructing control groups may be found in the literature published within relevant substantive areas. An educational evaluator should consult the literature about what affects learning in that substantive area, the literature on fertility should be consulted in designing a study of a family planning campaign, and so on.

While one might be tempted to construct control groups using any and all factors mentioned in the relevant scientific literature, some degree of restraint is advised. Using more than a few variables for selecting constructed controls is usually not very efficient, nor is it necessary. In general, candidates for constructed control characteristics tend to be highly intercorrelated. If one selects controls for an educational intervention on the basis of intelligence measures, one also introduces a control on parental background, since intelligence and parental background tend to be fairly strongly related.

Matching

The procedures used in selecting constructed control groups are referred to as methods of *matching*. Matching may be accomplished by selecting groups that resemble the major relevant characteristics of the group exposed to the program. For example, if children in a particular school are the target participants in an intervention, the constructed control group should be one or more schools whose demographic profiles of students mirror that of the participating school (see Exhibit 6-D).

Exhibit 6-D: Use of Constructed Controls in the Education Voucher Demonstration

The Education Voucher Demonstration was designed to introduce free-enterprise concepts into the educational process. Under the voucher concept, parents freely select a school for their child and receive a credit or voucher equal to the cost of the child's education that is paid directly to the school upon enrollment. It was presumed that this form of financing education would foster competition among the schools and improve the quality of education by making schools more responsive to students' needs. An initial external evaluation at the conclusion of the first year found, however, a relative loss in reading achievement for students in six public schools that participated in the voucher demonstration. The purpose of this study was to reexamine these findings from the first year of the voucher demonstration.

A constructed control group design was devised as follows. Schools were divided into three groups: (1) voucher schools with a traditional academic orientation, (2) voucher schools with an innovative orientation, and (3) nonvoucher comparison schools. The comparison schools were selected from the same districts and were comparable in terms of ethnic and socioeconomic composition, welfare status, etc. Both gain-score analysis and analysis of variance were used to analyze the data. The results indicate that the deleterious reading effect of the voucher demonstration was confined to only a few schools with programs featuring nontraditional, innovative curricula.

SOURCE: Adapted from P. M. Wortman, C. S. Reichardt and R. G. St. Pierre, "The First Year of the Education Voucher Demonstration: A Secondary Analysis of Student Achievement Test Scores." *Evaluation Quarterly*, 2 (May 1978): 193.

An alternative is to select from one or more schools those children who are similar to the target participants. The options are either *individual* or *aggregate matching*. In individual matching, the effort is to draw a "partner" for each target student from the unexposed pool of students. For example, if age, sex, number of siblings, and father's occupation were deemed the relevant matching variables, the roster of unexposed children would be scrutinized to locate the closest equiva-

Exhibit 6-E: An Evaluation of the Effects of Public Housing Using Constructed Controls with Individual Matching

This quasi-experiment was designed to assess the impact of moving into good-quality public housing from slum housing on family, health, student achievement, occupational attainment and housing satisfaction.

Taking advantage of the opening of a new housing project in Baltimore, the authors chose families who could be matched on twenty-six different characteristics and who were admitted to the new housing project with families on the waiting list who were not to be admitted. 396 families were admitted to the housing project and 633 families were constructed controls, the surplus being obtained since a greater attrition rate was anticipated among control families.

All of the families were followed by eleven interviews between 1955 and 1958. Interviews covered inventories of illnesses experienced by the families, their social-psychological adjustment, and the school performance of school-age children. In addition, an initial interview before admission to the public housing project was undertaken with participating families and with control families.

Only minor differences were found between participants and controls: Those in public housing were more satisfied with their housing and liked their neighbors more, but there were few discernible effects on illness or the school performance of children.

SOURCE: Summary, by permission, of D. M. Wilner, R. P. Walkely, T. C. Pinkerton and M. Tayback, *The Housing Environment and Family Life.* Baltimore: Johns Hopkins University Press, 1962.

lent child for pairing. Criteria of closeness may be adjusted to make matching possible, for example, matching so the exposed and unexposed children are within six months of age, even though a smaller difference in the selection of pairs may be most desirable. (See Exhibit 6-E for an illustration of individual matching.)

The second approach is aggregate matching. In this case, individuals are not matched, but the overall distributions on each matching variable are made to correspond for the experimental and control groups. The same proportions of children by sex and age would be found in the participating and comparison groups, but the result may have been obtained by including a 12-year-old girl and an 8-year-old boy to balance the aggregate distribution of the experimental group, which included a 9-year-old girl and an 11-year-old boy. (See Exhibits 6-F and 6-G for examples of aggregate matching.)

Individual matching is usually preferable to aggregate matching. The drawbacks to individual matching are that it is more expensive, time-consuming, and difficult to execute for a large number of matched variables. One other possibility is matching on individual and aggregate characteristics, as illustrated in Exhibit 6-H. The methods employed for matching vary in complexity. Sherwood et al. (1975) document a multivariate matching technique and the resulting equivalence of the matched experimental and control groups. The shortcomings of matching designs for evaluation have been carefully explicated (Campbell and Boruch, 1975; Campbell and Erlebacher, 1970). Essentially, inappropriate applications occur when matching is carried out on the basis of premeasures of the outcome variables used to assess impact. Particularly when such measures are unreliable or fallible, the findings from the evaluation can be misleading or invalid, due to the shift in unreliable measurements obtained at two time points (known as regression toward the mean). However, matching on the basis of other variables is feasible and desirable (Sherwood et al., 1975).

Selecting Constructed Controls

Whenever there is very little a priori knowledge about the substantive area of an intervention, some general guides may be followed, based on what social scientists have found over the past several decades to be generalized features of individuals, families, communities, or other units that affect many areas of human behavior. A brief outline of such control variables is given in Table 6.2.

Note that the characteristics shown in the table are "nested." That is, characteristics for individuals may also be used to characterize higher units by forming averages, measures of dispersion, or other aggregate-

Exhibit 6-F: Evaluating Instructional Television in El Salvador Using Aggregate Matched Constructed Controls

As part of a project of educational reform, the El Salvador school system decided to introduce instructional television into grades 7-9.

To evaluate the effect of the project on learning, a joint team of researchers, from El Salvador and Stanford University, administered tests of general ability and reading achievement, as well as survey questionnaires (measuring such variables as occupational aspirations) to three samples of students, as described below. Students were tested and surveyed at regular intervals to track changes over time. The groups tested and surveyed were as follows:

Cohort A: 902 students who entered Grade 7 in 1969. 581 students (in twenty-eight classes) experienced a Reform curriculum including television instruction; 114 students (in four classes) were given the Reform curriculum but without television instruction; and 207 students (in nine classes) received the traditional curriculum (pre-Reform). The first two groups were chosen by the Ministry of Education, while the third was chosen at random from among a large pool of classes.

Cohort B: 707 students (in twenty-nine classes) who entered the seventh grade in 1970, all of whom experienced the Reform curriculum. 482 students (in eighteen classes) experienced televised instruction, while the remaining 225 students (in eleven classes) did not.

Cohort C: 600 students in twenty-three classes experiencing the Reform curriculum. 467 students in eighteen classes experienced educational television, while 133 students in five classes did not.

Comparisons were made among cohorts and within cohorts, depending on experience with educational television. Differences among groups in background (sex, place of residence, socioeconomic status of families) were held constant statistically.

Results indicated that students experiencing the Reform curriculum gained more in general ability than those experiencing the "traditional" curriculum, and those who received televised instruction did better than those who did not. Comparisons were made over a period of two years for cohort C and three years for cohorts A and B. However, results for achievement tests measuring knowledge acquired in specific subjects were less favorable to television instruction: Television classes gained more in the initial year of exposure, but subsequent years showed no clear pattern of differences.

SOURCE: Summary, by permission, of J. K. Mayo, R. C. Hornick and E. G. McAnany, *Educational Reform with Television: The El Salvador Experience*. Stanford, CA: Stanford University Press, 1976.

descriptive measures. An individual may be characterized by his or her calendar age, a family by the average age of its members, a factory by the average age of its employees (or the proportion between certain ages), and a city by the average age of its inhabitants (or by the proportion of persons who are in the economically productive age group).

Perhaps the best way to use the characteristics shown in Table 6.2 is to regard them as constituting a checklist designed to remind the evaluator of characteristics that are likely candidates for consideration in constructing control groups. In assessing the impact of an antismoking educational campaign directed at preadolescent schoolchildren, an experimental group of schools could be matched with a constructed control group of schools, ones comparable in parental socioeconomic status, student intellectual functioning, city size, and location.

The characteristics in Table 6.2, however, are no adequate substitute for a priori knowledge directly relevant to the phenomenon being studied. The characteristics shown in that table have been found generally useful, but they are not necessarily appropriate to all social problems. For example, a program that is designed to lower rates of fertility among unmarried adolescents is best evaluated using constructed controls who are chosen on the basis of some theoretical understanding of adolescents' motivations for allowing themselves to become pregnant, engage in sexual behavior, and so on.

Data Collection Strategies for Constructed Control Designs

The strategic considerations that enter into data collection for designs with constructed controls are not essentially different from those

Exhibit 6-G: Evaluation of Hospital Psychiatry with Constructed Controls

The goals of Individualized Patient Programming (IPP) were, first, to improve the effectiveness of an inpatient psychiatric program through frequent and regular feedback to treatment staff, and, second, to provide greater assurance that each person had an individually tailored program with clearly stated goals and treatment plans.

In order to evaluate IPP, the approach was introduced to one inpatient unit of a psychiatric hospital, and a similar unit in the same hospital was used as the constructed control. The two units were similar in terms of capacity, catchment region, types of patients, serving both sexes, median length of stay, number of wards, staffing, and so on, as well as several sociodemographic characteristics of the patients. Three process-dependent variables (reporting habits to staff, ward atmosphere, and client satisfaction) and two outcome-dependent variables (postdischarge community adjustment and rehospitalization rate) were analyzed.

Results indicated partial success for the program with lower rehospitalization rates for male patients.

SOURCE: Summary of B.S. Willer, "Individualized Patient Programming: An Experiment in the Use of Evaluation and Feedback for Hospital Psychiatry." *Evaluation Quarterly*, 1 (November 1977): 587-608.

Exhibit 6-H: A Nonrandomized Experiment with a Constructed Control and Before/After Survey Measures

The Dacca Family Planning Experiment was a comparative evaluation of family planning programs directed at both males and females. The primary purpose was to analyze differential changes in birth control practices resulting from three educational approaches to family planning — direct education with husbands only, direct education with wives only, and direct education with both. The effectiveness of each of these educational approaches was to be measured by comparing each to a fourth group, who received birth control services but no educational experimental program (the control).

The study population was to represent individuals not yet using birth control to any large extent.

The study populations were chosen from the four housing colonies maintained by the Central Government of Pakistan for its employees in Dacca. The type of housing provided was based on the salary of the employees, ranked into five classes. The study groups were defined as those having low levels of position in the government (Class III and IV workers ranging from sweepers to low-level clerks) and living in separate but similar housing colonies. Couples within the study groups were then screened to exclude ineligibles on the following criteria: one spouse not usually residing in the area at the time of the Before Survey; couples who could not understand Bengali (the language to be used during the interview); the husband with more than one wife at the time of the Before Survey; couples who had been married for less than two years; if the wife was over 50 years of age; if either spouse was sterilized.

Data were gathered through the Before Survey and the After Survey and through clinic records and home visit records. Both spouses in the three experimental groups were interviewed in both the Before and After surveys. The control group was only interviewed in the After Survey. The Before and After surveys contained questions on the following topics: demographic characteristics; fertility; knowledge of birth control; intended future fertility; the use of birth control; and attitudes toward learning about and future use of birth control.

This study concluded that certain educational approaches are more effective than others in meeting multiple goals among many types of target populations. The educational approach aimed at *both* males and females had, by far, the greatest impact in increasing knowledge about family planning. The program directed at both sexes was superior for almost all criteria of program success, including improving the attitudes regarding the acceptance of other people using family planning. This ap-

proach also had the greatest clinic attendance and acknowledged use of contraceptives. Only in the cases of older women,
upper-class women, and younger men did the program directed
at only one sex have a greater impact. (In these instances, the
program directed at the females had greater impact.) It appears
that educational efforts aimed at both sexes may be the most
effective in achieving the broadest range of cognitive, attitudinal,
and behavioral changes in family planning.

SOURCE: Summary, by permission, of L. W. Green et al., *The Dacca Family Planning Experiment.* University of California, Berkeley, School of Public Health, 1972.

discussed in connection with randomized experiments. The general
recommendation is the more before-and-after intervention measures of
outcome, the better. The two reasons for this recommendation in the
case of randomized controls apply here as well: First, the more measures, the more reliable are the readings that can be made on pre- and
postoutcomes. Second, the process by which the intervention may
work can be tracked more carefully over time.

NONRANDOMIZED STUDIES: STATISTICAL CONTROLS

Impact assessments using randomized controls or constructed control groups employ a strategy in which participants in a program are
matched in designated ways with nonparticipants. They may involve
many measures of outcomes, including pre- or postintervention measures, or both.

Now we move to a strategy in which only postintervention measures
are used, and a different approach is employed to compare participants
to nonparticipants. *Cross-sectional surveys* are undertaken. These surveys permit post hoc comparisons between participants and nonparticipants, and comparability between the two groups is established by
holding relevant factors constant *statistically.*

For example, in estimating the effects of attending Catholic schools
on adults, evaluators contrasted those who had attended parochial
schools with Catholics who had not (Greeley and Rossi, 1966; Greeley
et al., 1976). In this case it was possible to use constructed controls
because there were many parishes without parochial schools, and some

TABLE 6.2   Characteristics Useful in Devising Constructed Control Groups

I.   Characteristics of Individuals:
Age
Sex
Educational attainment
Socioeconomic status (income, wealth, property ownership)
Tenure (land and/or home ownership)
Marital status
Occupation (occupational prestige)
Ethnicity (race, cultural group, language group, national origin)
Intellectual functioning (IQ, cognitive ability, knowledge)
Labor force participation
II.   Characteristics of Families (or households):
Life-cycle stage
Number of members
Number of children
Socioeconomic status (household income or earnings, wealth, occupations followed, etc.)
Housing arrangements
Ethnicity
III.   Characteristics of Organized Units (schools, classes, unions, etc.):
Size differentiation
Levels of authority
Number of subunits
Number of distinctly different roles (occupations)
Industry class
Growth rate
Budget
IV.   Characteristics of Communities (territorially organized units):
Industry mix
Governmental organization
Population size
Territorial size
Growth rate
Population density
Location in relation to other territorial units (part of metropolitan area, independent city, town, etc.)

Catholics therefore did not have the opportunity to attend such schools. Since the authors were concerned with measuring occupational attainment in adulthood (among other outcomes), only postintervention measures (occupational attainment as measured in a sample survey of Catholic adults) were available.

Of course, there were a number of additional ways in which the parochial-school attenders could have differed from their secular-school counterparts. Attendance at parochial schools might have represented a stronger commitment to Catholicism among the parents of such adults, a commitment expressed by settling in parishes that had parochial schools. The parents of the parochial-school attendees may have been affluent as well, since usually only parishes with sufficient revenues can afford to establish schools, and only relatively wealthy parents can afford the tuition charges that are levied. We know from numerous studies that economic status is related to school achievement. These possible differences in family wealth must be taken into account by applying appropriate statistical controls. Essentially, cross-sectional impact assessment depends heavily on the use of statistical methods to factor out the differences between persons who have experienced an intervention and those who have not.

A cross-sectional study, then, is one in which observations are made at a single point in time, contrasting program participants with nonparticipants (or those who have participated to varying degrees). Usually, the target population is sampled and a survey administered to gather information on a large number of possibly confounding variables. Differences between levels of exposure to an intervention are observed, holding constant through statistical analyses other relevant differences between participants and nonparticipants.

It should be noted that impact assessments with constructed controls and those using statistical controls are identical in conceptualization. The main difference lies in screening for nonparticipant targets through deliberate selection (constructed controls) as opposed to screening targets through statistical techniques (statistical controls). Both methods seek to obtain comparability between participants and nonparticipants and both depend heavily on a priori knowledge about what characteristics might distinguish the two groups.

Whether one conducts an impact assessment with constructed controls or with statistical controls may hinge on the distribution of target participants and nonparticipants in the population under study. To cite an obvious example, it makes little sense to attempt to use surveys of the general population to find participants and nonparticipants in prison rehabilitation programs, because those who might be targets would be relatively rare in any population survey. Hence, surveys would not be an efficient way to estimate the impact of any program that is aimed at a very narrowly defined set of targets.

An additional consideration is whether or not it is possible to obtain before-and-after measures. If for one reason or another it is not possible to obtain or collect before measures on both experimental and constructed control groups, surveys may be an efficient way to proceed. For example, to gauge the effects of the GI Bill's tuition-financing programs on veterans of the Korean War, it is probably not possible to do anything more than survey surviving veterans, in the hope that it will be possible to hold constant the potential differences between those who used their benefits and those who did not.

Successive Statistical Adjustments

The logic of holding variables constant is illustrated in Table 6.3, a hypothetical impact assessment of a vocational training program for unemployed men between the ages of 35 and 40. The program is designed to upgrade the job skills of participants, enabling them to obtain better (i.e., higher-paying) jobs. The program was evaluated by taking a sample of 1,000 participants and interviewing them one year after they completed vocational training. In addition, another 1,000 men from the same age brackets were sampled from the general population of the large metropolitan area in which the program was operating. Since the program was small, almost all men approached for interviews in the general sample had not participated in the program.

TABLE 6.3   Illustrations of Statistical Adjustments in a Hypothetical Evaluation of the Impact of an Employment Training Project

Outcome Measure = Average hourly wage rates 1 year after completion of training program

I. Gross comparison between men 35-40 who have completed training program with sample of men 35-40 who did not attend training program:

	Participants	*Nonparticipants*
Average Wage Rate	$3.75	$4.20
N =	(1,000)	(1,000)

II. Comparison after adjusting for educational attainment:

	Participants		*Nonparticipants*	
	Less than High School Completion	Completed High School	Less than High School Completion	Completed High School
Average Wage Rate	$3.60	$4.10	$3.75	$4.50
N =	(700)	(300)	(400)	(600)

III. Comparison adjusting for educational attainment and employment at start of training program (or equivalent date for nonparticipants):

	Participants				*Nonparticipants*			
	Less than High School	Completed High School			Less than High School		Completed High School	
	All Unemployed		U	E	U	E	U	E
Average Wage Rate	$3.60	$4.10	$3.50	$3.83	$4.00	$4.60		
N =	(700)	(300)	(100)	(300)	(100)	(500)		

NOTE: U denotes unemployed; E, employed.

Both samples were asked for information about earnings, and hourly wage rates were computed for both groups.

In Panel I of Table 6.3, the average wage rates of the two groups are compared. Those who had participated in the project were earning, on average, $3.75 per hour; for those who had not participated, the corresponding average was $4.20. Clearly, those who had participated were earning considerably less than those who had not (only 89 percent of the wage rate of nonparticipants). However, these unadjusted comparisons are quite misleading, since participants and nonparticipants could have differed on a number of earnings-related variables other than their participation in the project.

Panel II of Table 6.3 takes one such difference into account by presenting average wage rates separately for two educational levels: those who had not completed high school and those who had. Note that 70 percent of those who *had* been participants *had not* completed high school, as opposed to 40 percent of the nonparticipants. When we compare the wage rates of persons of comparable educational attainment, the hourly wages of participants and nonparticipants approach one another: respectively, $3.60 and $3.75 for those who had not completed high school, and $4.10 to $4.50 for those who had completed high school. Obviously, holding educational attainment constant diminishes the differences between wage rates of participants and nonparticipants.

Panel III takes still another difference into account. Since all participants were unemployed at the time of enrollment in the training program, it is appropriate to compare participants with those nonparticipants who were also unemployed around the same time. In this panel, nonparticipants are divided into those who were unemployed and those who were not. This time, those who participated in the project earned more at each educational level than those who did not participate and were unemployed around the same time: respectively, $3.60 and $3.50 for those who did not complete high school and $4.10 and $4.00 for those who did.

Note that the introduction of successive statistical adjustments (controls) was not a haphazard procedure. There was justification for introducing each control based on a priori knowledge about the determinants of earnings. In any real example, of course, additional controls would have been entered — perhaps for previous occupations held, marital status, number of dependents, and race — all factors known to be related to wage rates. Again, the worth of making impact assessments through statistical controls is heavily dependent on such a priori knowledge.

It also should be noted that this evaluation design is ordinarily unable to account fully for the effects of self-selection and to remove such effects from estimates of net program impact. In the hypothetical example presented in Table 6.3, unemployed persons who participated were by that very fact differentiated from those who did not — perhaps by higher levels of motivation, a difference that is not possible to measure retrospectively with any strong degree of confidence.

The adjustments made in Table 6.3 were accomplished in a very simple way in order to illustrate the logic of successive statistical controls. More complex and sensitive statistical methods are available to take a number of adjustments into account simultaneously. Especially appropriate are the techniques of multiple regression and analysis of covariance, as well as multiple discriminant function analysis and log linear models. (Advanced texts should be consulted; e.g., Hanushek and Jackson, 1977.)

Complex Multivariate Methods

To illustrate the use of more complicated multivariate methods, Exhibit 6-I shows the results of an analysis designed to estimate the net impact of parole on postrelease employment of ex-felons released from Texas prisons during the first six months of 1976. The equation shown in that table expresses the number of weeks from date of release to date of first employment for ex-felons during the first year after release, as a function of parole and a number of variables that can be viewed as affecting either work or receiving parole.

The coefficients shown in the column marked "b" are unstandardized regression coefficients expressing the net number of weeks to first employment for each unit of each of the independent variables. The coefficient for having been released on parole is −3.45 weeks, meaning that persons released on parole found their first job 3.45 weeks sooner than other persons, *holding constant* all the other variables in the equation. In effect, the regression coefficient for parole is an *estimated net effect* for parole status, indicating that persons released on parole went to work sooner than those who were let go unconditionally.

The remaining variables in the equation were entered because there were good reasons to believe that the conditions they represent affected employment or parole status. Thus age, sex, race, education, marital status, having a physical handicap, having arranged a job prior to release, and being returned to Houston (a prime labor market in Texas at the time) were entered into the equation. All were variables available in the data set and expected to affect how quickly the released felons obtained employment. Indeed, we see that some of them were useful:

Exhibit 6-I: Regression of Number of Weeks Postrelease to First Employment on Selected Prerelease Characteristics and Parole Status for Texas Prison Releasees

Independent Variables	Dependent Variable Is Number of Weeks before First Job in Postrelease Year	
	b	SE
Released on parole	−3.45**	1.25
Age (years)	.01	.08
Male	−14.45***	2.72
Black	4.45**	1.53
Chicano	4.33*	2.07
Education (years)	−.16	.34
Married	−.01	1.89
Number of previous convictions	.08	.09
Gate money ($00's)	.00	.00
Handicap prison classification	7.36**	2.25
Released to Houston	−4.67**	1.44
Job arranged before release	−.20**	.06
Expected number of weeks between release and first job	2.81***	.76
Prison Behavior Code	−.03	.02
Constant	16.68*	6.50
R^2 =	.25***	
N =	(397)	

*statistically significant at .05
**statistically significant at .01
***statistically significant at .001

NOTE: The regression results shown above are computed from the control group in one of the TARP experiments. Note that because the table above is concerned only with members of the control group, the table, in effect, describes a cross-sectional survey and is equivalent to having drawn a random sample of all persons released from the state prisons of Georgia over a six-month period in 1976. (The details of the experimental treatment used in the TARP experiments are described in Exhibit 6-N.)

SOURCE: Unpublished tabulations from TARP experiment control group in Texas. (See P. H. Rossi, R. A. Berk and K. J. Lenihan, 1980, for full description of study.)

Males were likely to go to work much more quickly than females (about 14.5 weeks sooner); the physically handicapped took longer; those who returned to Houston got work faster in that very good labor market; and those who had arranged for a job prior to release also went to work sooner.

Another set of variables was entered, to hold constant the tendency to be granted parole and hence to represent the selection process used by the Texas parole board: the number of previous convictions, and a prison behavior code (actually, a sort of point system in which each incident of misbehavior in prison led to a score increase).

The worth of the analysis presented in Exhibit 6-I depends largely on how thoroughly the variables used capture (or *model*) the nonparole factors involved in going to work quickly and the kinds of factors taken into account in the granting of parole.

Examples of Statistical Control Use

Exhibits 6-J, 6-K, and 6-L illustrate varying levels of statistical sophistication in the analysis of cross-sectional data to assess impact. Exhibit 6-J is mainly of historical interest, since it was undertaken very early in the development of social research, before computers made it possible to make many calculations easily and cheaply. It is a study of the impact of desegregation in the U. S. Army during the Korean conflict in the early 1950s. Assessing impact consisted of comparing soldiers in integrated units with those who served in segregated units. Elaborate statistical controls were not practical, because the appropriate statistical techniques were hard to apply in that period and because self-selection was scarcely a factor (the army placed soldiers in their units, and switching from one to another was very difficult).

Exhibit 6-K describes an attempt to discern whether currency exchanges in Chicago pursued different pricing policies in black as opposed to white neighborhoods. Using service charges of currency exchanges as an outcome variable, and census data characterizing the racial and socioeconomic compositions of the tracts in which the exchanges were located as statistical controls, the analysis sought to detect consistent price differences indicative of a discriminatory pricing policy among the currency exchanges.

Exhibit 6-L represents an elaborate attempt to discern whether federal family planning programs had an impact on fertility. Taking advantage of the existence of a survey of all family planning clinics in the United States that included measures of the services delivered in each unit, the authors linked that information to vital statistics for the same areas. Modeling the fertility rates and adding enrollment in the family

Exhibit 6-J: The Effects of Integration in U.S. Army Units in Korea

The authors were commissioned by the U.S. Army in the early 1950s to assess the impact of integrating blacks into previously all-white army units serving in Korea during the Korean "conflict." The study was based on qualitative interviewing with officers and enlisted men as well as self-administered questionnaires from a large sample of soldiers. Impact was evaluated by comparing responses given by each of the following four groups: whites in all-white units, whites in integrated units, blacks in all-black units, and blacks in integrated units. The analysis is illustrated by the following table, in which soldiers in quartermaster corps units are compared in their responses to a question of how they viewed the future of race relations in the United States.

How Quartermaster Troops Answered the Question, "As time goes on, do you think that white and colored people in the United States will get along better together than they do today, not as well as they do now, or about the same as now?"

	Quartermaster			
	Whites in All-White Units	Whites in Integrated Units	Negroes in Integrated Units	Negroes in All-Negro Units
Answers:				
They will get along better together	13%	68%	85%	82%
They will get along about the same as now	65	23	13	15
They will not get along as well as now	22	7	1	2
No answer	0	2	1	1
N (100%) =	(68)	(99)	(73)	(144)

In general, both whites and blacks in integrated units were more favorable to members of the other race, leading to the conclusion that actual experience serving in integrated units led to more favorable attitudes.

SOURCE: From L. Bogart, *Social Research and Desegregation of the United States Army* p. 176. Reprinted by permission of the author.

Exhibit 6-K: Racial Discrimination in Chicago's Storefront Banks

The main objective of Chicago currency exchanges is to serve residents in areas of the city so poor that they cannot attract a bank. Currency exchanges, for the most part, charge 1 to 2 percent of the face amount to cash checks and write money orders and $.20 to $.30 to remit utility payments. The purpose of this study was to evaluate the extent and form of price differentials in Chicago currency exchanges according to the racial or ethnic composition of the areas they serve.

A sample of forty-three exchanges were selected from the yellow pages of the telephone directory (every tenth exchange was chosen). The racial composition of census tracts in which exchanges were located was obtained by dichotomizing the census tracts into two groups: "3 percent or less" and "7 percent or more." Multiple regression analysis was used to analyze the data. Service charge, the dependent variable, was regressed on amount of service, percentage black in census tract, percentage Spanish-speaking in census tract. The latter also was analyzed as a squared term: interaction of percentage black and amount of service, and interaction of percentage Spanish and amount of service.

It was found that each percentage change in the racial composition from white to black results in an increase in service charge of $.0016. Although this seems to be a trivial amount, it translates into a 20 percent added surcharge for a mostly black area. The authors conclude that exchanges are exploiting Chicago's residential race segregation by charging higher prices to blacks, although they caution that their findings are exploratory.

SOURCE: Summary of W. Bridges and J. Oppenheim, "Racial Discrimination in Chicago's Storefront Banks." *Evaluation Quarterly,* 1 (February 1977): 159-171.

planning units as an element in the model, they discerned a significant impact of family planning units on fertility by counties. The impact they found is proportional to the level of activity of the family planning units in question.

Exhibit 6-L: Impact of United States Family Planning Programs on Fertility

The primary objective of U.S. family planning clinic programs in 1968-1969 was "to enable Americans freely to determine the number and spacing of their children, with priority for serving low-income persons." This study evaluated whether these programs had a significant impact on the fertility of those who participated in them. Sources of data were the 1970 census, National Center for Health Statistics, and Alan Guttmacher Institute (program service statistics). Units of analysis were called "statistical analysis units" (SAUs) which were either a county or a number of small counties. There were 778 "white" SAUs (each SAU had at least 20,000 white women) and 237 "black" SAUs (each had at least 10,000 black women).

The main program variable was enrollment in the family planning clinics (from the service records), and the outcome variable was fertility rate (from the census, measured in different ways). Statistical controls were introduced for population density, education, migration, marital status, in-school status, race, labor force, age, and parity in a linear, additive, multiple regression model.

The authors found that the program had strong negative effects on the fertility rates of both white and black married women in all subgroups defined by age and socioeconomic status, after controlling for the other factors. (A cost-benefit analysis of the program produced favorable ratios. That analysis is summarized in Exhibit 8-C.)

SOURCE: Summary, by permission, of P. Cutright and F. S. Jaffe, *Impact of Family Planning Programs on Fertility: The U.S. Experience*. New York: Praeger, 1977.

Note that this fertility study was an evaluation of a full-coverage program. Under the relevant federal legislation, all areas of the country were eligible for funds that would support family planning clinics. For one reason or another, some areas elected not to participate, and there was some variation in effort among participating local government units. This variation provided the opportunity to discern the effects of such clinic efforts. Of course, one must assume that the factors held constant in the statistical analysis also hold constant local variations in willingness to start up fertility clinics (i.e., the self-selection processes).

All of the studies cited above required researchers to call on a priori knowledge of the intervention in question and the phenomenon concerned. For Bogart and his colleagues, it was essential to know that soldiers had little choice about the units in which they served. For Bridges and Oppenheim it was important to conceive of the currency exchanges as largely responsive to their customers' socioeconomic levels; this enabled them to adjust service rates in order to discern if the racial composition of their clientele was also a factor in pricing policies. Finally, Cutright and Jaffe drew on their knowledge of how demographic and socioeconomic variables influence fertility.

In sum, statistical control is an excellent procedure to apply when one can enter as controls variables and conditions that take into account competing explanations of program outcomes. The procedure is especially important for problems in which it is not possible to undertake randomized experiments, or even to envisage them.

Note that Cutright and Jaffe (Exhibit 6-L) did not use a sample survey in the traditional sense. It is cross-sectional in that it is composed of one-shot measurements of fertility and program services. It uses the results of a survey of service agencies but melds that survey with census data and vital statistics.

Limitations on the Use of Cross-Sectional Studies

Cross-sectional approaches to impact assessment have some advantages and some limitations. On the positive side, cross-sectional studies can usually be accomplished quickly and are therefore quite cost-effective methods for estimating net project effects. The approach is also useful if one is unwilling or unable to take the time necessary to make before-and-after measurements. Under some circumstances, especially when randomized experiments or quasi-experiments are completely out of the question, cross-sectional studies may be the only approach to employ in impact assessment. One should be aware, however, that cross-sectional studies rely heavily on a priori knowledge of the processes involved.

On the negative side, cross-sectional studies are quite vulnerable to "specification errors" (to use the econometric term). Specification errors are mistakes in specifying the appropriate theoretical structure that can rule out competing explanations. For example, in the analysis of the effects of parole on subsequent recidivism (shown in Exhibit 6-I), if the analysts have failed to take into account an important factor in how parole boards judge whether or not prisoners are eligible for parole, the analysis presented in that table may simply be wrong. To be more specific, if it turns out that parole boards released only prisoners who undertook vocational training in prison, the effects that are claimed for parole in Exhibit 6-I may simply reflect the fact that parolees were better prepared to obtain jobs, and hence, parole effects simply mask vocational training effects that have nothing to do with being on parole per se.

Perhaps the most common specification error made in cross-sectional analyses is to have an inadequate model of the process of self-selection. The risk is particularly great in any cross-sectional study where beneficiaries have exercised the option of participating or not in the program.

Several econometricians (Barnouw et al., 1980; Heckman, 1980) have recently advocated the use of cross-sectional data, provided that the processes of self-selection can be appropriately modeled. They suggest that research on the processes of self-selection can lead to the development of well-fitting models of self-selection, and have worked out the conditions under which such adjustments for self-selection may be made appropriately.

Under some unusual circumstances it is possible to model very accurately the selection process by which persons (or other targets) are exposed to a treatment. For example, in the demobilization following World War II, it might have been possible to design a study of the effects of earlier as opposed to later release from the army. Soldiers were released according to a point system which took into account length of service, overseas time, decorations, and number of dependents. Since the time order of demobilization was largely determined by the points earned by a soldier, it would have been possible to use this variable in a statistical control study to show whether or not being released earlier or later after September 1945 had any effect on how fast and at what level soldiers obtained employment. Properly conducted, this hypothetical study could have been as powerful as a randomized experiment in providing the basis for unbiased estimates of the effects of early or late demobilization. (This approach is also known as a regression discontinuity design; see Cook and Campbell, 1979.)

Although one may attempt to put in measures that appear to take such self-selection into account, the measures used are often inadequate or poor, resulting in underadjustment for self-selection and hence overestimates of net program effects. Indeed, the controversy over the result of the Head Start evaluation (Campbell and Erlebacher, 1970) centers on whether or not the Westinghouse analysts properly adjusted for the differences between Head Start participants and non-participants.

Cross-sectional designs can be used for both partial-coverage programs and some types of full-coverage programs — namely, where the treatment was varied in some known way. The family planning center assessment conducted by Cutright and Jaffe (Exhibit 6-L) is a good example of a full-coverage program that varied in activity from area to area, including some regions where the activities of family planning clinics were essentially zero. By estimating the effects of differing levels of clinic activity, the study was able to relate how much of that activity was associated with how many averted births.

In the same way, several attempts have been made to estimate the effects of state gun-control legislation on gun-related crime rates (e.g., assaults with firearms and murders with firearms). Because the 50 states vary in the extent to which guns are regulated through systems of permits and registrations, the investigators (see Exhibit 6-M) attempted to relate the level of regulation to relevant crime rates. It turned out that

Exhibit 6-M: Using Cross-Sectional Studies of Interstate Variations in Gun-Control Legislation to Discern the Effects of Gun-Ownership Restriction on Crime Rates

For a variety of historical reasons, the fifty states vary widely in the extent to which there are gun-ownership registration laws and in the restrictions placed on both the ownership of weapons and their use. Since whether or not such legislation affects crime rates is a matter of some considerable controversy, several analyses have been undertaken to estimate the net effects on crime rates of variations in such legislation, as follows.

Geisel et al. (1969) attempted to relate a set of crime, accident, and suicide rates that involved the use of firearms to a combined index that expressed the extent to which each of the state's legislation in force in 1960 restricted the sale and ownership of guns. A regression model was devised that took into account state average per capita incomes, median educational attainment of adult residents, the sex ratio, police per 1,000 residents, proportion black in each state, population density, median age, and licensed hunters per capita in that state. The dependent variables consisted of gun homicide rates, gun assault rates, gun accident rates, and gun suicide rates. The resulting coefficients for gun regulations purportedly showed that the stricter were the regulations, the lower were the rates of each of the gun-related incidents. The authors further estimate that if each state's legislation were brought up to the strictness of New Jersey's laws, several hundred deaths per year could be averted.

In a study that disputes the findings of Geisel and his associates, Murray (1975) addresses himself to the same problem, using much the same data. However, an alternative specification of the regression model is used: State legislation is measured by the presence or absence of specific regulatory provisions, rather than an overall restrictiveness measure; 1970 Census data and 1970 crime, accident, and suicide rates are used; and additional state characteristics are used, including percentage unemployed, percentage of the population below the poverty line, and the proportion of the population who were immigrants. Murray's regression analysis did not yield significant coefficients for state gun-control legislation, from which finding Murray argues that gun-control legislation does not affect gun-related crimes, accidents, and suicide.

SOURCE: J. D. Wright, P. H. Rossi, K. Daly and E. Weber-Burdin, *Weapons, Crime and Violence in America*. Amherst, MA: Social and Demographic Research Institute, 1981.

the results are extremely sensitive to specification errors, some studies finding some effects and others finding none. The main differences among studies were the characteristics of states held constant in the analysis, illustrating dramatically the dangers of specification error inherent in cross-sectional designs.

Among the better-known cross-sectional studies of full-coverage programs is the Coleman Report (Coleman et al., 1966), in which variations among a set of schools in staffing levels, finances, student composition, and physical plants are assessed for impact on student learning. Coleman's original assessment was that differences in these

242 • COMPARATIVE DESIGNS

variables among U.S. schools in the early 1960s were not related very strongly to student achievement. Holding such things as student background variables constant, he found that students achieved no more in schools spending a great deal per capita on public education than in those whose expenditures were considerably less. Similar findings hold for student-to-teacher ratios, the adequacy of physical plants, and the training of teachers.

The Coleman Report was not universally acclaimed as a definitive assessment, however. Many educators and educational researchers disputed Coleman's findings. A two-year-long seminar led by Mosteller and Moynihan (1972) produced a spate of reanalyses, all testing alternative specifications on the same data. The vulnerability of one-shot surveys to criticisms on grounds of specification errors is again illustrated.

Hence, cross-sectional studies of impact share with quasi-experiments a built-in vulnerability to criticism. Since one can make only a persuasive, *not* a definitive, case for having correctly specified the analysis to account for potentially competing explanations of program effects, cross-sectional studies are always open to the criticism that alternative analyses would lead to different results.

Supplementary Use of Statistical Controls

Although a randomized experiment or a quasi-experiment using constructed controls may be analyzed properly only by straight comparisons between experimental and control groups, frequently evaluators also use statistical controls in their analyses. Much is to be gained by doing so.

Sometimes programs may be more effective with some types of beneficiaries and less so with others. Hence, separate analyses of, say, males and females may find that the program has been differentially effective with the two sexes. For example, in the TARP experiment (Rossi et al., 1980), a separate analysis was made of female ex-felons in the expectation that the very different situations of the two sexes (men and women are typically imprisoned for quite separate kinds of offenses and return to equally distinct home circumstances) would lead to differential impacts from the experimental intervention of unemployment insurance eligibility upon release from prison. It was found in this experiment that the benefit eligibility had a stronger work disincentive effect for women ex-felons because they were more responsible for dependent children and apparently preferred caring for their children to working, given unemployment benefit eligibility.

The use of statistical controls in randomized experiments also helps to increase the statistical power of such experiments. By holding constant preintervention factors that are related to the outcomes of interest,

Exhibit 6-N: A Mixed Randomized Experiment and Statistical Control Approach to the Analysis of a Criminal Justice Intervention

Two identical randomized experiments were designed to test the impact on recidivism of providing eligibility for unemployment insurance payments to released prisoners, each with 2,000 released prisoners, conducted in Georgia and Texas. Prisoners released from state prisons during the period January 1976 to June 1976 were randomly assigned to experimental groups (which offered eligibility for thirteen or twenty-six weeks of unemployment insurance benefits) or to control groups (which were simply followed through the year beyond release). The outcome measure was arrests on property-related charges over the year after release.

Direct comparisons between experimentals and controls led to the conclusion that the treatment had no discernible effect on subsequent arrests on property-related charges. The addition of statistical controls, however, brought to light a fairly complex process at work. The payments had both a direct positive effect, reducing arrests, and a negative indirect effect on arrests, reducing employment and thereby increasing arrests. These two effects cancelled each other out, leaving the experimental groups with the same arrest rates as the controls.

The introduction of statistical controls to this randomized experiment's results led to an important policy discovery, namely that policies providing modest financial support to released prisoners would reduce recidivism if they did not at the same time create a work disincentive. Since unemployment insurance benefits are usually made only to those who are unemployed as a condition of eligibility, this procedure, if modified, might lead to a program with positive benefits in the reduction of property crimes.

SOURCE: Summary of P. H. Rossi, R. Berk and K. Lenihan, *Money, Work and Crime.* New York: Academic, 1980.

the intervention effects are estimated with less measurement error. In statistical terms, the error sum of squares is thereby reduced, resulting in smaller standard errors for intervention estimates. For example, while the comparison of a straight control group to an experimental group in the LIFE experiment (Rossi et al., 1980) showed that the experimental group experienced 8 percent fewer arrests than did the control group, this difference hovered at the .05 level of significance. A regression analysis in which a number of preexperiment characteristics of the released prisoners were employed led to a lowering of the standard error for the intervention and a decrease in the associated level of significance to .02.

A final advantage of using statistical controls in randomized experiments is the potential for detecting interaction effects. In an analysis of a criminal justice intervention (Exhibit 6-N), for example, it was found that the program simultaneously produced two effects that tended to counteract each other — a finding that was completely obscured in the straight, one-way comparison between experimental and control groups.

The use of statistical control techniques in cross-sectional studies, quasi-experiments, or randomized experiments clearly requires both an intimate understanding of the substantive processes underlying the intervention and its presumed outcome, and a thorough mastery of multivariate statistical methods. While a general understanding of the logic behind statistical controls can be attained by almost anyone, the proper employment of the techniques involves considerable technical training, substantive knowledge, and access to high-capacity computers.

DESIGN TRADEOFFS

This chapter described three research approaches to the estimation of the net impacts of programs. The most rigorous approach is the randomized controlled experiment, and we recommend it highly in appropriate circumstances. We recognize, however, that for many programs randomized experimental designs are impracticable or inappropriate. Indeed, there are many circumstances in which constructed control approaches or statistical controls used in connection with cross-sectional surveys are preferable and certainly more practical.

We cannot stress enough the importance of a priori knowledge in any assessment of impact. Without valid knowledge about social processes in general and the processes involved in a particular program, it is difficult to avoid making serious errors in impact study designs, especially ones that involve constructed or statistical controls.

7

Single-Group Designs for Impact Assessment

In this chapter we deal with methods for making impact assessments with single-group designs. These are especially relevant for full-coverage programs with constant treatments. These are the circumstances in which it is not possible to use randomized, constructed, or statistical controls. The first approach we discuss is the use of participants as their own controls, an option if participants have been observed for some period of time prior to the intervention. An especially powerful use of reflexive controls is through time-series analyses employing before-intervention trends to project what would have happened without the intervention. The remaining two approaches are primarily judgmental: comparing outcomes with existing standards or norms (generic controls), or using judgments of experts, administrators, or participants (shadow controls).

KEY CONCEPTS

Generic Controls:	Established measures of social processes, such as published test norms, that are used as comparisons with the outcomes of interventions.
Reflexive Controls:	Outcome measures taken before interventions on participating targets as control observations.
Shadow Controls:	Expert and participant judgments used to establish net impact.
Time-Series Analyses:	Relatively long series of measurements on outcomes used to predict set of future outcomes.

*P*articularly in the evaluation of established programs, there are many instances of full or almost full coverage that prevent identifying and recruiting a comparison group for control purposes. Even when it is possible to identify such a group, there are times when the evaluation budget prevents doing so. While evaluations using single-group designs may encounter difficulty in estimating net effects, with proper safeguards, they may provide useful knowledge of program impact. Indeed, in some cases, sufficient data and appropriate analysis result in relatively rigorous evaluations.

REFLEXIVE CONTROLS

As noted in Chapter 5, using before-intervention outcome measures of participant targets instead of a comparison group is known as using *reflexive controls*. The term is simply a way of describing the use of targets as their own controls.

Before-and-After Studies

For full-coverage programs in which it is impossible to define randomized or constructed control groups or to locate nonparticipants through surveys, using reflexive controls may be the only approach available. Reflexive control evaluation may also be an economical first step, especially if there is no reason to believe that targets' scores on outcome measures would have changed without the intervention. For example, if targets are at their minimum on a wage scale before an intervention to increase earnings, the impact of a program to raise wages may be estimated by a reflexive control study, although we would not know with much certainty whether the changes reflected net impact. The essential justification for using a reflexive control design is that the targets remain identical in relevant ways before and after participation; in other words, the preintervention and postintervention outcome scores would have been the same without the intervention (i.e., net impact would equal gross impact).

It should also be obvious that reflexive control designs are highly vulnerable to misestimation of net effects. The major problem with targets as their own controls is that, by definition, the reflexive groups are observed at different points in time. Preintervention observations are made on units that are younger than they will be when the intervention is fully implemented. To the extent that the outcome variables are either age-related or are influenced by the extraintervention experiences these units accumulate after program exposure, the use of reflexive controls is not advised. When assessing the effects of a fertility reduction project addressed to women of childbearing age, simply knowing their fertility behavior in an earlier period is clearly inadequate. Fertility behavior at any point in time is not independent of prior fertility behavior. Moreover, some women in the reflexive group observations may be completing their fertility and would not be expected to bear children in a subsequent period.

Yet for many processes, maturational effects are not very important, especially over short periods of time. For instance, an educational campaign to change adults' beliefs about the nutritional components of certain types of foods is not likely to compete with maturational processes.

A second problem with reflexive controls arises out of potential differences in secular drift trends in the two periods involved. If observations of the reflexive control group are made during a period of depressed crop yields, a comparison with crop yields during a project period of more normal yields would be misleading. Similarly, a program to reduce crime will appear more effective if it coincides with other efforts to increase policing; or an employment training program will appear ineffective if it is accompanied by a prolonged period of rising unemployment and depressed economic conditions.

A third problem results from differences in interfering events between the two time periods. An *interfering event,* as defined previously, represents an unusual, one-time occurrence that affects outcome measures. Examples include serious natural disasters, a political crisis, and health epidemics. Any event that might affect output measures could interfere with the proper use of reflexive control observations.

An unusual example of the use of reflexive controls is shown in Exhibit 7-A. Shlay and Rossi (1981) obtained data on a sample of census tracts in the Chicago metropolitan area to assess the effects of zoning regulations on population and housing growth in the tracts. They used zoning laws and regulations applicable in 1960 to each of the tracts to form a measure of how restrictively each tract was zoned. Using the relevant 1960 population and housing census measures to predict by regression analysis what would be the population and housing stock in 1970, and entering the zoning restrictiveness measures in the regression, Shlay and Rossi arrived at estimates of the effects of zoning restrictions on the growth of housing and population in the census tracts.

Note that the analysis shown in Exhibit 7-A depends heavily on the existence of variation from census tract to census tract in the 1960 zoning regulations. Hence, each tract serves as its own control in pre-

---

Exhibit 7-A: **Estimating the Effects of Zoning Regulations on the Growth of Housing and Population Stocks in the Chicago SMSA, 1960-1970**

Using samples of census tracts drawn from within the city of Chicago and from within the rest of the Chicago SMSA, Shlay and Rossi ascertained from local municipal records the zoning regulations in force in each of the census tracts in 1960. A set of indices were constructed for each tract reflecting the extent to which the zoning regulations restricted residential use of tract land, ranging from the most exclusionary use pattern, in which only single family homes on large tracts were permitted, to the least exclusionary usage, in which any type of land use, including industrial and commercial uses, was permitted.

Using 1960 and 1970 Census values for housing and population characteristics, a regression equation was run that predicted 1970 characteristics of the tracts on the basis of 1960 values and the zoning index. The investigators found that zoning regulations did change the growth rates from what would have been expected on the basis of normal growth, and affected the nature of the tract populations' socioeconomic and life-cycle distributions.

SOURCE: A. Shlay and P.H. Rossi, "Keeping Up the Neighborhood: Estimating Net Effects of Zoning." *American Sociological Review*, December 1981. Reprinted by permission.

---

dicting growth in the intercensal period, and tracts are contrasted according to the amount of restrictions placed on land uses in each. The "maturational trends" in tract growth, like age-related changes in individuals, are taken into account by estimating such trends for the entire set of tracts and by considering zoning the cause of deviations from such maturational trends, as represented by predicted 1970 values of housing and population stocks.

Before-and-after studies of full-coverage interventions are relatively rare, mainly because before-intervention measures of full-coverage programs, unfortunately, are usually unavailable and because proper analysis depends heavily on treatment variation (as shown in Exhibit 7-A). Full-coverage programs with constant treatments tend more often to be assessed using generic or shadow controls, as we will discuss in a later section of this chapter.

Time-Series Analyses of Full-Coverage Programs

For many phenomena that are of public concern (e.g., fertility, mortality, and crime) or of administrative concern (e.g., proportions of college students dropping out at the end of their first year), there are often extensive *time series* — measures of outcomes taken weekly, monthly, quarterly, or at longer intervals. Such time series provide relatively firm bases upon which to build estimates of what would have happened in the absence of an intervention.

When a relatively long time series of preintervention observations exists, it is often possible to model long-standing trends in the target group, projecting those trends through the intervention and observing whether or not the postintervention period shows significant deviations from them. The use of such general time-trend modeling procedures as ARIMA (McCleary and Hay, 1980; Pyndyck and Rubinfeld, 1976; Cook and Campbell, 1979; Hibbs, 1977) can identify best-fitting trends by taking into account long-term linear patterns and seasonal variations. One must also allow for the degree to which any value or score on a measure is necessarily related to previous ones (technically referred to as autocorrelation). It should be noted, however, that the procedures involved are highly technical and require a fairly high level of statistical sophistication.

Exhibits 7-B and 7-C illustrate the use of existing time series in evaluations to assess the impacts of a gun-control law and of a water conservation project. Note that in both cases the evaluation is made possible by the existence of relatively long series (with approximately 120 time points) of measures on outcome variables. Thus, Exhibit 7-B uses information collected over several years on violent crimes reported to the police — homicide, assault, and armed robbery — to establish an expected trend for such crimes in the absence of the gun-control law that went into effect in 1975. Comparison of the rates experienced after enactment with the expected rates provides a measure of net outcome. Exhibit 7-C illustrates the same procedures, employing water usage rates before and after the enactment of fairly stringent regulations designed to lower water consumption. It should also be noted that both studies use a prior knowledge about the factors that affect the outcome measures in order to rule out possibly competing explanations.

As in the case of other types of statistical controls, time-series analyses are vulnerable to specification error. For example, the analysis

Exhibit 7-B: A Time-Series Analysis of the Effect of the Massachusetts Gun Control Law

In April 1975, the state of Massachusetts formally put into operation a gun-control law that mandates a one-year minimum sentence on conviction of carrying a firearm without a special license. This study evaluated the deterrent effect of the law. Gun-related offenses of homicide, assault with a gun, and armed robbery for the city of Boston were examined for shifts or changes in their levels in time periods prior to, concurrent with, and after the enactment of this law.

Multiplicative empirical-stochastic models with an embedded shift parameter were employed to analyze the time-series data of the monthly occurrences of homicide, assault with a gun, and armed robbery for the city of Boston from January 1966 through October 1975.

The authors found that the gun-control law has effected a statistically significant decrease in both armed robbery and assault with a gun in the time period. However, no statistically significant changes in the homicide rate were observed. The authors attributed the lack of effect on homicide to the large proportion of residential homicides and to the fact that future impact of gun control on homicide in general may not show up for several years, if ever.

SOURCE: Summary of S. J. Deutsch and F. B. Alt, "The Effect of Massachusetts' Gun Control Law on Gun-Related Crimes in the City of Boston." *Evaluation Quarterly,* 1 (November 1977): 543-567.

presented in Exhibit 7-B has been disputed by Hay and McCleary (1979), who claimed that the ARIMA model used by Deutsch and Alt was incorrect. Applying an alternative ARIMA model, Hay and McCleary found that some of the effects of the Massachusetts Gun Law assessed by Deutsch and Alt disappeared when a "more correct" model was applied. (See also Deutsch, 1979, for a continuation of this debate.) The point to bear in mind is by now an old refrain to the reader: Statistical controls, either those of cross-sectional analyses or those used in modeling time-series trends, are no better than the a priori thinking that goes into their construction.

Exhibit 7-C: A Time-Series Analysis of the Impact of a Water Conservation Campaign

In 1972 the Goleta Water Board declared a moratorium on new water hookups in an effort to maintain the level of demand within the limits of supply until alternative sources for water could be assessed. In addition, other conservation measures were taken to reduce water consumption, including the enactment of local laws to prohibit waste and an educational campaign. The purpose of this study was to assess the effectiveness of the Goleta County Water District's program to decrease water consumption.

The effectiveness of the program was measured by two dependent variables: domestic and commercial sales, and production. In order better to assess program impact, in addition to the moratorium, rainfall, season, and population were also treated as exogenous variables in a regression model. Monthly data for these variables were available from 1966 to 1976.

By holding other relevant variables constant, the authors were able to illustrate that the presence of the moratorium had a statistically significant influence on water use. The findings indicated an average 15 percent reduction in water consumption for the three years following the implementation of the moratorium.

SOURCE: Summary of J. E. Maki, D. M. Hoffman and R. A. Berk, "A Time Series Analysis of the Impact of a Water Conservation Campaign." *Evaluation Quarterly,* 2 (February 1978): 107-118.

Simpler methods of examining time-series data before and after an intervention can provide crude but useful clues to impact. If the confounding influences on an intervention are known, and there is considerable certainty that their effects are minimal, time series are useful for establishing net program effect. The chart shown in Exhibit 7-D presents auto accident rates in Great Britain before and after the enactment and enforcement of drastically changed laws dealing with the treatment of persons involved in accidents and in the penalities for driving while under the influence of alcohol. The chart indicates that the legislation had a discernible impact: Accidents declined after it went into effect, and the decline was especially dramatic for accidents occurring over the weekend. (Statistical analyses verified that the clearly apparent effects were also significant.)

When time series exist for interventions at different times and in different places, more complex analyses must be undertaken. In the study on water conservation districts described in Exhibit 7-C, Berk and his associates (1981) employed a multiple time series of water consumption to compare the relative efficacy of pricing policies versus educational campaigns in reducing domestic and commercial water consumption.

Time-series analyses are quite powerful designs for estimating the effects of constant-treatment, full-coverage programs. We strongly recommend them for circumstances in which appropriate statistical series exist.

GENERIC CONTROLS

All of the approaches discussed in Chapter 6 and the first part of this chapter are based on the use of observations especially undertaken for the purpose of estimating what would have happened without the intervention that is being tested. These procedures are stressed because, in most intervention situations, we rarely have firm knowledge about what ordinarily happens in the course of social action. In contrast, many of the physical sciences (e.g., chemistry) publish large handbooks that provide standardized values for wide varieties of physical processes. For example, it is not necessary for the industrial chemist to ascertain *de novo* typical BTU values for various fuels, since there are several handbooks in which such values are listed, based on the pooled

Exhibit 7-D: An Analysis of the Impact on Traffic Accidents of Compulsory Breathalyzer Tests for Drivers Involved in Accidents

In 1967 the British government enacted a new policy that allowed police to give breathalyzer tests at the scenes of accidents. The test measured the presence of alcohol in the blood of suspects. Heavier penalties were also instituted for drunken driving convictions. Considerable publicity was given to the provisions of the new law, which went into effect in October 1967.

The chart below plots the vehicular accident rates by various periods of the week before and after the new legislation went into effect. Visual inspection of the chart clearly indicates that a decline in accidents occurred after the legislation, which affected most times of the week, but had especially dramatic effects for weekend periods. (Statistical tests also verified what can be seen from visual inspection.)

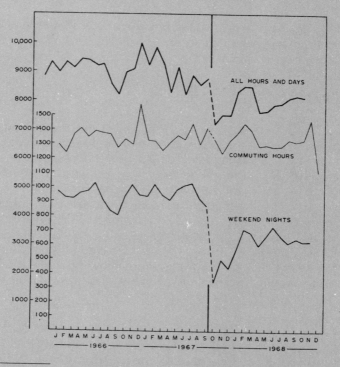

SOURCE: From H. L. Ross, D. T. Campbell and G. V Glass, "Determining the Social Effects of a Legal Reform: The British Breathalyzer Crackdown of 1967." *American Behavioral Scientist,* 13 (March/April 1970): 500.

experiences of perhaps scores of investigators. For the social researcher, however, there are few comparable compilations. We do not know, for instance, the typical experiences of persons on urban labor markets. Even more important, we do know that such "typical" experiences change from season to season and from year to year, fluctuating with the business cycle and with the mix of workers on the market.

Despite the general absence of such standardized values, there are a few areas of human behavior where such generic controls are available. As discussed in Chapter 5, *generic controls* are measures of social and human processes generally recognized as well established. Existing generic controls include measures of vital processes (e.g., death rates, birthrates, sex ratios, proportions of persons in various labor force categories) and derivatives of these measures. In addition, there are published standards or norms for various psychological tests (including tests of intelligence, achievement of various skills, personality, and the like). The information provided by generic controls, with proper safeguards, can be used to estimate what would ordinarily happen without an intervention.

For example, the effects of fluoridated water on dental caries were discovered by noting that the incidence of dental disorders varied among localities, and that such variation was correlated with the amount of fluorides naturally found in the drinking water. This correlation was discovered because dental epidemiologists had a fairly firm notion of the normal rates of carie formation. Similarly, the detection of epidemics rests heavily on the epidemiologist's knowledge of ordinary incidence rates for various diseases. Likewise, the efficacy of occupational health measures is judged against expected death rates from various causes in the general population.

In considering educational interventions, it is tempting to use the norms of achievement-test publishers as generic controls. But doing so may result in serious errors; there is so much variance in achievement that is associated with socioeconomic level, ethnic background, and similar factors that published norms are usually too general to be useful. Thus, in evaluating whether or not a new teaching program in education is effective, it is probably not appropriate to compare the gain in achievement-test scores of a sample of inner-city children against the published norms of the test constructor. The ordinary rates of learning for such children are likely to differ greatly from such general norms. Similarly, it is probably a mistake to compare the earnings of 34-year-old males as reported in the Census Bureau's Current Population Survey to those of 34-year-olds who have just completed a vocational training course. Generic controls, in short, are usually unavailable in sufficient detail for evaluators to be confident that the standards in question are appropriate for a particular use.

Absolute standards are a special form of generic controls, sometimes applied in circumstances in which goals are very explicit. For example, a goal for an income maintenance program may be to see that every person over 18 receives a minimum monthly income of $500. Such a specific goal may be viewed as constituting a "generic control," and a program can be assessed by whether or not that goal is achieved. Similarly, the objective of a prisoner rehabilitation program may be to reduce recidivism to zero, also a measurable attainment. However, few programs are willing to commit themselves to such absolute goals, nor is it likely that any goal so absolutely specified can be achieved by an intervention.

We wish to stress that generic controls should be used only under circumstances in which other types of controls are not available. It is tempting to consider their use in other evaluation contexts. Certainly, generic controls are inexpensive and take virtually no time to collect, especially in comparison to the expense involved in using randomized or constructed controls. However, even when randomized, constructed, or statistical controls cannot be collected, generic controls should be used only with the utmost caution, with intense scrutiny of whether or not the generic controls in question are comparable to participants in every critical way.

SHADOW CONTROLS

For most social programs, it is difficult to find any generic control observations. Norms simply do not exist for vocational training, income maintenance, or counseling programs, for example. However, there are persons with expertise in various human service areas on whose judgment it may be possible to rely when constructing estimates of whether or not a given gross outcome is sufficient evidence for significant net impact. In addition, it is also possible to turn to the participants themselves to obtain assessments of whether or not a program has affected them significantly. Judgments of experts, program administrators, and participants are called *shadow controls,* a name chosen to reflect their usual lack of a substantial evidential basis.

Despite the fact that shadow controls ordinarily can be used only with extreme caution, there are some circumstances in which their use is justified. One such circumstance is the case of an extraordinarily successful program, as the following illustrates.

One may find that a two-month-long vocational training program to produce drivers of heavy-duty trucks has enabled 90 percent of its participants (selected from among persons without such skills) to qualify for appropriate drivers' licenses. Such a finding suggests that the program has been quite successful in reaching its goal of imparting vocational skills. We can make this judgment because it seems highly unlikely that so large a proportion of any group of previously unskilled persons who wanted to become truck drivers would be able to qualify for such licenses in a two-month period on their own. The worth of this judgment depends heavily on knowing something about truck-driving and the special skills required to be proficient in it, plus some knowledge of the driver's license tests. A priori knowledge of high validity is clearly important in such judgments.

The obverse outcomes could also lead to firm judgments. If all of the truck-driving program's participants failed the license examination, that finding would be fairly clear evidence of program failure. But even this judgment cannot be made without some knowledge about truck-driving and the licensing tests. It may well be that all applicants fail on the first try, and that the crucial test is whether or not there is success on the second try.

Of course, it is likely the outcome results would be more ambiguous: It may well be that only 30 percent pass the licensing examinations. The typical finding raises the question of whether or not a comparable group receiving no training would have done as well. Usually, simple before-and-after measures on target participants only document the fact that a project is having an impact on participants that is consistent with project goals. But this is hardly definitive proof of net impact. Hence, for typical program results, using shadow controls is always risky.

Expert Judgments

If expert judgments are to be used as shadow controls, their worth depends heavily on the skills and knowledge of the experts in question. Those familiar with the field of adult vocational education and the typical outcomes of intervention projects in that field might be asked to draw on their experience in judging whether the 30 percent outcome described previously is greater or less than is ordinarily the outcome of successful adult vocational training. Clearly, the usefulness and validity of such judgments, and hence the worth of an evaluation using them, depend heavily on the judges' expertise and the development of firm knowledge in the field.

If expert judgments (or any shadow controls) are to be used, it is essential that their use be made explicit; that is, the bases upon which the expert judgments are made ought to be described as completely as possible. If an expert makes a judgment based on his or her own direct experiences, the extent of such experiences and the variations from instance to instance ought to be revealed. When possible, explicit references to other evaluation studies should be given so that one may check to see whether or not the circumstances of the other interventions are comparable to those of the one under judgment.

Often, the "shadow control" is a conclusion or construction based on the expert's understanding of the processes involved. Thus, to an expert in criminology, it may "stand to reason" that a given intervention will be effective, since it follows closely the leading paradigms in the field concerning the rehabilitation of ex-prisoners. While the judgment of an industrial engineer concerning the effectiveness of a production process may be quite enough upon which to base action, the judgment of a criminologist about rehabilitation simply does not command the same standing. Unfortunately, the very reason we have to employ rigorous impact assessment designs in the area of social programs is that the state of knowledge in the appropriate fields is inadequate. Although it "stands to reason" that many programs will succeed, they often do not pass the more rigorous tests of the better impact assessment designs.

The actual procedures employed by an expert to arrive at shadow controls may vary considerably. Typically, a well-known expert (or experts) in a relevant field is hired as a consultant and sent to visit the site of a program to examine closely its workings and to write a report summarizing experiences and assessments. (Exhibits 7-E and 7-F

Exhibit 7-E: The Use of Expert Judgment to Evaluate the Impact of Citizen Participation on Urban Renewal

Using interviews with major participants as well as data from the membership lists of a citizen's organization, the authors assessed the effectiveness of attempts to use a participatory process in the design of an urban renewal plan for the area around the University of Chicago. The assessment took several forms: First, planners were asked to identify those features of the completed plan that were affected by the participatory process; second, documentary records were examined for accounts of meetings between planners and citizens; and finally, detailed case studies were made of specific plan features, in an attempt to discern how the final plans were formed.

SOURCE: Summary, by permission, of P. H. Rossi and R. A. Dentler, *The Politics of Urban Renewal.* New York: Free Press, 1961.

provide typical examples of such judgmental assessments.) Visiting experts may examine project records; observe the project in operation; conduct interviews with participants; talk to project managers, staff, and other officials; and conduct interviews with former participants. In short, all of the means of informal social research may be employed.

The worth of an expert's judgmental assessment depends on the following two considerations: First, one must consider his or her state of knowledge about the substantive field. In a field where knowledge of how to achieve a particular outcome is quite advanced, an expert's appraisal may be very accurate. If little is known about an area (e.g., how to rehabilitate criminals), an expert's judgment of a particular project's effectiveness may not be worth more than that of any other person. Experts should also be familiar with the findings of other evalua-

Exhibit 7-F: Judgmental Expert Assessment Using Before-and-After Project Administrative Statistics

The Integrated Family Life Education (IFLE) Project in Ethiopia is an attempt to educate adults in appropriate practices in health, nutrition, agriculture, family planning, and civics. Adult education classes are the medium used, with many instructional materials carefully constructed and pretested, especially for the target population in question.

An outside evaluator, John Pettit, conducted a field visit to the project sites for a period of three weeks. Using administrative statistics derived from before-and-after measurements of literacy, subscription to proper sanity practices, etc., he was able to show that significant advances had been made by program participants. Interviews were undertaken with participants, community leaders, and staff workers on the project. The before-and-after measurements were made primarily to provide feedback information to project workers, but were also useful for evaluation purposes. For example, in one small village, participants using appropriate family practices were 5 percent at the start of the program and 32 percent at the end of a training cycle.

SOURCE: Summary, by permission, of C.D. Crone, "Evaluation: Autopsy or Checkup?" *World Education Reports*, 15 (October 1977): 3-13.

tions, including more systematic ones, of similar programs. For example, an expert asked to judge whether or not a community treatment center for released prisoners helps ex-felons obtain employment should be familiar with the many studies on the employment rates for ex-felons during months after release. Similarly, knowledge that few studies show much influence of classroom size on achievement, but strong positive effects on teachers' satisfaction ratings, should make one skeptical that a program based largely on such strategy is likely to do much for student achievement (although it may please the teachers).

Second, one must realize that it is only natural for a project administrator to attempt to present a project in the best possible light. Thus, one can expect the state of a project at the time of an announced visit to be better than at other periods, in ways ranging from the neatness and cleanliness of the headquarters to possibly well-rehearsed laudatory statements from participants.

Because in many circumstances judgmental assessments by experts are the only kinds of impact assessments that can be made, it is important that such experts be selected very carefully, with attention to their ability to surmount barriers to communication and their mastery of the state of knowledge in the discipline involved. At minimum, experts should consider the following sources of data:

1. *Administrative records.* Experts should collect information from administrative records (or have such tabulations made) on such topics as:
   a. size of project
   b. type of participants recruited
   c. attrition experience with participants
   d. postproject experiences of participants
   e. project costs per participant who completes program
   f. before-after measures of participant changes relevant to project goals

2. *Observations of project operation.* Projects that call for active work with participants (e.g., household visits, classroom sessions, media presentations) should be directly observed by the visiting experts.

3. *Interviews with participants.* Informal interviews with participants and/or former participants, at least some of which are spontaneous, can take up such issues as:
   a. recruitment of participants
   b. motivation of participants
   c. participant satisfaction with project
   d. participant progress toward attaining project goals

4. *Interviews with relevant context.* Informal interviews with local officials, administrators of competing programs, administrators

·of important local institutions (e.g., school superintendents, police chiefs) and local powerful individuals or representatives of local powerful institutions (e.g., large landlords, bankers, political officials) should cover the following topics:

a. worth of project
b. extent to which project is viewed as help or threat to community
c. interest in continuing project when demonstration period is over

Despite the weaknesses of expert judgments, there are circumstances in which this approach may be the only one that can be used. This is certainly the case for full-coverage, constant-level interventions of long standing. Also, the urgency of the need for impact assessment may force reliance on expert judgments; a lack of resources may prohibit the mounting of a relatively expensive, full-scale impact assessment using control groups or a cross-sectional approach. Moreover, other controls may be feasible in principle but prohibitively tedious to put into practice.

Exhibit 7-G presents an unusual study in which the time elapsed since program enactment is more than three decades. Salamon (1974) assessed the efficacy of a 1930s land-reform policy by examining land titles to see if the people who settled in the 1930s were still holding the land. Finding that there was some continuity over time, Salamon concluded that the policy was effective in creating a landed black middle class.

Of course, this conclusion is a result of his judging whether the proportion of settlers or their descendants still remaining on the land was greater or less than could be expected from the general tendency of landholdings to shift from generation to generation. That *any* of the original settlers or their descendants still remained is evidence of some impact, but the issue is whether this impact is any different from what would have happened in any event over the intervening three decades or more.

Salamon's case for the impact of the New Deal land-reform programs would have been considerably strengthened if he had been able to show that similar parcels of land in the same parts of the South did not show a comparable shift to black ownership over the period, and/or that nonprogram black-owned land tended to shift to white ownership. Undoubtedly, difficulties in ascertaining the races of parcel owners thirty-five years ago hindered the employment of this strategy.

Program-Administrator Judgments

Project administrators are routinely asked to assess their progress toward fulfilling project goals. In most cases it is doubtful that much

Exhibit 7-G: An Analysis of the Long-Range Effects of a New Deal Land-Reform Program

In the 1930s during the New Deal, a series of agricultural reforms were enacted, most of which were short-lived. One of the reforms involved purchasing land and selling it to small farmers for homesteading purposes at very favorable prices and financing terms. A few of the specific projects were started before protests from establishment agricultural interests brought about a cancellation of the program.

In the 1970s the author conducted an "evaluation" of the New Deal Land-Reform program by examining the current owners of parcels of land that were sold to black tenant farmers in eight land-resettlement projects in five states. Landownership records were searched to determine whether the land in question remained to any degree in the hands of persons related to or descended from the families to whom the parcels were originally sold in the 1930s.

Salamon concludes that the project was successful in creating a permanent, black middle class, since much of the land was still in the hands of the original settlers and their descendants.

SOURCE: Summary, by permission of John Wiley and Sons, Inc., of L. M. Salamon, "The Time Dimension in Policy Evaluation: The Case of the New Deal Land-Reform Experiments." *Public Policy,* Vol. 27, No. 2 (Spring 1979).

reliance can be placed on such reports as impact assessments, for fairly obvious reasons. First, it is a difficult task to undertake a judgmental impact assessment under the best of circumstances. It is too much to expect administrators with day-to-day responsibilities for the conduct of a project, often coupled with a lack of appropriate technical qualifications, to devote a great deal of time and care to an impact assessment.

Second, a properly conducted impact assessment takes as its guiding hypothesis that the project *has no effects,* a stance that runs exactly counter to the principle that should guide the administration of a project, namely that the intervention *does have important effects* on participants. To expect ordinary mortals to hold both hypotheses simultaneously is unrealistic.

TABLE 7.1   Administrative Records Useful for Project Description and as Aid in Impact Assessment

I. Participant Records:
1. Socioeconomic data on participants:
   age, sex, location, household composition, income, occupational data.
2. Critical dates:
   date of entry into project, attendance record, dates of leaving project.
3. Treatment records:
   exposure of participants to project, aid given, etc.
4. Follow-up data:
   addresses of participants, including future addresses and contacts to aid in follow-up beyond participation.
5. Critical event records:
   records of meetings with participants, important events in participants' lives (e.g., births, deaths, residential shifts, job changes).

II. Project Records:
1. Critical events in project history:
   dates of startup for important segments of project, encounters with helpful or hostile officials, important segments of program suspension.
2. Project personnel:
   biographical data on project personnel, shifts in personnel, instances of personnel training.
3. Changes in project implementation:
   problems encountered in project implementation changes instituted in project operations (including dates).

III. Financial Records:
   No attempt to describe such records will be made here, since one can assume that the typical local fiscal procedures required by project sponsors would be employed. The main issue to be emphasized is that financial records should be kept in a way that will facilitate cost-effectiveness or cost-benefit analyses, as described in Chapter 8.

Third, there is an understandable tendency for administrators to want to put their project in the best of all possible lights, a motivation that may act to downplay or actively suppress negative information on effectiveness.

About the best one can expect from an administrator's judgmental assessment is reasonably accurate descriptive statements about operational procedures. Hence, evaluators should look to administrators for reliable statistical, descriptive statements about a project, which requires a good set of administrative records. The kinds of records necessary have been described earlier in this chapter and in Chapter 4. Table 7.1 also lists administrative records useful to impact assessments. Clearly, portions of these records are not appropriate to all projects, and therefore Table 7.1 should be regarded as a checklist of suggested rather than essential records.

Participants' Judgments

Because the participants in social programs are the recipients of program services, one might be tempted to look to participant accounts of how well they were served by the program as approximations of net impact. While participants can tell us many useful things, it is overly optimistic to hope to get from them what it takes a highly skilled social researcher considerable effort to obtain. The problem is that it is difficult for any individual to assess imaginatively what would have happened to him or her if some specific event had not occurred. That is why individuals' accounts of how they "chose" their spouses or careers usually appear to be strings of chance events. Individuals simply do not have the varied experiences to be able to construct for themselves the appropriate control conditions or to "hold constant" their particular characteristics. Note that this is not a view of human beings as somehow naive and deficient, but a recognition that assessing net impact is a *comparative* task and that most persons simply do not have the breadth of experience necessary to make such comparisons.

Participant ratings of satisfaction with a program or with services, however, are interesting and important in their own right. In the first place, some programs stipulate participant satisfaction as one of their goals. Fine-tuning is often designed to rid programs of the "bugs" that irritate participants: Retirement benefit programs attempt to deliver retirement income in a way that is most satisfying to beneficiaries, including automatic bank deposits or special pick-up provisions. Public service programs may be particularly concerned with client satisfaction as an index of service-unit functioning. Exhibit 7-H provides a summary of a study conducted for the Kerner Commission on Urban Disorders. The study attempted to find out how blacks in big-city ghettos related to the police and welfare departments of those cities, testing these levels of satisfaction as reasons for the urban disorders of the 1960s.

In the second place, participant surveys may provide clues on how to increase target involvement, especially when full program participants are contrasted with program dropouts. Participant assessments of programs offer useful information but cannot replace impact assessments conducted according to the research designs described in Chapter 6 and in this chapter.

We have devoted much space in this chapter to the use of shadow controls in impact assessment, primarily because this approach is used fairly often and is fraught with considerable danger. In evaluating social programs, it is doubtful that experts can do more than establish gross outcomes. Net impact estimates made by experts appear to be fragile

Exhibit 7-H: An Analysis of Client Satisfaction with Agency Performance

As part of a study of urban service delivery systems in fifteen metropolitan areas, samples of residents were asked whether they were currently on welfare and, if so, their level of satisfaction "with the way you are treated by welfare workers or officials." In addition, caseworkers in local welfare agencies were interviewed concerning their attitudes toward clients, and information was obtained on their caseloads and other aspects of their jobs.

Considerable variation was found among the cities in the levels of satisfaction expressed by welfare clients toward their local welfare departments. Particularly interesting was the finding that welfare clients were most satisfied with their welfare departments in departments in which caseloads were very high and in which caseworkers, as a consequence, had infrequent contact with their clients. The correlation across the fifteen cities was .66, possibly indicating that frequent contact with caseworkers was a source of irritation to clients.

In the same study, ratings were also obtained from black residents concerning police maltreatment. An index of maltreatment complaints (insulting remarks, unfair arrests, etc.) had a high correlation with police self-reports of potentially abrasive actions frequently undertaken. These findings suggest that client assessments of services may turn out to be an important source of evaluation of urban services.

SOURCE: Summary, by permission, of P. H. Rossi, R. A. Berk and B. K. Eidson, *Roots of Urban Discontent.* New York: John Wiley, 1974.

and heavily subject to error. In short, we do not recommend this approach; it is decidedly second-best.

A NOTE ON APPLICABILITY

The approaches discussed in this chapter vary widely in their rigor. Impact assessments using reflexive controls, especially in time-series studies, may be as rigorous as the best of the approaches described in

Chapter 6. In contrast, the use of generic or shadow controls to estimate net impact is beset with uncertainties. Indeed, the latter controls should only be used when other approaches are either impossible or so constrained by the demands of time and budget that the choice is really between doing nothing at all or using judgmental methods.

8

Measuring Efficiency

Knowledge of the implementation and outcome of programs is indispensable, but in many cases it is just as critical to be informed about how program outcomes compare to their costs. Efficiency assessments (cost-benefit and cost-effectiveness analyses) provide a frame of reference for relating costs and program results, the latter measured either in monetary terms or in terms of actual outcomes. Useful analyses can be undertaken to decide on resource allocations and to influence policymakers, planning groups, and political constituencies who determine the fate of social intervention efforts.

Cost-benefit and cost-effectiveness studies may be undertaken during the program-planning phase. Such *ex ante* efforts have great utility, although the required empirical information and estimates necessary to undertake them often may not be available. While opportunities to conduct ex ante analyses are limited by these practical considerations, it is often feasible to undertake either cost-benefit or cost-effectiveness analyses as part of the assessment of project outcomes. These *ex post* analyses are important and powerful inputs into planning and decision-making processes.

AUTHORS' NOTE: This chapter was originally written by Sonia Rosenbaum, with subsequent modifications for the second, revised edition by Peter H. Rossi and Howard E. Freeman.

KEY CONCEPTS

Accounting Perspectives: Perspectives underlying decisions on which categories of goods and services to include as costs or benefits in an analysis.

Benefits: Net project outcomes, usually translated into monetary terms. Benefits may include both direct and indirect effects.

Benefit-to-Cost Ratio: The total discounted benefits divided by the total discounted costs.

Costs: Inputs, both direct and indirect, required to produce an intervention.

Cost-Benefit Analysis: The economic efficiency of a program expressed as the relationship between costs and outcomes, usually measured in monetary terms.

Cost-Effectiveness Analysis: The efficacy of a program in achieving given intervention outcomes in relation to the program costs.

Discounting: The treatment of time in valuing costs and benefits; that is, the adjustment of costs and benefits to their present values, requiring a choice of discount rate and time frame.

Ex Ante Analysis: Analysis undertaken prior to program implementation to estimate net outcome in relation to costs, usually undertaken as part of program planning.

Ex Post Analysis: Analysis undertaken subsequent to knowing net outcome effects.

Internal Rate of Return: The calculated value for the discount rate necessary for total discounted program benefits to equal total discounted program costs.

Net Benefits:	The total discounted benefits minus the total discounted costs (also called *net return*).
Opportunity Costs:	The value of opportunities foregone because of an intervention project.
Shadow Prices:	Imputed or estimated costs of goods and services when these goods and services are not valued in the current marketplace.

- Policymakers must decide which of a variety of educational programs to emphasize: basic primary education for young children, secondary education for adolescents, or vocational education for adults. All these have been shown to have substantial net impact in completed evaluations. How should the nation's educational resources be allocated?

- A government agency is reviewing national disease control programs currently under way. If additional funds are to be allocated to disease control programs, which programs would show the biggest payoffs per expenditures?

- Evaluations in the criminal justice field have established the effects of various alternative programs aimed at reducing recidivism. Which program is most cost-effective to the criminal justice system? Given the policy choices, how would altering the current pattern of expenditures maximize the efficiency of correctional alternatives?

- Members of a private funding group are debating whether to promote a program of low-interest loans for home construction or to initiate work-skills training for married women to increase family income. How do they decide?

These examples illustrate some common resource allocation dilemmas faced by planners, funding groups, and policymakers everywhere. They must continually choose how to allocate scarce resources in order to put them to their optimal use. Consider even the fortunate case where two or more pilot projects have been shown to be effective in producing the desired net impacts. To decide which one to fund on a larger scale, one needs to take into account the relations between cost and outcome of each. While other factors, including political considerations, come into play, the preferred program often is the one that produces the most impact on the most targets for the same expenditure. This simple principle is the foundation of *cost-benefit* and *cost-effectiveness* analyses, techniques that provide systematic approaches to resource allocation.

PERSPECTIVES ON RESOURCE ALLOCATION ANALYSIS

The application of resource allocation techniques to decisions about social programs is comparatively new. The basic procedures and concepts underlying resource allocation analysis stem from work undertaken in the 1930s to establish decision-making criteria for public investment activities. In the United States, early applications were to water resource development, and in England to transportation investments. After World War II, stimulated by the World Bank, cost-benefit analysis was applied to both specific project activities and national programs in lesser developed as well as industrialized countries. The idea of judging intervention efforts and national programs in terms of their efficiency (profitability, in a business sense) has gained widespread acceptance.

Even in application to industrial and technical development programs of an engineering type (e.g., roads, dams, communication networks) and to economic efforts (e.g., taxation and import-export regulations), cost-benefit analysis is still an emerging field. Concepts and techniques are constantly being revised and improved, and there are unresolved controversies about the assumptions that underlie different frameworks for cost-benefit analysis. Evaluators undertaking cost-benefit or cost-effectiveness analyses of social interventions must be aware of the stage of development of the appropriate substantive field and recognize the constraints of the two approaches.

Program Efficiency

Cost-benefit and cost-effectiveness analyses can be viewed both as conceptual perspectives and as sophisticated technical procedures. It bears emphasis that in many evaluations, formal, complete efficiency analyses are either impracticable or unwise. First, the required technical procedures may be beyond the resources of the evaluation project, may call for technical sophistication not available to the project's staff, or may be unnecessary, given either the very minimal or the extremely high efficacy of the intervention. Second, political or moral controversies that would result from placing economic values on particular input or outcome measures could obscure the relevance and minimize the potential utility of an otherwise useful and rigorous study. To some minds, these considerations may deny the wisdom of undertaking an efficiency study. Third, expressing the results of evaluation studies in efficiency terms may require different costs and outcomes to be taken into account, depending on the perspectives and values of sponsors, stakeholders, and evaluators themselves, again obscuring the relevance and utility of an evaluation. In brief, there often is no single, "correct" and simple efficiency analysis. The limitations of these studies are acknowledged by even the strongest advocates of cost-benefit analyses (Thompson, 1980; Stokey and Zeckhauser, 1978).

At the same time, the pertinence of efficiency analysis is undeniable. Social programs, almost without exception, are conducted under resource constraints. They almost invariably operate under circumstances where maintaining continuing support depends on convincing policymakers and funders that the "bottom line" (i.e., dollar benefits or the equivalent) justifies the program. Often, choices between competing programs are, at least in part, based on relative payoffs in economic terms. Even when efficiency studies are not undertaken, program decisions that take into account evaluation findings often are framed in terms of presumed output-to-input results.

The Uses of Efficiency Analyses

The employment of cost-benefit and cost-effectiveness techniques may be appropriate at two pivotal points in program efforts. In the planning and design phases, ex ante cost-benefit analyses may be undertaken on the basis of *anticipated* costs and benefits of programs. Such analyses, of course, assume that programs will be successful in implementing the delivery of the interventions involved *and* in achieving positive net outcomes of estimable magnitudes; these estimates are not necessarily empirically based.

In the impact assessment phase, after a program has been shown to have a significant impact, ex post cost-benefit and -effectiveness assessments may be undertaken to assess whether the costs of the intervention can be justified by the magnitude of net outcomes. In ex post analyses, costs and outcomes are based on studies of the types described in previous chapters on planning, monitoring, and impact evaluations.

The Concepts of Cost-Benefit and Cost-Effectiveness

A comprehensive *cost-benefit* analysis requires estimates of the benefits of a program, both tangible and intangible, and the costs of undertaking the program, both direct and indirect. Once specified, the benefits and costs are then translated into a common measure, usually a monetary unit. Obviously, many factors besides economic efficiency are brought to bear in policymaking, planning, and program implementation, but considerations of economic efficiency are almost always critical, given universally scarce resources.

Cost-benefit analysis requires the adoption of a particular economic perspective; in addition, certain assumptions must be made in order to translate program inputs and outputs into monetary figures. As noted, there is disagreement in the field on which procedures to utilize. Moreover, the assumptions underlying definitions and measures of costs and benefits strongly influence the resulting conclusions. All the requisite data for cost-benefit calculations are seldom available. Noble (1977), for example, has been able to document, using a large number of studies on rehabilitation, inadequate analytic and conceptual models, insufficiency of existing data, and the extreme sensitivity of cost-benefit results to their underlying but untested assumptions. Consequently, sensible policy priorities simply cannot be based on cost-benefit calculations in the field of rehabilitation.

Even if specific applications and conclusions of the approach can be questioned, its strength lies in the dicipline with which it forces the evaluator, policymaker, planner, and manager to articulate economic considerations that might otherwise remain implicit or unstated.

Cost-benefit analysis is least controversial when applied to technical and industrial projects, where it is relatively easy to place a monetary value on benefits as well as costs. Examples include engineering projects designed to reduce the costs of electricity to consumers, highway construction to facilitate transportation by means of roads, or irrigation programs to increase crop yields. However, estimating benefits in monetary terms is frequently more difficult in social programs, where, in the best of circumstances, only a portion of the known program outputs may be reasonably valued. For example, it is possible to translate future occupational gains from an educational project into monetary values. The issues are more complex in such social interventions as fertility control programs or health services projects, since one must ultimately place a value on human life in order to monetize program benefits fully (Zeckhauser, 1975).

For these reasons, *cost-effectiveness* analysis, rather than cost-benefit analysis, is often seen as a more appropriate technique. Cost-effectiveness requires monetizing only program costs; benefits are expressed in outcome units. For example, the cost-effectiveness of distributing free textbooks to rural primary schoolchildren could be expressed as follows: Each 1,000 project dollars increased reading scores by an average of one grade level.

For cost-effectiveness analysis, then, the outputs, or benefits, are expressed in terms of the costs of actual substantive outcomes. That is, the efficacy of a program in attaining its goals is assessed in relation to the monetary value of the resources or costs put into the program. Consider another example: Alternative educational interventions may be analyzed by measuring the educational gains, expressed in test scores, and then relating them to program costs. A cost-effectiveness analysis allows comparison and ranking of choices among potential programs according to the magnitudes of their effects relative to their costs. Put differently, the comparison is stated in terms of units of effectiveness for achieving particular outcomes. Actual program operations and impact — and hence inputs and outputs — replace, to a considerable extent, estimates and assumptions. Moreover, retrospective analyses can yield useful insights and experiences, or methodological procedures that can then be applied to future programs.

Efficiency analyses, for the most part, can be considered an extension of impact evaluation, not an alternative. It is impossible to engage in cost-benefit or cost-effectiveness calculations for programs whose impacts are entirely unknown and unestimable. It is senseless to do so for ineffective programs, that is, when impact evaluations discover no significant net effects. When applied to efficacious programs, efficiency analyses are useful in making policy decisions, planning expanded projects, and reviewing programs at different points in time. Moreover, cost-benefit analysis can be useful in determining the degree to which different levels of interventions produce different levels of benefits (Shortell and Richardson, 1978).

COMPONENTS OF COST-BENEFIT ANALYSIS

In simplest terms, an intervention is efficient if its benefits are greater than its costs. Therefore, efficiency analysts must calculate those benefits and costs.

Benefits

A program's *benefits* are its *net outcomes,* both tangible and intangible. For example, the benefits of a public health project may include reductions in illness and mortality, and increased economic productivity; the benefits of a vocational training project may include increased future earnings and economic productivity for participants, as well as the value of work done during training; and the benefits of a housing project may include increased quantity and quality of housing, and reduced health hazards.

Costs

Costs are somewhat easier to calculate. They are the program *inputs,* both direct and indirect — that is, the resources required to conduct the program. Important to the determination of project costs is the economists' notion of *opportunity costs,* or the value of foregone opportunities. From the target's point of view, participation in a program (e.g., vocational training) often means foregoing regular earnings, and is therefore treated as a cost.

The concept of opportunity costs reflects the problem of limited resources, whether money or time, when individuals or the community must choose only one of several alternatives. The cost of the choice can be measured by the utility or worth of the most likely foregone options. The actual estimation of opportunity costs often is complex.

In addition to the opportunity costs, program costs include expenditures for personnel, administration, equipment, facilities, supplies or materials, and any other labor and operating costs incurred. However, which specific components to include in the calculations and how to value them depend on the accounting perspective taken. In other words, the preceding "list" of project costs is an oversimplification of the calculations actually required. A summary of the costs and benefits of an Upward Bound study is reproduced in Exhibit 8-A.

Comparing Costs and Benefits

After listing as exhaustively as possible all the program benefits and costs, the next problem is to attach monetary values to them. In cost-benefit analyses, the time factor must be taken into account. The technique for doing so is known as *discounting,* which will be discussed later.

The final calculation simply consists of comparing cost and benefit totals, either directly to ascertain net benefits, or, more usually, as the ratio of benefits to costs. The results of cost-benefit analyses can be expressed in terms of several different ratios, depending on the criteria involved in reaching decisions on a program and the objectives and values of decision makers (see Thompson, 1980: Ch. 5). Alternatively, one can calculate the anticipated rate of return. A comparison of benefit-to-cost ratios (or the other summary measures) across different programs therefore provides the necessary data on the relative efficiency of project alternatives. See Exhibit 8-B for an illustration of a cost-benefit study for a family planning program.

Having reviewed the framework underlying analyses of costs to benefits in particular and of economic efficiency in general, we turn to certain technical issues and to an elaboration of the concepts.

METHODOLOGY OF COST-BENEFIT ANALYSIS

In order to carry out a cost-benefit analysis, one must first decide which perspective to take in calculating costs and benefits. What point of view should be the basis for specifying, measuring, and monetizing benefits and costs? In short, costs to and benefits for *whom?* Benefits and costs must be defined from a single perspective, since mixing points of view results in confused specifications and overlapping or double

Exhibit 8-A: List of Costs and Benefits for the Upward Bound Evaluation

Upward Bound was a program of remedial education at the high school level, developed in the 1960s. The purpose was to identify high-potential disadvantaged youths who would not be likely to go to college and to provide them with special college-preparatory education. Data from a large evaluation of students who had entered the program over a number of years were available. The evaluation also included information on older siblings of the respondents who had not participated. From the point of view of the participants, the benefits and costs were defined as follows:

Benefits

1. Increased after-tax lifetime incomes, measured on the basis of expected ultimate educational attainment of participants and the control group.
2. Stipends paid to participants during the program.
3. Increase in scholarships and college attendance grants to Upward Bound students.

Costs

1. Additional tuition costs required of Upward Bound students because of higher rates of college attendance.
2. Additional expenses of Upward Bound students while in college.
3. Earnings foregone by Upward Bound students while in college.
4. Transfer income over the lifetime foregone by Upward Bound students (e.g., unemployment and welfare).

SOURCE: Adapted, with permission, from W. I. Garms, "A Benefit-Cost Analysis of the Upward Bound Program." *Journal of Human Resources,* 6 (Spring 1971): 206-220.

accounting. This is not to say that cost-benefit analyses for a single program cannot be undertaken from various perspectives. Separate analyses, based on different perspectives, often provide information on benefits-to-costs as they impact on relevant stakeholders.

Accounting Perspectives

Three accounting perspectives may be used for the analysis of social projects: those of (1) individual targets, (2) program sponsors, and (3) communal aggregates, or the society involved. The *individual* accounting perspective takes the point of view of the unit that is the program target — that is, the person, group, or organization that receives the intervention or services. Cost-benefit analyses using the individual target perspective often produce higher benefit-to-cost ratios than those using other perspectives. Another way of stating this is that if the sponsor or society bears the cost and subsidizes a successful intervention, the individual program participant benefits the most. For example, an educational project requires relatively few costs to participants. The cost to targets is primarily time spent on the project, since books and materials usually are furnished. Benefits to the participants may include

Exhibit 8-B: The Costs and Benefits of a Family Planning Program: Cost-Benefit Ratios and Net Return Summaries

A cost-benefit analysis of the family planning program in the United Arab Republic estimated the benefits and costs of a prevented birth as follows.

Benefits

1. The main effect — the consumption expenditures that would have been required for an averted birth and which are now available to the population.
2. The wage productivity effect — the increase in output resulting from better nutrition of smaller-size families.
3. The increase in total public savings resulting from the diversion of resources that would have been required to educate the averted birth.

Costs

1. The magnitude of the loss of output resulting from a smaller labor force as the result of the delayed effects of lower fertility.
2. The costs of averting a birth through the provision of family planning services.

The final summary table is reproduced here. When two figures appear in a column, they reflect alternative assumptions made in the calculations.

	Egyptian Pounds per Prevented Birth	
	10% Discount Rate	15% Discount Rate
Benefits		
Consumption	222-351	109-206
Wage productivity effect	16-21	9-14
Public savings effect	37	24
Total	275-409	142-244
Costs		
Productivity	79-91	24-31
Family planning services	4-20	4-20
Total	83-111	28-51
Difference between benefits and costs (row 4 minus row 7)	164-326	91-216
Benefit-cost ratios (row 4 / row 7)	2.5-4.9	2.8-8.7

SOURCE: From G. C. Zaidan, *The Costs and Benefits of Family Planning Programs*. Washington: World Bank, 1971, pp. 2, 45. Reprinted by permission of the copyright holder.

improvements in earnings as a result of increased education, greater job satisfaction, and increased occupational options, as well as transfer payments received while participating in the project.

The *program sponsor* accounting perspective takes the point of view of the funding source in valuing benefits and specifying cost factors. The funding source may be a private agency or foundation, a government agency, or a for-profit firm. Under this perspective, the cost-benefit analysis most closely resembles what frequently is termed *private profitability analysis*.

The program sponsor accounting perspective is most appropriate where there are clear policy choices involving alternative programs that a government or other sponsor may fund, and under fixed budgetary conditions where new revenues will not be generated to fund additional projects.

From the program sponsors' point of view, for example, benefits from an educational project in terms of local, state, and federal governments are decreases in expenditures that no longer have to be made, such as public assistance subsidies or other forms of direct government spending. Another major sponsor (government) benefit is increased revenues as a result of the participants' improved earnings subsequent to the training (i.e., if trainees obtain better jobs and earn more, they will have to pay higher taxes). The costs to government are for operation, administration, instruction, supplies, facilities, and any additional subsidies or transfers paid to the participants during the training. Exhibit 8-C shows a cost-benefit calculation of short-term benefits to the government in terms of births averted by family planning programs.

Exhibit 8-C: Cost-Benefit Analysis of Family Planning Programs

A recent national evaluation of government-provided family planning programs aimed at low-income women in large population centers in the United States was carried out to assess the effects on fertility rates from 1970 to 1975. The evaluation linked data on enrollments at the family planning clinics to census data. A careful analysis showed that there was a significant reduction of fertility among groups served by the program, even net of other relevant variables such as age, race, and marital status. (This evaluation illustrates the potential use of cost-benefit based on available data.)

As a final step in the study, benefit-cost ratios were estimated from the point of view of the government and based on unwanted and unintended births averted. All the cost and benefit figures reflect expenditures and savings to the government in terms of births averted.

The calculations used to establish program impact suggest that during the six years in question, participation in the family planning clinics resulted in a total of almost 1.1 million births averted, ranging from 72,000 in 1970 to 324,000 in 1975. These amount to the direct effects of the program for women served, and do not include possible secondary effects of unserved persons who also might have benefited.

Available data were used to measure the following benefits to the government, which are listed as costs saved to the government by averting unwanted births: (1) medical care associated with pregnancy and birth which is borne by all sorts of multilevel government programs for the low-income population; (2) public assistance during the first year for children born to women already on public assistance; and (3) selected social services for public assistance recipients and their newborn for one year. The authors argue that these costs seriously understate savings in short-term costs of unwanted births, such as additional forms of public assistance and social services, and public housing, as well as opportunity costs of income lost due to the mother's giving up employment during portions of the pregnancy and early childrearing periods. These categories were excluded because data were not available to allow specifying the proportions of low-income women who would fall into each category and the resulting government expenditures. Estimates of national costs of public assistance for the three categories listed above took into account the fact that during the period in question, 16 to 19 percent of the patients in family planning clinics under evaluation were receiving public assistance. Thus, the estimated saving in government expenditures for these categories of costs ranged from $639 in 1970 to $1,238 in 1975 for each birth averted. These savings estimates were multiplied by the estimated number of births averted for each year, then totaled across the six years. Estimated savings were $1,076 million ($1.1 billion), a figure that therefore represents total benefits.

Costs were simply the federal appropriations for family planning clinic services, readily available from government records, and which amounted to $584 million in total (ranging from $33 to $160 million during the six-year period).

The benefit-cost ratio or total estimated savings to total costs for the program is 1.8 (1,076/584). If calculated separately for each year, the lowest ratio is 1.3, the highest 2.5 in 1975. This is interpreted to mean that one dollar invested by the federal government in family planning in one year saved federal, state, and local governments approximately $1.80 a year later. These savings are in addition to long-term savings, and the health, social, and demographic benefits to government and individuals from the prevention of unwanted and unintended births.

SOURCE: Summary, by permission, from P. Cutright and F.S. Jaffe, *Impact of Family Planning Programs on Fertility: The U.S. Experience.* New York: Praeger, 1977.

The *communal* accounting perspective takes the point of view of the community or society as a whole, usually in terms of total income. It is therefore the most comprehensive, but also the most difficult to apply. Taking the point of view of society as a whole implies that special efforts are being made to account for secondary project effects. A program will ordinarily have effects on groups not directly involved with the intervention, and these must be considered when examining the larger economy. Moreover, in the current literature, communal cost-benefit analysis has been expanded to include equity considerations, or the distributional effect of programs among different subgroups. These considerations imply that cost-benefit calculations need to be disaggregated by subgroups or that some criterion or appropriate weighting scheme be employed to assign more or less value to benefits according to who receives them (see, for example, Squire and van der Tak, 1975).

Exhibit 8-D: Communal Costs and Benefits of Upward Bound

Benefits
1. Increased before-tax lifetime incomes for program participants. (Before-tax incomes are used to reflect societal productivity.)

Costs
1. Direct cost of the Upward Bound Program to the government, including all resources expended, except student stipends.
2. Direct cost of program to participating colleges.
3. Extra costs of education incurred by society because of the higher rate of college attendance by Upward Bound students.
4. Extra living costs required by college attendance attributable to the program.
5. Before-tax earnings foregone by Upward Bound students while in college.

SOURCE: Adapted, with permission, from W. I. Garms, "A Benefit-Cost Analysis of the Upward Bound Program." *Journal of Human Resources,* 6 (Spring 1971): 206-220.

Exhibit 8-D lists the communal costs and benefits of Upward Bound, which can be compared to the list in Exhibit 8-A showing individual costs and benefits.

Although the components of a communal cost-benefit analysis appear to include most of the costs and benefits that also appear in calculations utilizing the individual and program sponsor perspectives, the items are valued and monetized differently. For example, communal costs for a project include opportunity costs in terms of alternative investments foregone by the community in order to fund the project in question. These are obviously not the opportunity costs an individual incurs as a consequence of project participation. Communal costs also include outlays for facilities, equipment, and personnel, usually valued in a way different from the program sponsor perspective. Finally, these costs do not include transfer payments, since they also would be entered as benefits to the community and would simply cancel each òther out.

Table 8.1 shows some of the basic components of cost-benefit analyses for the different accounting perspectives. (In the illustration, the program sponsor is a government agency.) The list is not to be taken as complete, but as an illustration only. Specific items included in real analyses vary.

Table 8.2 provides a simplified, hypothetical example of benefit-cost calculations for a training program from the three accounting perspectives. Again, the monetary figures are gross oversimplifications, since a real analysis would require far more complex treatment of the measurement issues involved. The example is merely intended to illustrate the previous discussion. Note that the same components may enter into the calculation as *benefits* from one perspective and as *costs* from another, and that the result of the calculation (in this case the ratio of benefits to costs and the difference between benefits and costs, or net benefit) will vary, depending on the accounting perspective utilized.

**Measuring Costs
and Benefits**

The specification, measurement, and valuation of costs and benefits — procedures that are central to cost-benefit analysis — raise two distinct problems. First is the identification and measurement of all program costs and benefits; second is the expression of all costs and benefits in terms of a common denominator, that is, their translation into monetary values.

The problem of identifying and measuring costs and benefits is most acute for ex ante appraisals, where there are scanty or no data with

TABLE 8.1   Components of Cost-Benefit Analyses for Different Perspectives

	Individual	*Program Sponsor*	*Communal*
Benefits	Increase in earnings (net of taxes)	Increase in tax revenues	Increase in earnings (gross of taxes)
	Additional benefits received (e.g., direct transfers, fringe, and noneconomic benefits)	Decrease in expenses of public assistance, and other subsidies	Increase in other income (e.g., fringe benefits, excluding direct transfers)
		Value of work done within the project	Decrease in expenses of alternative projects no longer applicable
			Value of work done
Costs	Opportunity costs (earnings foregone net of taxes)	Taxes lost	Opportunity costs (gross of taxes)
	Loss of direct subsidies no longer applicable (alternative projects)	Project costs (e.g., capital, administrative, instructional, direct subsidies)	Project costs excluding direct subsidies or transfer payments)
	Extra costs related to participation (e.g., fees, materials)		

which to make estimates. However, data often are limited in ex post cost-benefit analyses as well. For many social interventions, the information from an evaluation (or even a series of evaluations) may in itself prove insufficient to carry out a retrospective cost-benefit analysis. Thus, evaluations often provide only some of the necessary information, and the analyst frequently will have to use additional sources or judgments.

The second problem, again for many social programs, is the difficulty of translating benefits and costs into monetary units. Social programs frequently do not produce results that can be accurately valued

TABLE 8.2 Hypothetical Example of a Training Project Cost-Benefit Calculation from Different Accounting Perspectives

Benefits/Costs[a]

1. Earnings improvement of trainees (before taxes)	$100,000
2. Earnings improvement of trainees (after taxes)	80,000
3. Value of work done in training project	10,000
4. Project costs for facility and personnel	$50,000
5. Project costs for equipment and supplies	5,000
6. Trainee stipends (direct transfer payments)	12,000
7. Earnings foregone by trainees (before taxes)	11,000
8. Earnings foregone by trainees (after taxes)	9,000
9. Taxes lost: (7) minus (8)	2,000

	Individual	Program Sponsor	Communal
Benefits	(2) 80,000	(1)-(2) 20,000	(1) 100,000
	(6) 12,000	(3) 10,000	(3) 10,000
	92,000	30,000	110,000
Costs	(8) 9,000	(4) 50,000	(4) 50,000
		(5) 5,000	(5) 5,000
		(6) 12,000	(7) 11,000
		(9) 2,000	
	9,000	69,000	66,000
B/C Ratio	$\frac{92,000}{9,000} = 10.22$	$\frac{30,000}{69,000} = .44$	$\frac{110,000}{66,000} = 1.67$
Net Benefit	83,000	−39,000	44,000[b]

a. Assume that these figures represent present values: see subsequent section.
b. Note that net social benefit can be split into net benefit for trainees plus net benefit for the government, which in this case is negative: 83,000 + (−39,000) = 44,000.

by market prices. For example, many would argue that the benefits of a fertility control project, of a literacy campaign, or of training in improved health practices cannot be monetized in ways acceptable to the various stakeholders. Exhibit 8-E exemplifies the problems of measurement for a methadone program. For example, what value should be placed on fear and anguish (Item 1)? In such cases, cost-effectiveness analysis might be a reasonable alternative, since benefits do not have to be valued in terms of money, only quantified by outcome measures.

Because of the advantages of expressing benefits in monetary terms, a number of approaches have been specified for monetizing outcomes or benefits (Thompson, 1980: 149-151):

Money Measurements. The least controversial approach is the estimation of direct monetary benefits. For example, if keeping a health center open for two hours after work reduces targets' absence from work (for which they do not receive wages) by an average of 10 hours

Exhibit 8-E: Measuring the Benefits of a Methadone Treatment Program

The Direct Benefits of Methadone Treatment

1. *Benefits to Potential Victims*
   a. decrease in private protection expenditures
   b. decrease in the value of damage to victim resources
   c. decrease in the value of forced transfers
   d. decrease in the negative value placed on fear and mental anguish

2. *Benefits to Taxpayers*
   a. decrease in criminal justice expenditures
   b. decrease in medical expenditures for narcotic-related illnesses

3. *Benefits to Methadone Patients*
   a. decrease in expenditures on heroin
   b. increase in legal earnings, minus the decrease in illegal earnings

The Empirically Measurable Direct Benefits of Methadone Treatment

1. decrease in criminal justice expenditures
2. decrease in medical expenditures for narcotic-related illnesses
3. decrease in expenditures on heroin
4. increase in legal earnings

SOURCE: From T. Hannan. "The Benefits and Costs of Methadone Maintenance," *Public Policy,* 24 (Spring 1976): 200, 201. Reprinted by permission.

per year, then, from an individual perspective, the annual benefit can be calculated by multiplying the average wage by 10 hours by the number of employed targets.

Market Valuation. Another relatively uncontroversial approach is to monetize gains or impacts by valuing them at market prices. If crime is reduced in a community by 50 percent, one can estimate benefits in terms of housing prices by adjusting current values on the basis of such prices in communities with lower crime rates and similar social profiles.

Econometric Estimation. A more problematic approach is to estimate the presumed value of a gain or impact in market terms. For example, the increase in receipts from greater business taxes due to a reduced fear of crime could be determined by calculating relevant revenues of similar communities with lower crime rates, and then estimating the tax returns that would ensue. The estimation may require complex analytical efforts and problematic assumptions, making such pricing tentative at best.

Hypothetical Questions. A still more problematic approach is to estimate the value of intrinsically nonmonetary benefits by directly questioning the targets. For instance, a program to prevent dental disease may decrease participants' cavities by an average of one at age 40; thus, one might conduct a survey on how much people think it is worth to have an additional intact tooth as opposed to a filled tooth. Such estimates presume that the monetary value obtained realistically expresses the worth of an intact tooth. Of course, hypothetical valuations of this kind are open to considerable skepticism.

Observing Political Choices. The most tentative approach is to estimate benefits on the basis of political actions. If states are consistently willing to appropriate funds for high-risk infant medical programs at a rate of $50,000 per child saved, this figure could be used as an estimate of the monetary benefit of such a program. But since political choices are complex, shifting, and inconsistent, this approach is generally very risky.

In summary, for the results of a cost-benefit analysis to be valid and reliable and reflect fully the economic effects of a project, all relevant components must be included. When important benefits are disregarded because they cannot be measured or monetized, the project may appear less efficient than it is; if certain costs are omitted, the project will seem more efficient. The results may be just as misleading if estimates of costs or benefits are either too conservative or too generous.

Pricing Methods

Benefits and costs need to be defined and valued differently, depending on the accounting perspective used. When the communal perspective is taken, project effects and therefore benefits and costs must be valued by considering the impact on the entire community, region, or country. For many programs, the outputs simply do not have market prices (e.g., the reduction of pollution or the work of a housewife), yet their value must be estimated.

The preferred procedure is to use "shadow prices," also known as "accounting prices," to reflect better than actual market prices the real costs and benefits to society. *Shadow prices,* in other words, are derived prices for goods and services that reflect national benefits and costs.

Distributional Considerations

Traditionally, the effectiveness of social interventions is predicated on the notion that an effective intervention makes at least one person better off and nobody worse off. But this may not be the case. Lowering the minimum wage for teenagers, for instance, may increase their employment but reduce work opportunities for older adults.

The basic means of incorporating equity and distributional considerations in the cost-benefit analysis involves a system of weights whereby benefits are valued more if they produce the anticipated positive effects. If a lowered teenage minimum wage increases total family incomes of the most disadvantaged households but decreases the family incomes of the moderately disadvantaged, the dollars gained and lost could be weighted differently, depending on the degree of disadvantage to the families. Some accomplishments are worth more to the community, both for equity reasons and for the increase in human well-being, and should therefore be weighted more heavily.

The weights to be assigned can be determined by the appropriate decision makers, in which case value judgments will obviously have to be exercised; they may also be derived by using certain economic principles and assumptions. There are a number of formal approaches, including Guttentag's decision theoretic approach (discussed in Chapter 3). In any case, it is clear that weights cannot be applied indiscriminately. Analysts will undoubtedly develop further refinements as they continue to deal with the distributional effects issue.

An intermediate solution to considerations of equity in cost-benefit analyses is to make calculations for separate subgroups of the society, instead of calculating a single aggregate measure. Disaggregation has been done for income groups (e.g., Hansen and Nelson, 1976) and levels of achievement (e.g., Wolfe, 1977). A great deal of attention has been devoted to such distributional issues in analyses of the effects of schooling, particularly because the costs of subsidized education are in part borne by taxpayers who do not have children in school, and the benefits are received by those who are less well off (Ribich and Murphy, 1975). Finally, it has even been suggested that intergenerational considerations must be considered to resolve the equity of returns to education (Conlisk, 1977).

Secondary Effects (Externalities)

Projects may have external or spillover effects, that is, side effects or unintended consequences that may be either beneficial or detrimental. Since such effects are not deliberate outcomes, they may be omitted from cost-benefit calculations if special efforts were not made to include them.

A secondary effect for a training program, for example, might be the spillover of the training to relatives, neighbors, and friends of the participants. Among the more commonly discussed negative externalities of industrial or technical projects are pollution, noise, traffic, and destruction of plant and animal life.

For many projects, two secondary effects are likely: *displacement* and *vacuum* effects. For example, an educational or training project may produce a group of newly trained persons who enter the labor market, compete with workers already employed, and displace them (i.e., force them out of their jobs). Project participants may also vacate jobs held previously, leaving a vacuum that other workers might fill.

Externalities may be difficult to find and measure (see Klarman, 1974, for a review of the difficulties of specifying indirect and intangible benefits of health services). But once found, the cost-benefit analysis should attempt to incorporate them into the calculations.

Discounting

The last major element in the methodology of efficiency analyses concerns the treatment of time in valuing program costs and benefits. The technique is known as *discounting*, and consists of reducing costs and benefits that are dispersed through time to a common monetary base, or adjusting them to their *present values*.

Intervention programs vary in duration, and successful ones in particular produce benefits that are derived in the future, sometimes long after the intervention has taken place. The effects of many programs are expected to persist through the participants' lifetimes. Often the evaluator has to extrapolate into the future to measure impact and ascertain benefits, especially since program benefits are gauged as projected income changes for participants. But costs are usually highest at the beginning of an intervention, when many of the resources must be expended; they either taper off or cease when the intervention ends. Even a fixed cost expended at two different time points, or a constant benefit derived at various times, cannot be considered equivalent. Ex post cost-benefit analyses, and not just ex ante appraisals, often extrapolate into the future to carry out a complete analysis. Otherwise, the evaluation would be based only on the restricted period of time for which actual program performance data were available.

Costs and benefits occurring at different points in time must be brought into a common measure, or made commensurable. In other words, the time patterns for costs and benefits of a program must be taken into account. Instead of asking, "How much *more* will my invest- ment be worth in the future?" standard economic practice is to ask, "How much *less* are benefits derived in the future worth than those derived in the present?" The same goes for costs. The answer depends on what we assume to be the rate of interest, or the *discount rate,* and the time frame chosen. Exhibit 8-F provides an example of discounting.

The choice of the time period on which to base analysis depends on the nature of the program and whether the analysis is ex ante or ex post. All else being equal, a program will appear more beneficial the longer the time horizon chosen.

The choice of discount rate relates to the accounting perspective. There is no authoritative approach. One is to fix the rate on the basis of the *opportunity costs of capital,* that is, what an amount can be expected to gain if invested elsewhere in the private market or in the public sector. Another approach, under the communal perspective, is to use the *social discount rate,* which presumably reflects a community's time preference. Also, a program sponsor such as a government group might make an administrative decision on a given rate to be used for all calculations. Recent manuals recommend that a more sophisticated *accounting rate of interest* be computed that is linked to the shadow wage rate (Little and Mirrlees, 1974), or takes into account distributional impacts (Squire and van der Tak, 1975).

The results of a study are thus particularly sensitive to the choice of discount rate. Therefore, in practice this complex and controversial issue is usually resolved by carrying out discounting calculations based on several different rates. Finally, instead of applying what may seem to be an arbitrary discount rate or rates, one may calculate the program's *internal rate of return,* or the value that the discount rate would have to be for program benefits to equal program costs.

When to Do Ex Post Cost-Benefit Analysis

It is important to consider a number of factors in determining whether to undertake a cost-benefit analysis. In some evaluation con- texts, the technique is feasible, useful, and a logical component of a comprehensive evaluation; in others, its application may rest on dubi- ous assumptions and be of limited utility. Optimal requisites for an ex post cost-benefit analysis of a program include the following:

- The program has independent or separable funding.
- The program is beyond the development stage and it is certain that net effects are significant.

Exhibit 8-F: Discounting Costs and Benefits to Their Present Values

Discounting is based on the simple notion that it is preferable to have a given amount of capital in the present rather than in the future. All else equal, capital can be saved in a bank to accumulate interest, or can be used for some alternative investment. Hence it will be greater in the future. Put differently, a fixed amount payable in the future is worth less than the same amount in the present. Conceptually, discounting is the reverse of compound interest, since it tells us how much we would have to put aside today to yield a fixed amount in the future. Algebraically, discounting is the reciprocal of compound interest, and it is carried out by means of the simple formula:

$$\text{Present Value of an Amount} = \frac{\text{Amount}}{(1 + r)^t}$$

where r is the discount rate and t stands for the number of years. Hence, the total stream of benefits (and costs) of a program expressed in present values is obtained by adding up the discounted values for each year. An example of such a computation follows:

A training program is known to produce increases of $1,000 per year in earnings for each participant. The earnings improvements are discounted to their present values at a 10 percent discount rate and for five years.

YEAR	1	2	3	4	5
	$\frac{\$1,000}{(1 + .10)^1}$	$\frac{\$1,000}{(1 + .10)^2}$	$\frac{\$1,000}{(1 + .10)^3}$	$\frac{\$1,000}{(1 + .10)^4}$	$\frac{\$1,000}{(1 + .10)^5}$
	$909.09	$826.45	$751.32	$683.01	$620.92

Over the five years, total discounted benefits equal $909.09 + $826.45 + ... + $620.92, or $3,790.79. Thus, improvements of $1,000 per year for five years are not worth $5,000, but only $3,790.79. At a 5 percent discount rate, the total present value would be $4,329.48. In general, benefits calculated using low discount rates will appear greater than those calculated with high rates, all else being equal.

- Program impact and magnitude of impact are known or can be validly estimated.
- Benefits can be reduced to monetary terms.
- Decision makers are considering alternative programs, rather than simply whether or not to continue the existing project.

COST-EFFECTIVENESS ANALYSIS

Cost-benefit analysis allows the comparison of the economic efficiency of program alternatives, even when the interventions are not aimed at common goals. After initial attempts in the early 1970s to use cost-benefit analysis in social fields, however, some evaluators became uneasy about directly comparing cost-benefit calculations for, say, family planning, health, housing, or educational projects. As noted, sometimes it is simply not possible to obtain agreement — for example, on the monetary value of a life prevented by a fertility control project, or a life saved by a health campaign — and then compare the results.

Cost-effectiveness analysis does not require that benefits and costs be reduced to a common denominator. Instead, the effectiveness of a program in reaching given goals is related to the monetary value of the resources going into the program (Levin, 1975). In cost-effectiveness analyses, programs with similar objectives are evaluated and the costs of alternative programs for achieving the same goals are compared. One can compare programs aimed at lowering the fertility rate, different educational methods for raising achievement levels, or various interventions to reduce infant mortality. Exhibit 8-G summarizes the concepts used in cost-effectiveness analyses of corrections programs.

Cost-effectiveness allows comparison and rank-ordering of programs in terms of their costs for reaching given goals, or the various inputs required for different degrees of goal achievement. But since the benefits are not converted to a common denominator, one can neither ascertain the worth or merit of a given intervention, nor compare which of two or more programs in different areas produces better returns. One can only compare the relative efficiency of programs' goals with respect to each other, where efficiency is a function of minimal costs. Exhibit 8-H summarizes a cost-effectiveness analysis of correctional program alternatives in terms of cost per reduction in recidivism.

Cost-effectiveness can be viewed as an extension of cost-benefit analysis to projects with multiple and noncommensurable goals. Cost-effectiveness is based on the same principles and utilizes the same methods as cost-benefit analysis. The assumptions of the method, as

Exhibit 8-G: Cost-Effectiveness Analysis Concepts for Corrections Programs

Any correctional program is made up of these major components: First, there are tasks or activities performed on a day-to-day basis within the program. Second, there are outputs or intermediate products or subgoals that result from the daily activity in the program. Finally, there are outcomes, or final products or goals, which represent what a program seeks to achieve. In a prison, for example, the major day-to-day activity is "taking care of" inmates. An output or intermediate product is "treatment," which begins when an inmate enters the facility and is regarded as completed when the inmate leaves. But treatment is not an end in itself. Treatment is provided in order to achieve a goal or outcome, which in this article is assumed to be reduced recidivism. [The following] table outlines alternative ways of conceptualizing the distinction between inputs, outputs, and outcomes.

	Focus of Analysis		
	How	What	Why
Alternative Conceptual- izations	Activity, task, inputs	Objectives, subgoals, intermediate products, outputs	Goals, final products, outcomes
Example	Group counseling, food and clothing, recreation	"Treatment" or "rehabilitation"	Reduced recidivism
Cost Measure	Input cost	Output cost	Outcome cost
Example	Cost per day	Cost per case	Cost per reduced arrest

SOURCE: From C. M. Gray, C. J. Conover and T. M. Hennessey, "Cost Effectiveness of Residential Community Corrections: An Analytical Prototype." *Evaluation Quarterly*, 2 (August 1978): 378.

well as procedures required for measuring costs and discounting, for example, are the same for either approach. Therefore, the concepts and methodology introduced previously with regard to cost-benefit analysis can also be regarded as a basis for understanding the cost-effectiveness approach.

Exhibit 8-I shows the use of cost-effectiveness analysis to compare an experimental educational television program with a proposed reform of an existing formal school system. It shows in simple terms the use of cost-effectiveness ratios to compare alternative projects in terms of costs to produce measured cognitive gains.

SUMMARIZING A COMPLEX FIELD

In this chapter we have provided an overview of cost-benefit analysis by examining its logic, assumptions, concepts, and procedures. Cost-benefit analysis requires that program costs and benefits be known, quantified, and transformed to a common measurement unit; that they be projected into the future to reflect the lifetime of a program; and that future benefits and costs be discounted to reflect their present values. Cost-effectiveness analysis has been suggested as a feasible alternative in the many instances where benefits cannot be calibrated in monetary units. Also, we have stressed that ex post analyses are more appropriate than ex ante studies for evaluating human service programs.

In terms of ex post efficiency estimation, cost-benefit and cost-effectiveness analyses should be viewed as components of a comprehensive evaluation, since solid evidence of net impact is the basis for the formulation of benefits and effectiveness. Competent analysis can provide extremely valuable information about a program's economic efficiency and is important in planning, program implementation, and policy processes. As shown in Exhibit 8-J, cost-benefit and -efficiency analyses often provide important information not available from impact assessments alone.

We have provided only a general overview of the efficiency approach. As should be apparent, considerable technical sophistication characterizes much of the work surrounding it. As a style of thinking about program results, however, it has great value for the evaluation field.

Exhibit 8-H: Cost-Effectiveness of Residential Community Corrections

An analysis of the relative cost-effectiveness of a community corrections program for adult and juvenile offenders, in comparison with traditional probation and incarceration methods, is based on the reduction of recidivism. Different measures of recidivism are employed, as well as duration. The results are summarized in the following table:

Correctional Alternative	Cost per Client Treated	Net Offense Reduction Due to Treatment		Cost per Reduced:		Cost per Reduction in:	
			Offense Sustained	Nonstatus Offense	Seriousness of Offenses	Severity of Offenses
Juvenile Probation							
Very short run	$ 504	÷ 4.3 =	$ 117	$ 180	$ 4	$ 81
Short run	504	÷ 4.3 =	117	180	4	81
Long run	661	÷ 4.3 =	154	239	4	107
Residential Clients—							
No Prior Institutionalization							
Very short run	739	÷ 4.2 =	176	352	14	101
Short run	836	÷ 4.2 =	199	398	16	114
Long run	3,649	÷ 4.2 =	869	1,738	68	500

Correctional Alternative	Cost per Client Treated	Net Offense Reduction Due to Treatment		Cost per Reduced:		Cost per Reduction in:	
				Offense Sustained	Nonstatus Offense	Seriousness of Offenses	Severity of Offenses
Residential Clients—							
Prior Institutionalization							
Very short run	1,132	÷ 6.2	=	183	1,415	25	166
Short run	1,281	÷ 6.2	=	207	1,601	28	188
Long run	5,592	÷ 6.2	=	902	6,990	123	822
Juvenile Institutions							
Very short run	621	÷ 6.3	=	99	222	8	65
Short run	2,597	÷ 6.3	=	412	928	34	412
Long run	12,641	÷ 6.3	=	2,006	4,515	165	1,317

SOURCE. From C. M. Gray, C. J. Conover and T. M. Hennessey, "Cost Effectiveness of Residential Community Corrections: An Analytical Prototype." *Evaluation Quarterly*, 2 (August 1978): 394.

Exhibit 8-I: Cost-Effectiveness Analysis of Educational Television and Educational Reform Projects

Data from an experimental evaluation of educational television (ETV) and an educational reform program introduced in El Salvador by AID allow a cost-effectiveness comparison of the two alternatives for expanding basic schooling (in this case at the seventh-grade level). Educational gains were measured by means of standard achievement tests administered at the beginning and end of the school year in 1972. Educational reforms involved expanded curriculum and materials and retrained teachers, with and without ETV. Actual costs for the reform and ETV programs were calculated: The annual cost per student of the reform program without ETV was $16, and the cost of ETV alone was $22. The following table summarizes the results of the cost-effectiveness analysis:

	Gain	Gain Over Traditional
Mathematics		
Gain for traditional classes	1.95	—
Gain for experiment ETV class	5.70	3.7
Gain for experiment control group (reform but no ETV)	5.20	3.2
Science		
Gain for traditional classes	1.34	—
Gain for experiment ETV class	4.20	2.9
Gain for experiment control group (reform but no ETV)	5.10	3.8
Social Studies		
Gain for traditional classes	2.61	—
Gain for experiment ETV class	6.40	3.8
Gain for experiment control group (reform but no ETV)	3.10	1.5

The cost-effectiveness ratios for the different subjects are the following:

	ETV	Reform Only
Math	3.7/$22 = .17	3.2/$16 = .20
Science	2.9/$22 = .13	3.8/$16 = .24
Social Studies	3.8/$22 = .17	1.5/$16 = .10

Only in social studies is the cost-effectiveness ratio for ETV larger than for reform only. Therefore, the author argues for investing in the curriculum and teaching reforms, and not installing ETV.

SOURCE: Reprinted from M. Carnoy, "The Economic Costs and Returns to Educational Television" in *Economic Development and Cultural Change*, 23 (1975) 237-238. By permission of the University of Chicago Press © 1975 The University of Chicago.

Exhibit 8-J: Effects and Costs of Day-Care Services for the Chronically Ill

Long-term, adult day-care settings not now covered by Medicare were studied in a randomized experiment to test the effects on patient outcomes and costs of using these new services. This article reports findings for day care. Patients' physical, psychosocial, and health functions were assessed quarterly, and their Medicare bill files were obtained. Medicaid data were obtained on most patients, but few used many Medicaid-covered, long-term care services. Multistage analysis was performed to mitigate effects of departures from the randomized design. Day-care patients showed no benefits in physical functioning ability at the end of the study, compared with the control group. Institutionalization in skilled nursing facilities was lower for the experimental group than for the control group, but factors other than the treatment variable appeared to explain most of the variance. There was a possibility that life was extended for some day-care patients. The new services averaged $52 per day, or $3,235 per year. When costs for existing Medicare services used were added, the yearly cost of the experimental group was $6,501, compared with $3,809 for the control group — an increase of $2,692, or 71 percent.

SOURCE: Adapted, with permission, from William Weissert, Thomas Wan, Barbara Livieratos, and Sidney Katz, "Effects and Costs of Day-Care Services for the Chronically Ill: A Randomized Experiment," *Medical Care*. Vol. 18, No. 6, 1980: 567-584.

9

The Context of
Evaluation Research

Policy and management decisions related to programs occur with or without evaluations. Evaluations can impact on the decision-making process only if influentials know of and respect evaluation results, and if the evaluations are timely and relevant to program concerns. Further, the contexts in which evaluations are undertaken and the organizational arrangements under which evaluation groups do their work influence both the quality and utility of evaluations.

While evaluations do make long-term contributions to the knowledge of how and how not to design and implement intervention efforts, it is their direct and relatively immediate contributions to program implementation and outcome that provoke support and advocacy for evaluation research. Appropriately, there continues to be skepticism among decision makers, planners, program staff, and target participants themselves on the advantages of social interventions. At the same time, this skepticism fortunately is counterbalanced by our aspiration to improve our own lives and those of our brothers and sisters throughout the world. State-of-the-art evaluation is one means of speeding up efforts to contribute to human and social progress.

KEY CONCEPTS

External Validity:

Extent to which the design of a study allows findings to be generalized.

Internal Validity:

Extent to which the design and execution of a study allow definitive statements of outcome.

Policy Significance:

Extent to which findings are meaningful in the context of program costs, alternative interventions available, and the press for intervention actions.

Statistical Power:

Estimate of the likelihood that a net effect will be observed if it exists, given the statistical properties of measures and the statistical procedures employed.

Statistical Significance:

Probability that a result is due to chance.

Evaluation, as we have repeatedly emphasized, is not just a technical activity. It is research designed to aid the processes of policy formation, program design and implementation, and management. Hence, it is also a political activity. By that phrase, we mean that evaluations always are conducted within contexts in which there are many interested parties with stakes in the outcomes of the efforts. These stakeholders affect both the evaluator's ability to carry out evaluations effectively and the ways in which evaluation results are employed by policymakers, planners, funders, and managers. In this chapter we discuss some of the issues that stem from the fact that evaluations take place within more or less politicized environments, and require relations with persons who have their own viewpoints and professional and personal interests.

Evaluation activities are also conducted within organizations — a vast range of organizations, including universities, for- and not-for-profit corporations, and human-service-provider settings. These organizations, depending on their missions and the persons within them, have an impact on the type, quality, and utility of evaluations.

Unfortunately, evaluators still have too little systematic knowledge about themselves and their efforts — how others use their work and its relation to the larger, political context in which it is conducted. That knowledge, however, is growing, and recent years have seen a number of studies that allow at least some generalizations.

INTERPRETING EVALUATION FINDINGS

The procedures described in the preceding chapters provide data intended *to aid in the making of judgments* about the effectiveness of interventions. The italicized phrase is intended to stress the fact that such findings are not the only considerations that should go into such judgments. The findings of evaluation efforts are not self-evident as far as their practical implications are concerned, and other elements — beyond the strictly methodological — have to be taken into account by the evaluator during a study. In this sense, the conventional posture of social researchers requires modification (Cronbach et al., 1980). Some of the additional elements of decision-making will be discussed briefly in this chapter. The questions that need to be raised are:

- *How large a positive effect is needed?* Where should a significance level be set to discern whether or not a program's net outcome is different beyond chance from no outcome at all?

- *How generalizable is the outcome?* Will the positive results obtained in an evaluation still be reached if a program is continued or applied to different circumstances?

- *How relevant are the findings to policy and program interests?* Are differences not only real but of sufficient magnitude to warrant commitment of resources on an ongoing, long-term basis?

Setting the Level of Statistical Significance

The result of a quantitative assessment of a program's impact is an estimate of the net outcome of the program. How large should such an estimate be before one accepts the results as plausible? First, one must determine whether the net outcome is different from zero. Since findings are usually not exactly zero, we need to know with some degree of confidence whether or not the results are different from zero.

To aid in making such judgments, we turn to statistical theory. Using an appropriate statistical model, we can determine how often net outcomes of given sizes in a series of replications of a given randomized experiment will occur if the true outcome of the experiment is zero (or some other specified magnitude). For example, in a given experiment we may learn that a net outcome of at least a certain size could occur by chance in, say, 5 of 100 trials of the experiment when the intervention actually has no effect. If we accept the results as indicating that the program *has* an effect, we are actually betting that this particular experiment is *not* one of 5 percent in which the true effect is zero; that is, we are assuming that the results are *not* simply due to chance (i.e., the result of the randomization procedure). If we reject the hypothesis that the experiment has an effect, we risk making the opposite error of claiming a particular outcome that actually was program-induced to be a chance finding (see Crane, 1976).

In traditional social research, the levels of statistical significance are usually set at .05 and .01. The level set can be thought of as the degree of risk that the findings are due to chance. In other words, the appropriate statistical model says the findings would occur by chance five times in 100 trials (.05) or once in 100 trials (.01), depending on the level set. While it may be comforting to rely on tradition, this judgment in applied social research should be made with caution — reflecting the fact that the judgment errors could have serious consequences. Instead, in some cases one might apply stricter levels of statistical significance (e.g., .0001), accepting as indicating a statistically significant effect only those net outcomes occurring by chance once in 10,000 trials. In still other cases one might decide to apply very lenient thresholds (say, .20), in which one accepts net outcomes that would occur by chance once every 5 trials as reasonable evidence of a real program effect.

A sophisticated approach to the acceptance-rejection determination is embodied in the concept of *statistical power*. Statistical power refers to the likelihood that a net effect will be observed if it exists, given the statistical properties of the measure and the statistical procedures employed. For example, given an estimated value for the correlation between pre- and posttest scores for experimental and control groups, and given also sample size estimates, the probability of detecting a real result of a given size can be calculated. This is known as the *power* of the results of a statistical analysis. Conversely, calculating the statistical probability of results allows estimating appropriate sample size, given the use of a particular statistical procedure.

Setting the levels of statistical significance for a program evaluation involves making judgments about the relative importance of two types of errors:

- *Type I error, or false positives:* Making a positive decision when the correct decision should have been negative; that is, concluding that a program has an effect when it actually does not.

- *Type II error, or false negatives:* Making a negative decision when the correct decision should have been positive; that is, failing to detect a real program effect.

The probability of making a Type I error is equal to the level of significance set for the test. One can minimize false positives by setting a very strict criterion for statistical significance, but that only increases the probability of making a false negative error. *The two types of errors are inversely related,* and it is possible to minimize both types of error simultaneously only at enormous cost. In every evaluation project, one should decide a priori which of the two types of errors is more important, designing the study and particularly any statistical analysis accordingly. The judgment of whether false positives or false negatives are more important to minimize is clearly a value judgment and is based on the substantive area of the evaluation, not on theory or statistics.

Let us illustrate the circumstances under which false positives and false negatives dominate. In testing the equipment of an airplane for safety, it is clear that false positives are more serious than false negatives. In short, it is more important to avoid certifying as safe an airplane that might fail under usage (i.e., avoid false positives) than it is to avoid rejecting as unsafe one that would not fail in usage. One can make this judgment under the principle that preserving life is more important than developing and manufacturing airplanes inexpensively. Analogous decisions are involved with medical interventions.

In contrast, the opposite situation may obtain in a relatively low-cost program such as an educational television intervention: Since effective educational programs of any type are difficult to design and the negative effects of adopting an ineffective project are not very serious (especially in the absence of other educational alternatives), it follows that false positives are less costly than false negatives. It may be better to adopt a pool of educational projects that, in statistical terms, are problematic in their effectiveness in the hope that at least *some* are actually effective.

In intervention efforts, the following principles may be useful to follow:

- For projects that risk some harm to individuals, households, or communities, it may be more important to minimize false positives than false negatives.

- For projects in which there is little chance of doing harm to individuals, households, or communities, and there are few effective interventions, false negatives may dominate false positives.

The notion of harm should be interpreted quite broadly to include all sorts of costs that might be inflicted were the intervention to go into effect as a statutory program. Expensive projects, ones that might have some negative side effects, and those that involve treatments that are in some sense risky to the targets, are examples of potentially harmful interventions.

The first implication of these principles is that the levels of statistical significance that should be applied to potentially harmful programs should be set more strictly than for benign, less costly treatments. A second implication is that the former programs should be assessed using the more powerful of the research designs discussed in the previous chapters.

If a project might do some harm, it is especially important to make sure that it is rejected when, in fact, it is ineffective. A project to cure mental patients by subjecting them to dangerous treatment (e.g., psychosurgery or extensive use of psychopharmacological preparations) should be more carefully tested than a project to increase popular acceptance of a safe nutritional supplement.

Statistical significance testing, however, provides only a minimal basis for judging the worth of modifying a delivery system or advocating a particular intervention strategy. Significance tests depend on sample sizes, their distributions, and the tests used, and very small differences may be significant at even an extreme level (e.g., .0001). In a sense, all that tests produce is an estimate of whether or not the differences are real, that is, the degree to which it is possible that the findings occurred by chance. Findings must be judged also by the *magnitude* of effects found, a topic we discuss subsequently under policy significance.

The Generalizability of Evaluation Findings

Impact assessments typically are conducted using "samples" of target populations: subsets of the target populations that are chosen either as a matter of convenience or in some more structured way to maximize their representativeness. An important issue that arises once an evaluation has been conducted is the extent to which its findings can be generalized to the entire target population. This issue in evaluation research is often put in terms of the tradeoff between *internal* and *external* validity (Campbell and Stanley, 1966; see also our discussion in Chapter 5).

The *internal* validity of a design is its capability, through derived data, to make definitive statements about whether or not the program produced the net intervention outcomes. When properly conducted, randomized controlled experiments have high internal validity because such designs enable an investigator to ascertain whether the intervention being tested has an appropriate effect. Because controlled experiments rule out extraneous causes of the effects, such designs offer greater assurance that the intervention was the "cause" of the difference noted between experimental and control groups. The other designs discussed in Chapter 5 show decreasing amounts of internal validity.

In contrast, *external* validity refers to the ability of a research design to allow inferences or generalizations about effects beyond the specific groups and contexts being tested. A particular research design has high external validity to the extent that the design permits generalizations to some relevant population beyond the group used in the evaluation itself. Hence, an important consideration in designing any evaluation is whether the targets selected from the population form an unbiased sample of that population. A well-designed and well-executed randomized controlled experiment in a single secondary school may clearly show a paraprofessional training project to be very effective. However, if the students selected to participate in the experiment are chosen without regard to how well they represent secondary students in the population in question, it is difficult to generalize that paraprofessional training projects will be effective in other secondary schools. In short, the external validity of the experiment would be poor.

Similarly, a project designed to decrease unemployment through the adoption of a more efficient computer job listing in government employment agencies can be tested by sending specifically trained demonstration agents to a number of employment offices. If the offices are chosen according to appropriate sampling procedures, it is possible to make generalizations about effectiveness in the entire country, within the limits of sampling variation. If the sample is chosen unsystematically — say, by selecting offices from those that volunteer to try out the new procedures — generalization to all employment offices is problematic. This is because offices that volunteer may be more predisposed to use the new method as assiduously as possible and hence provide results that overestimate the potential responsiveness of all offices to the new procedures.

Because randomized experiments are difficult to do well on a large scale and with fair samples of target groups, they are likely to be carried out with greater attention to issues of internal than external validity. For example, because of the expense of studying an adequate number of communities, the six income maintenance experiments undertaken in the United States and Canada were carried out in a small number of "typical" urban and rural communities; but there was no systematic attempt to choose such communities on the basis of their representativeness of all urban and rural communities in the United States (Rossi and Lyall, 1976). Impact assessments that use statistical controls, in contrast, are ordinarily designed with more attention to problems of external validity. Representative samples of target populations are frequently selected, and participants are identified within them.

Whether or not to emphasize internal or external validity in designing an impact assessment is an issue that must be faced *early* in the research design stage. For a project that is quite innovative (and possibly expensive), it may be worthwhile to emphasize internal validity. The implementation of such a project would lead to a great loss in resources if it turns out to be ineffective, even in the most favorable circumstances. In contrast, for a project that is known to be effective for some types of targets, the main issue may be whether it would be effective over a broader range of targets. For example, in an income transfer payment program that is very expensive and worthwhile only if enacted at a fairly high level of payment, it may be expedient to conduct a carefully designed randomized controlled experiment in a prototypical situation before undertaking a full impact assessment. Where there is less likelihood of ineffectiveness but the issue is effectiveness with all subgroups in a target population, less restrictive designs may be employed with more representative samples.

Another important consideration (which, in a sense, may be considered a matter of external validity) is the extent of a program's replicability or transferability. A prototype or pilot intervention designed to test the applicability of a counseling program run by dedicated and skillful counselors may have poor external validity, because it would be difficult to institute the program on a widespread basis. That is, it may be very unlikely that sufficiently dedicated and skillful persons can be found to run the program over the entire nation at the same level as that tested.

In general, pilot or prototype runs may be different from mass-produced programs not because the targets used are unrepresentative, but because the treatment in the pilot run is delivered in a way that cannot be replicated on a large scale. There are many examples of the difficulty of generalizing from pilot runs to mass-produced programs. In education, many teaching techniques work well in the hands of their advocates but fail when mandated by schoolwide policies. This external validity problem further underscores the importance of monitoring, as discussed in Chapter 4.

The Issue of Policy Significance

Although an evaluation outcome may produce results that all would agree are statistically significant and generalizable, the net outcome may still not be of any *policy significance*. That is, there are situations in which the findings may pass most of the tests we have discussed in this chapter but are too small to be relevant to policy, planning, and managerial action. For example, the *Sesame Street* evaluation discussed in Chapter 6 found that children viewing the program were statistically significantly different from nonviewers in their knowledge of the alphabet. Substantively, the difference amounted to only several letters, and hence may have had little policy significance (Cook et al., 1975).

The issue of what the magnitude of a difference must be to have policy significance varies from field to field. In education, an important gain is sometimes defined as one whose magnitude is at least one-half a standard deviation. One formal way of providing data for such judgments is to conduct cost-benefit and cost-effectiveness analyses, as discussed in the previous chapter. Doing so allows judgments to be made on the basis of whether resources are effectively expended compared with the costs and benefits of alternative projects.

Another, more diffuse criterion is to make judgments of the social worth of the change in outcome. Small magnitudes of change have policy significance when social worth is high; large ones have significance when social worth is low. Thus, a program of nutritional education that reduces clinically observable cases of malnutrition in children by 2 percent may be policy-significant; a consumer education project that reduces the purchase of unnecessary small household appliances by 10 percent may not.

The availability of alternative interventions also needs to be taken into account. For example, in a country with high saturation of television sets and a formal educational system that requires extensive resources and a long period to modify, small gains from educational television may be policy-significant; the same magnitude of change would not be viewed positively if rapid changes at low cost were possible in the formal educational system.

Policy significance also emerges as an issue in another guise. Too often a prospective program may be tested without sufficient understanding of how the policy issues are seen by those decision makers who will have to approve the enactment of the program into statutes. Hence, while the evaluation of the program in question may be flawless, its findings may prove irrelevant. In the New Jersey-Pennsylvania Income Maintenance Experiment, the experiment designers posed as their central issue the following question: How large is the work disincentive effect of an income maintenance plan? By the time the experiment was completed and congressional committees were considering various income maintenance plans, the key issue was not the work disincentive effect. Rather, members of Congress were more concerned with how the many different forms of welfare could be consolidated into one comprehensive package, without ignoring important needs of the poor and without creating many inequities.

Since the ultimate purpose of impact assessment, as with evaluative approaches generally, is to help decision makers form and adopt public policies, the research must be sensitive to the various policy issues involved. The goals of a project must resemble those articulated by policymakers in deliberations on the issues of concern. A carefully designed randomized experiment showing that a reduction in certain regressive taxes would lead to an improvement in worker productivity may be irrelevant if decision makers are more concerned with motivating entrepreneurs and attracting potential investments.

Responsible impact assessment design must necessarily involve, if at all possible, some contact with relevant decision makers to ascertain their interests in the project being tested. For an innovative project that is not currently being discussed by decision makers but is being tested because it may become the subject of future discussion, the evaluators and sponsors of the test of impact effectiveness must rely on their informed guesses about what policy issues might arise. For other projects, the processes of obtaining decision-maker opinions are quite straightforward. One may consult the proceedings of deliberative bodies (e.g., government committee hearings or legislative debates), interview decision makers' staffs, or consult decision makers directly.

Indeed, it is just this issue that has led to the development of evaluability assessments, discussed in Chapter 2.

Although we have geared this discussion toward impact evaluations, the same issues pervade delivery system (process and accountability) evaluations. For example, to fine-tune a program's target eligibility requirements, to increase coverage and reduce bias, one must examine statistical significance and magnitude of difference, estimating what results are due to the changed criteria for target coverage and bias or to chance.

Interpreting evaluation results, then, requires considerations that go beyond methodology. The fact that evaluations are conducted according to the canons of social research may make them superior to other modes of judging social programs, but evaluations provide only superfluous information unless they are designed to draw on the values and preferences involved in policymaking, program planning, and management. Their weaknesses, in this regard, tend to center on how research questions are stated and how findings are interpreted (Datta, 1980). To maximize the utility of evaluation findings, the evaluators must be sensitive to two levels of policy considerations.

First, programs that address problems perceived as critical require better (that is, more rigorous) assessments than interventions related to trivial concerns. Technical decisions, such as setting levels of statistical significance and magnitude, should be informed by the nature of policy and program considerations. It is always a matter of judgment and sensitivity. Even when formal efficiency analyses (Chapter 8) are undertaken, the issue remains. For example, the decision to use an individual, program, or community accounting perspective is determined by policy and sponsorship considerations.

Second, evaluation findings have to be assessed according to their generalizability, whether the findings are policy- and program-significant, and whether the program clearly fits need (as expressed by the many factors that are involved in the policymaking process).

REDUCING CONFLICT BETWEEN
EVALUATORS AND STAKEHOLDERS

To evaluate is to make judgments; to conduct an evaluation is to provide findings that can be used to make judgments. The distinction between making judgments and providing information upon which judgments can be based is useful and clear in the abstract, but it is often difficult to delineate in practice. Some stakeholders may perceive the results of an evaluation to be critical judgments and react accordingly.

Who are the parties typically involved in the use of evaluation results? Listed here are some of the stakeholder groups that either directly participate or become interested in the evaluation process and its results:

- *Policymakers and Decision Makers:* Persons responsible for deciding whether a program is to be instituted, continued, discontinued, expanded, or curtailed.
- *Program Sponsor:* Organization that initiates and funds the *program* to be evaluated.
- *Evaluation Sponsor:* Organization that initiates and funds the *evaluation.* (Sometimes the evaluation sponsor and the program sponsor are identical.)
- *Target Participants:* Persons, households, or other units who participate in the program or receive the intervention services under evaluation.
- *Program Management:* Group responsible for overseeing and coordinating the intervention program.
- *Program Staff:* Personnel responsible for actual delivery of the intervention (e.g., teachers).
- *Evaluators:* Group or individuals responsible for the design and/or conduct of the evaluation.
- *Program Competitors:* Organizations or groups who compete for available resources.
- *Contextual Stakeholders:* Organizations, groups, individuals, and other units in the immediate environment of a program (e.g., local government officials or influentials situated on or near the program site).

Although these nine groups do not completely exhaust all conceivable parties interested and/or involved in the "politics of evaluation," they are the stakeholders that typically participate in one way or another in the conduct and outcome of an evaluation. It is not completely clear how the interests of each are engaged and acted upon by a given evaluation outcome. In a particular situation, policy and decision makers may be pleased by a positive evaluation and frustrated by a negative one; in another situation their reactions may be the reverse.

Perhaps the only reliable prediction that can be made is that program sponsors, managers, and staff are most likely to regard positive evaluations favorably and to react with hostility to negative ones. Such reactions are quite understandable, since these groups usually have the most at stake in program continuation and it is their activities that are most clearly judged by the evaluation report.

All too often the novice evaluator, having completed a report and proudly announced the results, is devastated by a torrent of criticisms of and negative reactions to the findings. It is therefore useful to sensitize fledgling evaluators to the fact that their findings will often be greeted with skepticism, suspicion, and hostility (although knowing this may not assuage the novice's disappointment). An evaluator may frequently be at the center of ensuing controversies. Anticipating such reactions may make it possible to take steps to reduce the amount and intensity of potential conflict.

It should be noted that there are critics who reject evaluations, at their best, as we advocate them in this book, and as they are typically undertaken today. Ideology and distrust of quantitative methods are major reasons for such attitudes. Our view, however, is that if criticism of a particular evaluation is justified, it is because it and relevant political and bureaucratic issues have been mishandled, not because the fundamental approach of evaluation research is faulty.

Shared Understanding of Overall Design

It is important that the major interests that might be engaged in an evaluation understand both the assumptions and limitations of the evaluation and the methodology employed. This is particularly important with respect to the project's sponsor, management, and staff.

The evaluator should try to develop some consensus with these groups about the aims of the project to be evaluated, the methods to be employed, and the possibility that the evaluation may turn out in ways that could reflect negatively upon them (see Chapter 2). As Berk and Rossi (1976) observe, effectiveness of evaluation data may be enhanced by partisan participation in evaluation design activities (see Exhibit 9-A). This process of building consensus and commitment should begin *before* evaluation is undertaken (Wholey, 1977).

Groups that have a stake in the outcome of an evaluation should be made aware of the ways evaluation results can be useful to them. For example, a monitoring evaluation can provide project managers information that facilitates staff supervision and project modification. Put differently, evaluation is undertaken because there are stakeholders that want and need information about project operation and effects. Therefore, the evaluator also needs to build understanding and ensure commitment by informing the relevant groups of the ways they can profit from an evaluation (see Chapter 2 on evaluability assessment).

Intervention Goal Specification

One major and common point of conflict is whether the terms of evaluation were properly chosen — especially whether or not the goals of a program were correctly specified. As we noted in Chapters 2 and 3, it is important to recognize that a program need not have one goal or a small set of goals in order to be evaluated. We stand by the criteria we stressed in earlier chapters — that the goals be clear and that they be measurable. Despite the complexities involved, it is sometimes prudent to evaluate a program from the different viewpoints of policymakers, program administrators, and various clients and other community members. The extent to which it is worth increasing the complexity of an evaluation design by measuring the multiple goals of these diverse groups must be resolved on an individual, evaluation-by-evaluation basis. It is worth repeating that the process of deciding on the terms of evaluation and accommodating a range of viewpoints into the evalua-

Exhibit 9-A: Partisan Contributions to Design

The effectiveness of evaluation data is often further enhanced when program partisans can be encouraged to participate in the research design and when relevant measures are in metrics which policymakers take as valid. For example, in a classic parole study by Kassebaum, Ward, and Wilner (1971), the evaluation design was so tight that it was almost impossible to escape its inevitable conclusions. The treatment was several different kinds of group therapy thought to maximize what its advocates called a "Therapeutic Community." A randomized experiment was used, testing therapeutic programs that met as closely as possible the optimum specifications desired by program supporters. In other words, the researchers in effect asked what program advocates would want in the best of all possible worlds, provided for those needs, and then assessed this "ideal" program. In addition the outcome measures included results (e.g., rearrest) that the State Adult Corrections Authority took as valid. Therefore, when the findings showed "no effect," it was much harder to dismiss them. Although the state prison system was not immediately changed, this and other research findings began a process that led to major alterations in state prison policy.

SOURCE: From R.A. Berk and P.H. Rossi, "Doing Good or Worse: Evaluation Research Politically Re-Examined." *Social Problems,* 23 (February 1976): 343. Reprinted by permission of the Society for the Study of Social Problems.

tion is an act that should be undertaken in consultation with the stakeholders involved *before* the evaluation begins.

Further, as we noted earlier, some writers have stressed the importance of using the theoretical knowledge of particular fields in order to develop a set of objectives (Chen and Rossi, 1980). It is argued that theory-driven sets of criteria may either minimize the chance that evaluations will be negative or fail to contribute knowledge about program implementation and impact. Others have advocated the use of formal decision analytic procedures, and still others such approaches as goal-attainment scaling (see Chapter 2). The point we are making should be clear: Goal specification is essential, at least to ensure elegance in design.

Dissemination

Evaluation results and interim reports have to be presented in a timely fashion, early enough so that procedures used in the project can be modified accordingly. This admonition applies particularly to evaluation monitoring. Plans for monitoring, in particular, should include provision for such feedback to relevant parties.

Evaluation results also have to be presented in an understandable fashion, attaining a combination of simplicity and accuracy, which is hard for some evaluators to reach. For especially complicated impact evaluations that have to be conducted by highly trained social scientists, it is often advisable to have professional writers or editors review or write reports addressed to project management and decision makers.

Dissemination is a matter not only of clearly communicating one's evaluation results, but also of understanding why the various stakeholders' goal priorities differ. The discussion in Exhibit 9-B relates this point to drug-treatment agencies, stressing the importance of verbal communication.

Note also that an assessment of "what is" is most useful when it points to "what might be better." An evaluation that concludes in a negative judgment without suggesting actions that might remedy defects is certainly more likely to be met with hostility than one that does offer positive recommendations.

Evaluation-Program Arrangements

Evaluators are best off when their position is as secure and independent as possible from the influences of project management and project staff. In the past, some experienced evaluators went so far as to state categorically that evaluations should never be undertaken within the same organization responsible for the administration of a project, but should always be conducted by an outside group.

Exhibit 9-B: Decision Makers' Judgment and Dissemination

If evaluation information is to impact on decision-making, major shifts in the priority actors in certain roles give to various criteria in judging treatment agencies may be required. For example, it appears that planners in this system will have to augment their concerns for issues of management efficiency, staff competence, and treatment philosophy, with a greater concern for client impact if client outcome data are greatly to influence their judgments regarding treatment agencies. Whether such shifts in the priority of criteria used in decision-making will occur when outcome data become available is an empirical question. If such shifts do not occur, evaluation information will not be heavily utilized by planners.

This suggests that evaluators interested in having the results of their work utilized should focus their attention on the constellation of decision criteria used by actors in the task environment of the system they are evaluating. Knowledge of the decision criteria used by different audiences in the absence of program evaluation information should prove useful in designing the evaluation to meet the information preferences of system decision makers. During the feedback of evaluation results, familiarity with the decision criteria actually used in the system should help guide developmental work aimed at encouraging and facilitating the use of information provided by the evaluation. In addition, it will provide a baseline for later assessment of the actual effect of evaluation results on decision-making.

A second implication regarding utilization of evaluation information derives from the finding that, generally, practitioners currently obtain their important evaluative information about agencies through personal contacts or oral feedback. The findings of other studies suggest that this reliance upon verbal information through personal contacts is common among decision makers. This pattern will not necessarily change when evaluation information becomes available. These results make apparent the importance of finding vehicles for feeding back evaluation information that include direct personal contacts and oral presentations. Even if this is accomplished, it is possible that oral presentations by evaluators may not be enough to result in utilization desired, unless evaluators can become perceived by decision makers as important and valued personal contacts and sources of information.

SOURCE: From J. D. Hawkins, R. A. Roffman and P. Osborne, "Decision-Makers' Judgments: The Influence of Role, Evaluative Criteria, and Information Access." *Evaluation Quarterly*, 2 (August 1978): 450-451.

One reason "outsider" evaluations may have seemed the desired option is that there were differences in the levels of training and presumed competence of insider and outsider evaluation staffs. These differences have narrowed. The career of an evaluation researcher has typically taken one of three forms. Until the 1960s, a large proportion of evaluation research conducted on health, social, rehabilitation, education, and welfare services was done by either university-affiliated researchers or research firms. Since the late 1960s, public service agencies in these program areas have been hiring researchers for staff positions to conduct more in-house evaluations. Also, the proportion of evaluations done by private, for-profit research groups has increased markedly. As research positions in both types of organizations have increased and the academic job market has declined, more persons well trained in the social and behavioral sciences have gravitated toward research jobs in public agencies (Polivka and Steg, 1978) and for-profit firms.

The current evidence is far from clear. In a study of correlates of evaluation quality, Bernstein and Freeman (1975) found that there was a somewhat greater likelihood for insider than outsider evaluations to be of high quality, a finding attributed to the greater ability of insiders than outsiders to influence the conduct of the intervention efforts studied.

In the discussion in Chapter 2, we noted the likelihood that accountability has the most utility if undertaken internally. Recent studies in The Netherlands of external and internal evaluations suggest why internal evaluations may have a higher rate of impact on organizational decisions. According to van de Vall and Bolas (1981: 479), of more importance than which category of researchers excels at social policy formation are those variables responsible for the higher rate of utilization of internal researchers' findings. The answer, they suggest, lies partly in a higher rate of communication between researchers and policymakers, accompanied by greater consensus, and partly in a balance between standards of epistemological and implemental validity: "In operational terms, this means that social policy researchers should seek equilibrium between time devoted to methodological perfection and translating results into policy measures." Van de Vall and Bolas's data suggest that currently in-house social researchers are in the more favorable position for achieving these instrumental goals than external researchers.

Given the increased competence of staff and the visibility and scrutiny of the evaluation enterprise, there is no reason now to favor one organizational arrangement over another. Nevertheless, there remain many critical points during an evaluation when there are opportunities for work to be misdirected and consequently misutilized (Cook et al., 1980).

We urge that all evaluators continue to cultivate clear understandings of their roles with sponsors and program staff. Evaluators' full comprehension of their roles and responsibilities is one major element in the successful conduct of an evaluation effort. (See Exhibit 9-C for others.)

POLITICAL TIME AND
EVALUATION TIME

Evaluations, especially of impact, take time. The tighter and more elegant the study design, the longer the evaluation usually takes. Large-scale social experiments that gauge the effects of major innovative programs may require four to eight years to complete and document. The political and program worlds often move at a much faster pace. Policymakers and project sponsors often want to know in a matter of weeks or months whether or not a program is achieving its goals. This disparity in time is another problem for evaluators.

Evaluators often encounter pressure to complete their assessments more quickly than the best methods permit, as well as to release preliminary results before they are completely firm. At times, evaluators are asked for their "impressions" of effectiveness, even when they have stressed that such impressions are liable to be useless in the absence of firm results.

Also, the planning and procurement procedures within organizations that sponsor evaluations make it difficult to undertake timely studies. In most cases, procedures must be approved at several levels and by a number of key stakeholders. As outlined in Exhibit 9-D, the typical evaluation done under contract to the U.S. Department of

Exhibit 9-C: Improving Evaluations

Evaluation researchers can help harmonize the productivity of evaluation research in the interests of the public good, the government good, *and* the private good by three major efforts. One is by obtaining wide *research community consensus on a hierarchy of preferred research designs and methods* of relatively common, often repeated, and typical evaluation research problems, and promulgating those standards through reformed procurement regulations specific to social research, so that all government sponsors and reviewers will be able to recognize minimum quality *and flexibility* standards for both valid research designs for evaluations *and* their administration. That will both raise the overall quality and provide external support for those evaluation researchers who find themselves in conflict with government reviewers or sponsors over the choice of the first- or second-best designs, and who most often lose.

A second area in which evaluation researchers can provide great help is *to collect, assess, screen and disseminate successful examples of effective evaluation research* that are valid, policy-relevant, and have had positive social impact, *and examples of* how they have effectively dealt with the regulatory constraints imposed.

A third arena for productive action is to work for the rational reform of government research procurement and administrative regulations designed specifically *for* social research, *by* social researchers, and *out of* social research knowledge.

SOURCE: From C. C. Abt, "The Public Good, the Private Good, and the Government Good in the Evaluation of Social Programs: How Inept Government Requirements Increase Costs and Reduce Effectiveness." *Evaluation Quarterly*, 2 (November 1978): 620-630.

Education requires three years from conception to completion. While both governmental and private-sector sponsors have tried to develop mechanisms to speed up the planning and procurement processes, the workings of their bureaucracies, legal requirements related to contracting, and the need to establish agreement on the evaluation questions and design hinder these efforts.

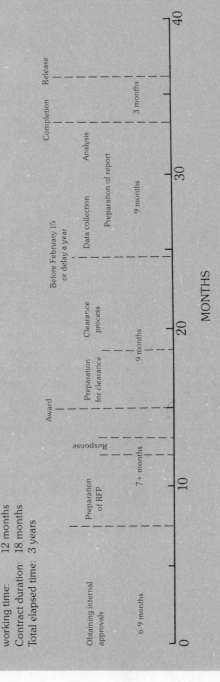

Exhibit 9-D: Typical Time Required for Undertaking a U.S. Department of Education Evaluation Contract

Total anticipated
working time: 12 months
Contract duration: 18 months
Total elapsed time: 3 years

Obtaining internal
approvals

6-9 months

Preparation
of RFP

7+ months

Response

Award

Preparation
for clearance

Clearance
process

9 months

Before February 15
or delay a year

Data collection

Preparation of report

9 months

Completion

Analysis

Release

3 months

MONTHS

SOURCE: Reproduced from *Program Evaluation in Education*, by Senta A. Raizen and Peter H. Rossi, National Academy Press, Washington, DC, 1981.

It is not clear what can be done to reduce the degree of pressure arising from the different time schedules of evaluation and decision-making. It is self-evident that a long-term study should not be undertaken if the information is needed before the evaluation can be completed. It may be better in such circumstances to rely on expert opinion or another of the more judgmental evaluation methods discussed in Chapter 7. It would clearly be better to have some information — as sound in technical quality as possible, given time constraints — than to have no information at all.

A more strategic approach is to confine technically complex evaluations to pilot or prototype projects for interventions that are not likely to be implemented on a large scale in the near future. Thus, randomized controlled experiments may be most appropriate to evaluate the worth of new programs (initially implemented on a small scale) before such programs appear upon the agendas of decision-making bodies. Extensive cross-sectional analyses may be applied to programs that have a history of steady support.

A final strategy for evaluators is to *anticipate* the direction of programs and policy activities, rather than be forced, within heavy time constraints, to fill the demands of other parties. One proposal that has attracted some attention is to establish independent evaluation institutes dedicated to examining, on a pilot or prototype basis, interventions that might one day be in demand. A national evaluation center could assess the worth of alternative social programs addressed to policy issues foreseen to be important a decade or more ahead. While this proposal has some attractive features, especially to professional evaluators, it is not at all clear that it is possible to forecast accurately what the next decade's social issues will be. As things stand now, we believe that the tension caused by the disparities between political and research time will continue to be a problem in the employment of evaluation as a useful tool for policymakers and project managers.

THE ROLES OF EVALUATIONS

At every point during a program, evaluation results can be useful in the decision-making process. In some cases, project sponsors may contract for an evaluation with the strong anticipation that it will critically influence continuation, modification, or termination of a project. In those cases, the evaluator may be under pressure to produce information quickly, so that decisions can be made expeditiously. In short, evaluators may have a receptive audience.

In other situations, evaluators may complete their assessments of an intervention only to discover that decision makers react slowly to their findings (Cox, 1977). Even more disconcerting are the occasions when a program is continued, modified, or terminated without regard to an evaluation's valuable and often expensive information.

Although in such circumstances evaluators may feel as though their labors have been in vain, the decision-making process is indeed complex. As we have noted, one can only expect that the results of an evaluation will be *but one* of the elements in decision-making. This is clearly revealed in the 1915 controversy over the evaluation of the Gary plan in New York City (see Exhibit 9-E).

There are many parties involved in a human service program, as we noted earlier. Program sponsors, managers and operators, and sometimes the participants often have very high stakes in the continuation of a program, and their unsupportable but enthusiastic claims may often count more than the results of an evaluation. The outcomes of a political process may be viewed as balancing a variety of interests; the outcome of an evaluation is simply a single argument on one side or another.

To imagine otherwise would be to claim that evaluators occupy a place in the political decision-making process that commands the power of veto, a role that would strip decision makers of their prerogatives. Under such circumstances evaluators would become philosopher kings whose pronouncements on particular programs would override those of all the other parties involved.

In any political system that is sensitive to weighing, assessing, and balancing the conflicting claims and interests of a number of constituencies, one can expect an evaluation to play the role of expert witness, testifying to the degree of a program's effectiveness. A jury of decision makers and other stakeholders may give such testimony more weight than uninformed opinion or shrewd guessing, but it is they, not the witness, who reach a verdict.

Studies of Utilization

The growth of the evaluation enterprise has been accompanied by a number of efforts to understand how and when evaluations are utilized. In part, this activity is related to the disappointment among evaluators and advocates of evaluation utility over the slight influence evaluations appear to have on policy and program activities. In Chapter 2 we suggested that an evaluation's results can be valuable in different ways: They can influence technical-administrative decisions, provide accountability evidence, validate programs, and contribute to general knowledge on social problems.

Exhibit 9-E: Politics and Evaluation

The Gary plan initially had been introduced into two New York schools on a pilot basis, and the Ettinger plan into a number of other schools. Superintendent Maxwell, resentful of interference in this professional domain and suspicious of the intent of Mitchel's administration, had already expressed his feelings about the Gary plan as it was operating in Angelo Patri's school: "Well, I visited that school [PS 45, Bronx] the other day, and the only thing I saw was a lot of children digging in a lot." Despite the superintendent's views, the Gary system had been extended to twelve schools in the Bronx, and there were plans to extend it.

The cry for more research before extending the plan was raised by a school board member. In the summer of 1915, Superintendent Maxwell ordered an evaluative study of the Gary plan as it had been implemented in the New York schools. The job was given to B. R. Buckingham, an educational psychologist in the research department of the New York City Schools and a pioneer in the development of academic achievement tests.

Buckingham used his newly developed academic achievement tests to compare two Gary-organized schools, six schools organized on the Ettinger plan, and eight traditionally organized schools. The traditionally organized schools came out best on the average, while the two Gary-organized schools averaged poorest. Buckingham's report was highly critical of the eager proponents of the Gary system, who made premature statements concerning its superiority to other forms of schooling.

No sooner had the Buckingham report appeared than a veritable storm of rebuttal followed, both in the press and in professional journals. Howard W. Nudd, executive director of the Public Education Association, wrote a detailed critique of the Buckingham report, published in the New York *Globe,* the *New York Times, School and Society,* and the *Journal of Education.*

Nudd counterattacked on technical grounds. First, he showed that at the time Buckingham conducted his tests, the Gary plan had been in operation in one school for only four months, and in the other for less than three weeks. He asserted that much of the equipment requested by Wirt had not been provided, and that the work of the Gary schools had been seriously disturbed by the constant stream of visitors who characteristically descend on a program that achieves visibility. In a detailed, school-by-school comparison, Nudd showed that in one of the Gary-organized schools 90 percent of the pupils came from immigrant homes where Italian was their first tongue, while some of the comparison schools were largely populated by middle-class, native American children. Moreover, pupils in one of the Gary schools had excellent test scores. When scores from that school alone were compared with those from other schools, the Gary school was seen to stand very well, indeed. When scores were averaged with the second Gary school, the overall result put the Gary plan well behind.

Buckingham had no answer to the contention of inadequate controls, but he argued that he was dealing not with two schools, six schools, and eight schools, but with measurements on over 11,000 children, and therefore his study represented a substantial test of the Gary scheme. He justified undertaking his study early on the grounds that the Gary plan, already in operation in twelve Bronx schools, was being pushed on the New York schools and superintendent precipitously. As noted above, there was pressure from the mayor's office to extend the plan throughout the New York schools, and to make any increase in the education budget contingent on wholesale adoption of the Gary system. Buckingham concluded that Superintendent Maxwell was obligated to undertake a study of the schools to determine their success in giving instruction in the "fundamental subjects," and not in terms of any other values or goals of the Gary plan.

The president of the Board of Education found it advantageous to cite Nudd's interpretation of the Buckingham report in debate at the Board of Education meeting. Superintendent Maxwell continued to cite the Buckingham study as evidence against the effectiveness of the Gary plan, even a year and a half later.

SOURCE: Adapted from A. Levine and M. Levine, "The Social Context of Evaluative Research: A Case Study." *Evaluation Quarterly*, 1 (November 1977): 520-523.

Types of Utilization

According to Leviton and Hughes (1979, 1981), evaluation findings can influence program planning and implementation in terms of instrumental, conceptual, or persuasive use. *Instrumental use* refers to documented and specific actions of decision makers and problem solvers (Rich, 1977). For example, evaluation data showing that patients of health maintenance organizations require fewer days of hospitalization than do hospital ambulatory patients have been used by advocates of the former approach testifying before congressional committees. *Conceptual use,* according to Rich (1977), is the use of evaluation to influence thinking about an issue without engaging the information for any specific, documentable purposes. An example is the current effort to control the costs of delivering health and welfare services, stimulated at least in part by evaluations of their efficacy and costs to benefits. *Persuasive use* refers to enlisting evaluation results in efforts either to defend or to attack political positions — in other words, to support or refute the status quo.

Disappointment about utilization of evaluations is largely related to the limited evidence that they have instrumental use. It is clear that most evaluations are initiated because of their potential for instrumental use, and the field's continued prosperity depends on maximizing such use. Certainly, evaluations over time may be important for their conceptual use, and in the long run, such use in itself may more than justify the costs and efforts required for studies. The fact remains, however, that the vast majority of evaluations are supported and sponsored by mission-oriented organizations that are not usually inclined to provide resources and evaluation opportunities without some reasonable expectation of direct, relatively short-term instrumental use. Thus, interest in evaluation centers on studies that maximize this mode of use.

Variables Affecting Utilization

In studies of the use of social research in general and evaluations in particular, five conditions appear to affect utilization consistently (Leviton and Hughes, 1981):

1. relevance
2. communication between evaluators and users
3. information processing by users
4. plausibility of evaluation results
5. user involvement or advocacy

The importance of these conditions and their relative contributions to utilization have been carefully studied by Weiss and Bucuvalas

(1980). They examined 155 decision makers in the mental health field and their reactions to 50 actual research reports. Decision makers, they found, apply both a *truth test* and a *utility test* in screening social research reports. Truth is judged on two bases: research quality and conformity to prior knowledge and expectations. Utility refers to feasibility potential and degree of challenge to current policy. Weiss and Bucuvalas's study provides convincing evidence of the complexity of the utilization process (see Exhibit 9-F).

Guidelines for Maximizing Utilization

Out of the research on utilization and the real-world experiences of evaluators, a number of guidelines for increasing utilization have emerged. These have been summarized by Solomon and Shortell (1981) and are briefly noted here for reference:

1. Evaluators must understand the cognitive styles of decision makers. For instance, there is no point in presenting a complex piece of analysis to a politician who cannot or will not consume such material. Thus, reports and verbal presentations tailored to a predetermined audience may be more appropriate than, say, academic journal articles.

2. Evaluation results must be timely and available when needed. Evaluation findings must therefore balance timing and accessibility of findings with thoroughness and completeness of analysis. Evaluators may have to risk criticism from some of their academic colleagues, whose concepts of scholarship cannot always be met because of the need for rapid results and crisp reporting.

3. Evaluations must respect stakeholders' program commitments. Evaluations are done for specific sets of individuals and organizations, and their usefulness demands wide participation in the evaluation design process to ensure sensitivity to stakeholders' interests. Differences in values and outlooks between clients and evaluators should be explicated at the outset of a study and be a determinant of whether or

Exhibit 9-F: Truth Tests and Utility Tests

In coping with incoming floods of information, decision makers invoke three basic frames of reference. One is the relevance of the content of the study to their sphere of responsibility, another is the trustworthiness of the study, and the third is the direction that it provides. The latter two frames, which we have called truth and utility tests, are each composed of two interdependent components:

Truth test: Is the research trustworthy? Can I rely on it? Will it hold up under attack? The two specific components are:

1. Research Quality: Was the research conducted by proper scientific methods?
2. Conformity to User Expectations: Are the results compatible with my experience, knowledge, and values?

Utility test: Does the research provide direction? Does it yield guidance — either for immediate action or for considering alternative approaches to problems? The two specific components are:

1. Action Orientation: Does the research show how to make feasible changes in things that can feasibly be changed?
2. Challenge to the Status Quo: Does the research challenge current philosophy, program, or practice? Does it offer new perspectives?

Together with Relevance (that is, the match between the topic of the research and the person's job responsibilities), these four components constitute the frames of reference by which decision makers assess social science research. Research Quality and Conformity to User Expectations form a single truth test in that their effects are contingent on each other: Research Quality is less important for the usefulness of a study when results are congruent with officials' prior knowledge than when results are unexpected or counterintuitive. Action Orientation and Challenge to the Status Quo represent alternative functions that a study can serve. They constitute a utility test, since the kind of explicit and practical direction captured by the Action Orientation frame is more important for a study's usefulness when the study provides little criticism or reorientation (Challenge to the Status Quo) than it is when Challenge is high. Conversely, the criticisms of programs and the new perspectives embedded in Challenge to the Status Quo add more to usefulness when a study lacks feasible prescriptions for implementation.

────────────

SOURCE: Adapted, with permission, from Carol H. Weiss and Michael J. Bucuvalas, "Truth Tests and Utility Tests: Decision-Makers' Frames of Reference for Social Science Research," *American Sociological Review*, Vol. 45 (April), 1980: 302-313.

not a particular evaluation is undertaken by a particular evaluation team.

4. Utilization and dissemination plans should be part of the evaluation design. Evaluation findings are most likely to be used if the evaluation effort includes "teaching" potential users the strengths and limitations of the effort, the degree to which one may expect definitive results, how the information from the evaluation can be effectively communicated by decision makers to their constituencies, and what criticisms and other reactions may be anticipated.

5. Evaluations should include the assessment of utilization. Evaluators and decision makers must not only share an understanding of the purposes for which a study is undertaken but also agree on the criteria by which its successful utilization may be judged. Under such conditions, however much informality is necessary, an effort should be made to judge the extent to which the uses of findings meet these expectations.

It should be evident that while these guidelines are relevant to the utilization of all program evaluations, the roles of evaluation consumers do differ and affect the uses to which information is put and consequently mechanisms to maximize utility. In particular, if evaluations are to influence legislation and far-reaching policies, they must be conducted and "packaged" in ways that meet the needs of potential users. From a study of congressional staff with major responsibilities for the development of educational legislation, Florio et al. (1979) compiled a useful summary of requirements, which we present in Exhibit 9-G.

Exhibit 9-G: Educational Inquiry: The Unmet Potential

The interviewees mentioned over 90 steps that could be taken to improve the use of educational studies in the formation of legislative policy. The most common themes, which reflect the current barriers to such use, are the ways in which research and assessment reports are presented and the failure to meet the needs demanded by the policy cycles in Congress.

The table summarizes the responses to the question of how to improve the use of available information.

Staffers struck a common theme of work and information overload problems associated with the job. They rarely have time to "evaluate the evaluations," let alone read through the "voluminous reports" that come across their desks. This was at the root of the repeated call for executive summaries in the front matter of reports, which would allow them to judge the relevance of the contents and determine if further reading for substance was necessary. Although 16 (61%) of the staffers complained of an information overload problem, 19 (73%) also indicated that they were often forced to generate their own data relevant to political and policy questions. As one staffer put it, "we have no overload of useful and understandable information."

The timing of the study reports and their relevance to questions and problems before the Congress were major barriers repeatedly mentioned by congressional staff. Mary Moore, senior policy analyst for the Assistant Secretary of Education (HEW) and one of the sources of policy-relevant information, compares the policy process to a "moving train." She suggests that information providers have the obligation to know the policy cycle and meet it on its own terms.

The credibility problem is also one that plagues social inquiry. Bertram Carp, Deputy Director of the White House Domestic Policy staff and former aide to Vice-President Mondale when he was a senator, said that "all social science suffers from the perception that it is unreliable and not policy-relevant." His comments were reflected by several of the staffers interviewed — for example, "research rarely provides definitive conclusions," or "for every finding, others negate it," or "educational research can rarely be replicated and there are few standards that can be applied to assess the research products." One went so far as to call project evaluations "lies," then reconsidered and called them "embellishments."

Again, it must be pointed out that the distinctions among different types of inquiry — research, evaluation, data collection, and so on — are rarely made by the recipients of knowledge and information. If project evaluations are viewed as fabrications, it reflects negatively on the entire educational inquiry community.

Even when policy-relevant research is presented in time to meet the "moving train," staffers complain of having "too much unassimilable information," or that "studies are poorly packaged," contain too much technical jargon, and are too "self-serving." Several said that researchers write for other researchers and rarely, except in congressionally mandated studies, tailor their language to the decision-making audiences in the legislative process. A theme underlying many of these observations is that the research and evaluation community *does* have the needed knowledge and information available. This indicates that there is less than a clear understanding of the limitations on the contributions which can be made by the educational inquiry community.

Improving the Use of Educational Studies

Format & Presentation (45)	*Relevance to Congressional Needs (25)*
Use executive summary (13)	Meet timing of legislative cycle and process (9)
Clarify language/eliminate jargon (7)	Have policy-relevant information (9)
Use charts and visual displays (6)	Demonstrate a greater understanding of the political arena in Congress (4)
Synthesize available findings (4)	Make appropriate information available throughout the legislative process (3)
Present data in concise fashion (4)	
Use examples of results (4)	
Make concrete recommendations (3)	
Provide references to more information (3)	
Index data (1)	

Credibility (22)

Develop direct relationships with staff early and throughout the conduct of a study (13)
Have sources with a strong reputation (5)
Have more accurate and unbiased information (3)
Do not have results that are overly cautious (1)

Note: Times are mentioned in parentheses.

SOURCE: Adapted, with permission, from David H. Florio, Michael M. Behrmann, and Diane L. Goltz, "What Do Policy Makers Think of Evaluational Research & Evaluation? Or Do They?", *Educational Evaluation and Policy Analysis*, Vol. 1, January 1979, pp. 61-87. Copyright 1979, American Educational Research Association, Washington, DC.

EPILOGUE

There are many reasons to expect continued support of evaluation activities. First, decision makers, planners, project staffs, and target participants are increasingly skeptical of common sense and conventional wisdom as sufficient bases upon which to design social programs that will achieve their intended goals. Decades of attempts to solve the problems represented by explosive population growth, the maldistribution of resources within and between societies, popular discontent, rising crime, continued educational deficiencies among adults and children, high drug and alcohol addiction rates, and apparently growing weaknesses in traditional institutions such as the family have led to a realization that these are obstinate and difficult issues to face. This skepticism has, in turn, led policymakers and decision makers to seek ways to learn more quickly and efficiently from their mistakes and to capitalize more rapidly on effective measures. To fund an evaluation is to express that skepticism, or at least to state implicitly that a proposed program may not be as effective an answer to a problem as hoped.

A second major reason for the growth of evaluation research has been the development of knowledge and technical procedures in the social sciences. The refinement of sample survey procedures has provided an important information-gathering method. When coupled with more traditional experimental methods in the form of field experiments, these procedures become a powerful means of testing social programs. Advances in measurement, statistical theory, and substantive knowledge in the social sciences have also added to the ability of social scientists to take on the special tasks of evaluation research.

Finally, there are the changes in the social and political climate of our times. We have come to insist that communal and personal problems are not fixed features of the human condition but are subject to change and amelioration through the reconstruction of social institutions. We believe more than our ancestors did that societies can be improved, and that the lot of all persons can be enhanced by the betterment of the disadvantaged and deprived. At the same time, almost worldwide, we are confronted with severely limited resources for welfare, health, and other social programs. It is tempting to wish away inflation, argue against domestic and international violence, and believe "moral reconstruction" will diminish the need for many communal programs — but it is catastrophically naive to think that these "actions" will solve our problems.

The prognosis is troublesome, in the short term at least, when we contemplate both the variety and number of concerns that require urgent action, and the level of resources that can be committed to their amelioration and control. It will become increasingly difficult to choose which problems to confront first, and which programs to implement in order to deal with them. Our position is clear: Systematic evaluations are invaluable to current and future efforts to improve the lot of humankind.

REFERENCES

Abt Associates
   1977   An Overview of the Experimental Housing Allowance Program Demand Experiments. Cambridge, MA: Abt Associates.

Abt, C. C.
   1978   "The Public Good, the Private Good, and the Government Good in the Evaluation of Social Programs: How Inept Government Requirements Increase Costs and Reduce Effectiveness." Evaluation Quarterly 2 (November): 620-630.

Adams, B. and B. Sherman
   1978   "Sunset Implementation: A Positive Partnership to Make Government Work." Public Administration Review 36 (January/February): 78-81.

Armor, D. J., J. M. Pouch, and H. B. Stambul
   1976   Alcoholism and Treatment. Santa Monica, CA: Rand Corporation.

Augustin, M. S., E. Stevens, and D. Hicks
   1973   "An Evaluation of the Effectiveness of a Children and Youth Project." Health Services Report 88 (December): 942-946.

Barnouw, B. S. and G. G. Cain
   1977   "A Reanalysis of the Effect of Head Start on Cognitive Development: Methodology and Empirical Findings." Journal of Human Resources 12 (Spring): 177-197.

Barnouw, B. S., G. G. Cain, and A. Goldberger
   1980   "Issues in the Analysis of Selectivity Bias," in E. W. Stromsdorfer and G. Farkas (eds.) Evaluation Studies Review Annual, Volume 5. Beverly Hills, CA: Sage Publications.

Bennett, C. A. and A. A. Lumsdaine
   1975   Evaluation and Experiment. New York: Academic.

Berk, R. A., T. Cooley, C. J. LaCivita, and K. Sredl
   1981   Saving Water: Lessons in Conservation from the Great California Drought, 1976-1977. Cambridge, MA: Abt Books.

Berk, R. A. and P. H. Rossi
   1976   "Doing Good or Worse: Evaluation Research Politically Re-Examined." Social Problems 23 (February): 337-349.

Bernstein, I. N. and H. E. Freeman
   1975   Academic and Entrepreneurial Research. New York: Russell Sage.

Blalock, H. M., Jr. and A. Blalock (eds.)
   1968   Methodology in Social Research. New York: McGraw-Hill.

Bogart, L. (ed.)
   1969   Social Research and the Desegregation of the United States Army. Chicago: Markham.

Bohrnstedt, G. W.
   1970   "Reliability and Validity Assessment in Attitude Measurement," pp. 80-99 in G. F. Summers (ed.) Attitude Measurement. Skokie, IL: Rand McNally.
   1982   "Measurement," in P. H. Rossi et al. (eds.) Handbook of Survey Research. New York: Academic.

Boruch, R. F.
  1975 "On Common Contentions About Randomized Field Experiments," pp. 107-142 in R. F. Boruch and H. W. Riecken (eds.) Experimental Testing of Public Policy: The Proceedings of the 1974 Social Science Research Council Conference on Social Experiments. Boulder, CO: Westview.

Boruch, R. F., A. J. McSweeney, and E. J. Soderstrom
  1978 "Randomized Field Experiments for Program Planning, Development, and Evaluation: An Illustrative Bibliography." Evaluation Quarterly 2 (November): 655-695.

Bozzo, R. M., E. L. Kane, and S. Mittenthal
  1977 Evaluation of the State of Delaware's Human Service Delivery System. Washington, DC: National Institute for Advanced Studies.

Bremner, R.
  1956 From the Depths: The Discovery of Poverty in America. New York: New York University Press.

Brewster, M. A., I. Crespi, R. Kaluzny, J. Ohls, and C. Thomas
  1980 "Homeowner Warranties: A Study of the Need and Demand for Protection Against Unanticipated Repair Expenses." American Real Estate and Urban Economics Association Journal 8(2): 207-215.

Bridges, W. and J. Oppenheim
  1977 "Racial Discrimination in Chicago's Storefront Banks." Evaluation Quarterly 1 (February): 159-171.

Cain, G. G.
  1975 "Regression and Selection Models to Improve Nonexperimental Comparisons," pp. 297-317 in C. A. Bennett and A. A. Lumsdaine (eds.) Evaluation and Experiment. New York: Academic.

Campbell, D. T.
  1969 "Reforms as Experiments." American Psychologist 24 (April): 409-429.

Campbell, D. T. and R. F. Boruch
  1975 "Making the Case for Randomized Assignment to Treatments by Considering the Alternatives: Six Ways in Which Quasi-Experimental Evaluations in Compensatory Education Tend to Underestimate Effects," pp. 195-296 in C. A. Bennett and A. A. Lumsdaine (eds.) Evaluation and Experiment. New York: Academic.

Campbell, D. T. and A. Erlebacher
  1970 "How Regression Artifacts in Quasi-Experimental Evaluations Can Mistakenly Make Compensatory Education Look Harmful," pp. 185-210 in J. Helmuth (ed.) The Disadvantaged Child, Volume 3: Education: A National Debate. New York: Brunner/Mazel.

Campbell, D. T. and J. C. Stanley
  1966 Experimental and Quasi-Experimental Designs for Research. Skokie, IL: Rand McNally.

Carlson, D. B. and J. D. Heinberg
  1977 How Housing Allowances Work. Washington, DC: The Urban Institute.

Carnoy, M.
  1975 "The Economic Costs and Returns to Educational Television." Economic Development and Cultural Change 23 (January): 207-248.

Caro, F. G. (ed.)
  1971 Readings in Evaluation Research. New York: Russell Sage.

Cernea, M. and B. J. Tepping
    1977 A System for Monitoring and Evaluating Agricultural Extension Projects. Washington, DC: World Bank.

Chelimsky, E.
    1978 "Differing Perspectives of Evaluation," pp. 19-38 in C. C. Rentz and R. R. Rentz (eds.) Evaluating Federally Sponsored Programs: New Directions for Program Evaluation 2 (Summer). San Francisco: Jossey-Bass.

Chen, H-t. and P. H. Rossi
    1980 "The Multi-Goal, Theory-Driven Approach to Evaluation: A Model Linking Basic and Applied Social Science." Social Forces 59 (September): 106-122.

Cicirelli, V. G. et al.
    1969 The Impact of Head Start. Athens, OH: Westinghouse Learning Corporation and Ohio University.

Coleman, J. S., T. Hoffer, and S. Kilgore
    1981 Public and Private Schools: High School and Beyond. Chicago: National Opinion Research Center.

Coleman, J. S. et al.
    1966 Equality of Educational Opportunity. Washington, DC: Government Printing Office.

Conlisk, J.
    1977 "A Further Look at the Hansen-Weisbrod-Pechman Debate." Journal of Human Resources 12 (Spring): 147-163.

Conner, R. F.
    1977 "Selecting a Control Group: An Analysis of the Randomization Process in Twelve Social Reform Programs." Evaluation Quarterly 1 (May): 195-244.

Cook, T. D., H. Appleton, R. F. Conner, A. Shaffer, G. Tamkin, and S. J. Weber
    1975 "Sesame Street" Revisited. New York: Russell Sage.

Cook, T. D. and D. T. Campbell
    1976 "The Design and Conduct of Quasi-Experiments and True Experiments in Field Settings," pp. 223-326 in M. D. Dunnette (ed.) Handbook of Industrial and Organizational Research. Skokie, IL: Rand McNally.
    1979 Quasi-Experimentation Design and Analysis Issues for Field Settings. Skokie, IL: Rand McNally.

Cook, T. D., J. Levinson-Rose, and W. E. Pollard
    1980 "The Misutilization of Evaluation Research: Some Pitfalls of Definition." Knowledge: Creation, Diffusion, Utilization 1 (June): 477-498.

Cook, T. D. and C. S. Reichardt
    1976 "Guidelines — Statistical Analysis of Nonequivalent Control Group Designs: A Guide to Some Current Literature." Evaluation 3 (May): 136-138.

Cook, T. D. and C. S. Reichardt (eds.)
    1979 Qualitative and Quantitative Methods in Evaluation Research. Beverly Hills, CA: Sage Publications.

Cooley, W. W. and G. Leinhardt
    1980 "The Instructional Dimensions Study." Educational Evaluation and Policy Analysis 2 (January): 7-25.

Cooper, A. M. and M. B. Sobell
    1979 "Does Alcohol Education Prevent Alcohol Problems? Need for Evaluation." Journal of Alcohol and Drug Education 25 (January): 54-63.

Costner, H. L. and R. K. Leik
1964 "Deductions from Axiomatic Theory." American Sociological Review 29 (December): 819-835.

Cox, G. B.
1977 "Managerial Style: Implications for the Utilization of Program Evaluation Information." Evaluation Quarterly 1 (August): 499-508.
1980 "Involuntary Patient Flow: A Computer Simulation of a Psychiatric Ward." Evaluation Review 4 (October): 571-584.

Crane, J. A.
1976 "The Power of Social Intervention Experiments to Discriminate Differences Between Experimental and Control Groups." Social Science Review 50 (June): 224-242.

Cronbach, L. J. and Associates
1980 Toward Reform of Program Evaluation. San Francisco: Jossey-Bass.

Crone, C. D.
1977 "Evaluation: Autopsy or Checkup?" World Education Reports 15 (October): 3-13.

Cutright, P. and F. S. Jaffe
1977 Impact of Family Planning Programs on Fertility: The U.S. Experience. New York: Praeger.

Datta, L.
1977 "Does It Work When It Has Been Tried? And Half Full or Half Empty? pp. 301-319 in M. Guttentag and S. Saar (eds.) Evaluation Studies Review Annual, Volume 2. Beverly Hills, CA: Sage Publications.
1980 "Interpreting Data: A Case Study from the Career Intern Program Evaluation." Evaluation Review 4 (August): 481-506.

Deutsch, S. J.
1979 "Lies, Damn Lies and Statistics: A Rejoinder to the Comment by Hay and McCleary." Evaluation Quarterly 3 (May): 315-328.

Deutsch, S. J. and F. B. Alt
1977 "The Effect of Massachusetts' Gun Control Law on Gun-Related Crimes in the City of Boston." Evaluation Quarterly 1 (November): 543-567.

Diaz-Guerrero, R., I. Reyes-Lagunes, D. B. Witzke, and W. H. Holtzman
1976 "Plaza Sésamo in Mexico: An Evaluation." Journal of Communication 26 (Spring): 145-154.

Edwards, W., M. Guttentag, and K. Snapper
1975 "A Decision-Theoretic Approach to Evaluation Research," pp. 139-182 in E. L. Struening and M. Guttentag (eds.) Handbook of Evaluation Research, Volume 1. Beverly Hills, CA: Sage Publications.

Elliott, D. C. et al.
1976 Research Handbook for Community Planning and Feedback Instruments, Volume 1 (rev.). Boulder, CO: Behavioral Research Institute.

Fairweather, G. W. and L. G. Tornatzky
1977 Experimental Methods for Social Policy Research. Elmsford, NY: Pergamon.

Feaster, J. G. and G. B. Perkins
1973 Families in the Expanded Food and Nutrition Education Program: Comparison of Food Stamp and Food Distribution Program Participants and Nonparticipants. Washington, DC: U.S. Department of Agriculture.

Federal Statistical System
1976 Social Indicators 1976. Washington, DC: U.S. Department of Commerce.

Festinger, L.
1964 "Behavioral Support for Opinion Changes." Public Opinion Quarterly 28 (Fall): 404-417.

Fisher, R. A.
1935 The Design of Experiments (1st ed.). London: Oliver & Boyd.

Florio, D. H., M. M. Behrmann, and D. L. Goltz
1979 "What Do Policy Makers Think of Evaluational Research and Evaluation? Or Do They?" Educational Evaluation and Policy Analysis 1 (January): 61-87.

Franke, R. H. and J. D. Kaul
1978 "The Hawthorne Experiments: First Statistical Interpretation." American Sociological Review 43 (October): 623-642.

Franklin, J. L. and J. H. Thrasher
1976 An Introduction to Program Evaluation. New York: John Wiley.

Freeman, H. E.
1977 "The Present Status of Evaluation Research," pp. 17-51 in M. Guttentag and S. Saar (eds.) Evaluation Studies Review Annual, Volume 2. Beverly Hills, CA: Sage Publications.

Freeman, H. E., R. E. Klein, J. Kagan, and C. Yarbrough
1977 "Relations Between Nutrition and Cognition in Rural Guatemala." American Journal of Public Health 67 (March): 223-239.

Freeman, H. E., P. H. Rossi, and S. R. Wright
1980 Doing Evaluations. Paris: Organisation for Economic Cooperation and Development.

Freeman, H. E. and C. C. Sherwood
1970 Social Research and Social Policy. Englewood Cliffs, NJ: Prentice-Hall.

Freeman, H. E. and M. A. Solomon
1979 "The Next Decade in Evaluation Research." Evaluation and Program Planning 2 (March): 255-262.

Gall, J. E., Jr. and D. D. Norwood
1977 Demonstration and Evaluation of a Total Hospital Information System. Hyattsville, MD: National Center for Health Services Research.

Garms, W. I.
1971 "A Benefit-Cost Analysis of the Upward Bound Program." Journal of Human Resources 6 (Spring): 206-220.

Geisel, M. S., R. Roll, and R. S. Wettick, Jr.
1969 "The Effectiveness of State and Local Regulation of Handguns: A Statistical Analysis." Duke Law Journal (August): 647-676.

Gibbs, J. P.
1966 "Suicide," pp. 281-321 in R. K. Merton and R. A. Nisbet (eds.) Contemporary Social Problems. New York: Harcourt Brace Jovanovich.

Goldman, J.
1977 "A Randomization Procedure for 'Trickle-Process' Evaluations." Evaluation Quarterly 1 (August): 493-498.

Gramlich, E. M. and P. P. Koshel
1975 Educational Performance Contracting: An Evaluation of an Experiment. Washington, DC: Brookings.

Gray, C. M., C. J. Conover, and T. M. Hennessey
1978 "Cost Effectiveness of Residential Community Corrections: An Analytical Prototype." Evaluation Quarterly 2 (August): 375-400.

Greeley, A. M., W. C. McCready, and K. McCourt
1976 Catholic Schools in a Declining Church. Kansas City: Sheed and Ward.

Greeley, A. M. and P. H. Rossi
1966 The Education of Catholic Americans. Chicago: Aldine.

Green, L. W., H. C. Gustafson, W. Griffiths, and D. Yaukey
1972 The Dacca Family Planning Experiment. Berkeley: University of California Press.

Guttentag, M. and E. L. Struening (eds.)
1975 Handbook of Evaluation Research, Volume 2. Beverly Hills, CA: Sage Publications.

Hannan, T.
1976 "The Benefits and Costs of Methadone Maintenance." Public Policy 24 (Spring): 197-226.

Hansen, W. L. and F. H. Nelson
1976 "The Distributional Efficiency of Benefits for a Student Financing Program with Payment Obligations Contingent upon Future Income." Proceedings of the Inaugural Convention of the Eastern Economic Association 2(3, Supplement, July): 83-98.

Hanushek, E. A. and J. E. Jackson
1977 Statistical Methods for Social Scientists. New York: Academic.

Hawkins, J. D., R. A. Roffman, and P. Osborne
1978 "Decision Makers' Judgments: The Influence of Role, Evaluative Criteria, and Information Access." Evaluation Quarterly 2 (August): 435-454.

Hay, R., Jr. and R. McCleary
1979 "Box-Tiao Time Series Models for Impact Assessment: A Comment on the Recent Work of Deutsch and Alt." Evaluation Quarterly 3 (May): 277-314.

Hayes, S. P., Jr.
1959 Evaluating Development Projects. Paris: UNESCO.

Heckman, J.
1980 "Sample Selection Bias as a Specification Error," in E. W. Stromsdorfer and G. Farkas (eds.) Evaluation Studies Review Annual, Volume 5. Beverly Hills, CA: Sage Publications.

Heumann, L. F.
1979 "Racial Integration in Residential Neighborhoods: Toward More Precise Measures and Analysis." Evaluation Quarterly 3 (February): 59-80.

Hibbs, D. A., Jr.
1977 "On Analyzing the Effects of Policy Interventions: Box-Jenkins and Box-Tiao versus Structural Equation Models," pp. 137-139 in D. R. Heise (ed.) Sociological Methodology 1977. San Francisco: Jossey-Bass.

Hornik, J., H. Gates, and C. Costanzo
1981 Technical Manual for Management Information System. Northampton, MA: Mental Patients Advocacy Project, Western Massachusetts Legal Services.

Hovland, C. I., A. A. Lumsdaine, and F. D. Sheffield
    1949 Experiments in Mass Communication, Volume III: The American Soldier.
          Princeton, NJ: Princeton University Press.

Ingle, H.
    1976 "Reconsidering the Use of Television for Educational Reform: The Case of El
          Salvador," pp. 114-139 in R. F. Arnove (ed.) Educational Television: Policy
          Critique and Guide for Developing Countries. New York: Praeger.

Irwin, J.
    1970 The Felon. Englewood Cliffs, NJ: Prentice-Hall.

Kagan, J., R. B. Kearsley, and P. R. Zelazo
    1977 "The Effects of Infant Day Care on Psychological Development." Evaluation
          Quarterly 1 (February): 109-142.

Kassebaum, G., D. Ward, and D. Wilner
    1971 Prison Treatment and Parole Survival. New York: John Wiley.

Kelling, G., T. Pate, D. Dieckman, and C. E. Brown
    1974 The Kansas City Preventive Patrol Experiment: A Technical Report.
          Washington, DC: Police Foundation.

Kennedy, S. D.
    1980 Final Report of the Housing Allowance Demand Experiment. Cambridge,
          MA: Abt Associates.

Kershaw, D. and J. Fair
    1976 The New Jersey Income-Maintenance Experiment, Volume I. New York:
          Academic.

Kiresuk, T.
    1973 "Goal Attainment Scaling at a County Mental Health Service." Evaluation
          1(1): 12-18.

Kish, L.
    1965 Survey Sampling. New York: John Wiley.

Klarman, H. E.
    1974 "Application of Cost-Benefit Analysis to the Health Services and the Special
          Case of Technologic Innovation." Journal of Health Services 4 (Spring):
          325-352.

Krug, A. S.
    1967 "The Relationship Between Firearms Licensing Laws and Crime Rates."
          Congressional Record 113, Part 15 (July 25): 200060-200064.

Lambert, C., Jr. and H. E. Freeman
    1967 The Clinic Habit. New Haven, CT: College and University Press.

Lash, T. W. and H. Sigal
    1976 State of the Child: New York City. New York: Foundation for Child De-
          velopment.

Levin, H.
    1975 "Cost-Effective Analysis in Evaluation Research," pp. 89-124 in M. Gutten-
          tag and E. L. Struening (eds.) Handbook of Evaluation Research, Volume 2.
          Beverly Hills, CA: Sage Publications.

Levine, A. and M. Levine
    1977 "The Social Context of Evaluation Research: A Case Study." Evaluation
          Quarterly 1 (November): 515-542.

Levine, R. A., M. A. Solomon, and G.-M. Hellstern (eds.)
   1981   Evaluation Research and Practice: Comparative and International Perspectives. Beverly Hills, CA: Sage Publications.

Leviton, L. C. and Hughes, E. F. X.
   1979   Utilization of Evaluations. Evanston, IL: Northwestern University Center for Health Services and Policy Research.
   1981   "Research on the Utilization of Evaluations: A Review and Synthesis." Evaluation Review 5 (August): 525-548.

Lieberman, H. M.
   1974   "Evaluating the Quality of Ambulatory Pediatric Care at a Neighborhood Health Center: Creative Use of a Chart Review." Clinical Pediatrics 13 (January): 52-55.

Little, I. M. D. and J. A. Mirrlees
   1974   Project Appraisal and Planning for Developing Countries. New York: Basic Books.

Lynn, L. E., Jr.
   1980   Designing Public Policy. Santa Monica, CA: Scott, Foresman.

Main, E. D.
   1968   "A Nationwide Evaluation of the MDTA Institutional Job Training." Journal of Human Resources 3 (Spring): 159-170.

Maki, J. E., D. M. Hoffman, and R. A. Berk
   1978   "A Time Series Analysis of the Impact of a Water Conservation Campaign." Evaluation Quarterly 2 (February): 107-118.

Marks, S. D., M. R. Greenlick, A. V. Hurtodo, J. D. Johnson, and I. Henderson
   1980   "Ambulatory Surgery in an HMO." Medical Care 18 (February): 127-146.

Mayo, J. K., R. C. Hornik, and E. G. McAnany
   1976   Educational Reform with Television: The El Salvador Experience. Palo Alto, CA: Stanford University Press.

McCleary, R. and R. Hay, Jr.
   1980   Applied Time Series Analysis for the Social Sciences. Beverly Hills, CA: Sage Publications.

McLaughlin, M. W.
   1975   Evaluation and Reform: The Elementary and Secondary Education Act of 1965/Title I. Cambridge, MA: Ballinger.

Mendenhall, W.
   1968   Introduction to Linear Models and the Design and Analysis of Experiments. Belmont, CA: Duxbury.

Mielke, K. W. and J. W. Swinehart
   1976   Evaluation of the Feeling Good Television Series. New York: Children's Television Workshop.

Miley, A. D., B. L. Lively, and R. D. McDonald
   1978   "An Index of Mental Health System Performance." Evaluation Quarterly 2 (February): 119-126.

Morris, L. L. and C. T. Fitz-Gibbon
   1978   How to Measure Program Implementation. Volume 4 in L. L. Morris (ed.) Program Evaluation Kit (8 volumes). Beverly Hills, CA: Sage Publications.

Mosteller, F. and D. P. Moynihan (eds.)
   1972 On Equality of Educational Opportunity. New York: Vintage Books.

Murray, D. R.
   1975 "Handguns, Gun Control Laws, and Firearm Violence." Social Problems 23 (October): 81-93.

Murray, S.
   1980 The National Evaluation of the PUSH for Excellence Project. Washington, DC: American Institutes for Research.

Namboodiri, N. K., L. F. Carter, and H. M. Blalock, Jr.
   1975 Applied Multivariate Analysis and Experimental Designs. New York: McGraw-Hill.

National Center for Health Services Research
   1977 Emergency Medical Services Systems Research Projects, 1977. Washington, DC: National Center for Health Services Research.

National Institute of Mental Health
   1976 A Working Manual of Simple Program Evaluation Techniques for Community Mental Health Centers. Washington, DC: Government Printing Office.

Nay, J. N., J. W. Scanlon, R. E. Schmidt, and J. Wholey
   1976 "If You Don't Care Where You Get To, Then It Doesn't Matter Which Way You Go," pp. 97-120 in C. C. Abt (ed.) The Evaluation of Social Programs. Beverly Hills, CA: Sage Publications.

Nicholson, W. and S. R. Wright
   1977 "Participants' Understanding of the Treatment in Policy Experimentation." Evaluation Quarterly 1 (May): 245-268.

Noble, J. H., Jr.
   1977 "The Limits of Cost-Benefit Analysis as a Guide to Priority Setting in Rehabilitation." Evaluation Quarterly 1 (August): 347-380.

Nunnally, J. C. and R. L. Durham
   1975 "Validity, Reliability, and Special Problems of Measurement in Evaluation Research," pp. 289-252 in E. L. Struening and M. Guttentag (eds.) Handbook of Evaluation Research, Volume 1. Beverly Hills, CA: Sage Publications.

Orshansky, M.
   1969 "Perspectives on Poverty: How Poverty Is Measured." Monthly Labor Review 92 (February): 37-41.

Patton, M. Q.
   1980 Qualitative Evaluation Methods. Beverly Hills, CA: Sage Publications.

Pierce, G. L. and W. J. Bowers
   1979 The Impact of the Bartley Fox Gun Law on Crime in Massachusetts. Boston: Center for Applied Social Research, Northeastern University.

Polivka, L. and E. Steg
   1978 "Program Evaluation and Policy Development: Bridging the Gap." Evaluation Quarterly 3 (November): 696-707.

Pressman, J. L. and A. B. Wildavsky
   1973 Implementation. Berkeley: University of California Press.

Price, D. R.
1978 "Sunset Legislation in the United States." Baylor Law Review 30(8): 401-446.

Pyndyck, R. S. and D. L. Rubinfeld
1976 Econometric Models and Economic Forecasts. New York: McGraw-Hill.

Quigley, P. A., L. Morris, and G. Hammett
1976 The Choctaw Home-Centered Family Education Demonstration Project. Tucson, AZ: Behavior Associates.

Raizen, S. A. and P. H. Rossi (eds.)
1981 Program Evaluation in Education: When? How? To What Ends? Washington, DC: National Academy Press.

Reeves, B. F.
1970 The First Year of Sesame Street: The Formative Research. New York: Children's Television Workshop.

Reiss, A. J., Jr.
1971 The Police and the Public. New Haven, CT: Yale University Press.

Ribich, T. I. and J. L. Murphy
1975 "The Economic Returns to Increased Educational Spending." Journal of Human Resources 10 (Winter): 56-77.

Rich, R. F.
1977 "Uses of Social Science Information by Federal Bureaucrats," in C. H. Weiss (ed.) Using Social Research for Public Policy Making. Lexington, MA: D. C. Heath.

Riecken, H. W. and R. F. Boruch (eds.)
1974 Social Experimentation: A Method for Planning and Evaluating Social Intervention. New York: Academic.

Robert Wood Johnson Foundation
1980 Annual Report. Princeton, NJ: Robert Wood Johnson Foundation.

Roethlisberger, F. J. and W. Dickson
1939 Management and the Worker. Cambridge, MA: Harvard University Press.

Roos, L. L., Jr., N. P. Roos, and B. McKinley
1977 "Implementing Randomization." Policy Analysis 3 (Fall): 547-560.

Ross, H. L., D. T. Campbell, and G. V Glass
1970 "Determining the Social Effects of a Legal Reform: The British Breathalyzer Crackdown of 1967." American Behavioral Scientist 3 (March/April): 494-509.

Rossi, P. H.
1978 "Issues in the Evaluation of Human Services Delivery." Evaluation Quarterly 2 (November): 573-599.
1979 "Critical Decisions in Evaluation Studies." New Directions for Testing and Measurement 1: 79-88.

Rossi, P. H., R. A. Berk, and B. K. Eidson
1974 Roots of Urban Discontent. New York: John Wiley.

Rossi, P. H., R. A. Berk, and K. J. Lenihan
1980 Money, Work and Crime. New York: Academic.

Rossi, P. H. and R. A. Dentler
   1961   The Politics of Urban Renewal. New York: Free Press.

Rossi, P. H. and K. Lyall
   1976   Reforming Public Welfare. New York: Russell Sage.

Rossi, P. H. and W. Williams (eds.)
   1972   Evaluating Social Programs. New York: Seminar.

Rossi, P. H., J. D. Wright, and A. Anderson (eds.)
   1982   Handbook of Survey Research. New York: Academic.

Rossi, P. H. and S. Wright
   1977   "Evaluation Research: An Assessment of Theory, Practice, and Politics."
          Evaluation Quarterly 1 (February): 5-52.

Rutman, L.
   1980   Planning Useful Evaluations: Evaluability Assessment. Beverly Hills, CA:
          Sage Publications.

Salamon, L. M.
   1974   The Time Dimension in Policy Evaluation: The Case of the New Deal
          Land-Reform Experiments. Durham, NC: Center for Urban and Regional
          Development Policy, Duke University. (Reprinted in Public Policy 27 (2),
          1979.)

Schatzman, L. and A. L. Strauss
   1973   Field Research: Strategies for a Natural Sociology. Englewood Cliffs, NJ:
          Prentice-Hall.

Schmidt, R. E., J. W. Scanlon, and J. B. Bell
   1978   Evaluability Assessment: Making Public Programs Work Better. Washington,
          DC: The Urban Institute.

Seitz, S. T.
   1972   "Firearms, Homicide and Gun Control Effectiveness." Law and Society
          Review 6 (May): 595-613.

Sewell, W. H. and R. M. Hauser
   1975   Education, Occupation and Earnings: Achievement in the Early Career. New
          York: Academic.

Sherman, L.
   1980   Experimental Interventions in the Treatment of Spouse Abuse. Washington,
          DC: Police Foundation.

Sherwood, C. C., J. N. Morris, and S. Sherwood
   1975   "A Multivariate, Nonrandomized Matching Technique for Studying the Im-
          pact of Social Interventions," pp.183-224 in E. L. Struening and M. Gutten-
          tag (eds.) Handbook of Evaluation Research, Volume 1. Beverly Hills, CA:
          Sage Publications.

Shlay, A. and P. H. Rossi
   1981   "Putting Politics into Urban Ecology: Estimating the Net Effects of Zoning."
          American Sociological Review 46 (October).

Shortell, S. M. and W. C. Richardson
   1978   Health Program Evaluation. St. Louis: C. V. Mosby.

Skipper, J. K., Jr. and R. C. Leonard
   1968   "Children, Stress and Hospitalization." Journal of Health and Social Be-
          havior 9 (December): 275-287.

Solomon, M. A. and S. M. Shortell
  1981 "Designing Health Policy Research for Utilization." Health Policy Quarterly 1: xx.

Squire, L. and H. G. van der Tak
  1975 Economic Analysis of Projects. Baltimore: Johns Hopkins University Press.

Stephan, A. S.
  1935 "Prospects and Possibilities: The New Deal and the New Social Research." Social Forces 13 (May).

Stokey, E. and R. Zeckhauser
  1978 A Primer for Policy Analyses. New York: Norton.

Stouffer, S. A. et al.
  1949 The American Soldier: Combat and Its Aftermath. Manhattan, KS: Military Affairs/Aerospace Historian.

Struening, E. L. and M. Guttentag (eds.)
  1975 Handbook of Evaluation Research, Volume 1. Beverly Hills, CA: Sage Publications.

Struyk, R. J. and M. Bendick (eds.)
  1981 Housing Vouchers for the Poor: Lessons from a National Experiment. Washington, DC: The Urban Institute.

Stuart, H. D. and A. M. Cruze
  1976 "Estimates of the Target Population for Upward Bound and Talent Search Programs." Durham, NC: Research Triangle Institute.

Suchman, E.
  1967 Evaluative Research. New York: Russell Sage.

Sudman, S.
  1976 Applied Sampling. New York: Academic.

Tessler, R. and D. Mechanic
  1975 "Consumer Satisfaction with Prepaid Group Practice: A Comparative Study." Journal of Health and Social Behavior 16 (March): 95-113.

Thompson, M.
  1980 Benefit-Cost Analysis for Program Evaluation. Beverly Hills, CA: Sage Publications.

UNCO, Inc.
  1975 National Childcare Consumer Study. Washington, DC: UNCO, Inc.

U.S. Department of Justice
  1977 Criminal Victimization Surveys in Boston: A National Crime Survey Report. Washington, DC: Government Printing Office.

van de Vall, M. and C. A. Bolas
  1981 "External vs. Internal Social Policy Researchers." Knowledge: Creation, Diffusion, Utilization 2 (June): 461-481.

Vanecko, J. J. and B. Jacobs
  1970 Reports from the 100-City CAP Evaluation: The Impact of the Community Action Program on Institutional Change. Chicago: National Opinion Research Center.

Watts, H. W., J. K. Peck, and M. Taussig
    1977 "Site Selection, Representativeness of the Sample, and Possible Attrition Bias," pp. 441-446 in H. W. Watts and A. Rees (eds.) The New Jersey Income-Maintenance Experiment, Volume III. New York: Academic.

Weiss, A. T.
    1975 "The Consumer Model of Assessing Community Mental Health Needs." Evaluation 2: 71.

Weiss, C. H.
    1972 Evaluating Action Programs: Readings in Social Action and Education. Boston: Allyn & Bacon.

Weiss, C. H. and M. J. Bucuvalas
    1980 "Truth Tests and Utility Tests: Decision-Makers' Frames of Reference for Social Science Research." American Sociological Review 45 (April): 302-313.

Weissert, W., T. Wan, B. Livieratos, and S. Katz
    1980 "Effects and Costs of Day-Care Services for the Chronically Ill: A Randomized Experiment." Medical Care 18(6): 567-584.

Westat, Inc.
    1976- Continuous Longitudinal Manpower Survey, Reports 1-10. Rockville,
    1980   MD: Westat, Inc.

Wholey, J. S.
    1977 "Evaluability Assessment," pp. 41-56 in L. Rutman (ed.) Evaluation Research Methods: A Basic Guide. Beverly Hills, CA: Sage Publications.
    1979 Evaluation: Promise and Performance. Washington, DC: The Urban Institute.
    1981 "Using Evaluation to Improve Program Performance," pp. 92-106 in R. A. Levine et al. (eds.) Evaluation Research and Practice: Comparative and International Perspectives. Beverly Hills, CA: Sage Publications.

Wholey, J. S., J. W. Scanlon, H. Duffy, J. S. Fukumoto, and L. M. Vogt
    1970 Federal Evaluation Policy. Washington, DC: The Urban Institute.

Willer, B. S.
    1977 "Individualized Patient Programming: An Experiment in the Use of Evaluation and Feedback for Hospital Psychiatry." Evaluation Quarterly 1 (November): 587-608.

Williams, W.
    1980 The Implementation Perspective. Berkeley: University of California Press.

Williams, W. and R. F. Elmore (eds.)
    1976 Social Program Implementation. New York: Academic.

Wilner, D. M., R. P. Walkely, T. C. Pinkerton, and M. Tayback
    1962 The Housing Environment and Family Life. Baltimore: Johns Hopkins University Press.

Wilson, J. Q. (ed.)
    1966 Urban Renewal: The Record and the Controversy. Cambridge, MA: MIT Press.

Winer, B. J.
    1971 Statistical Principles in Experimental Design. New York: McGraw-Hill.

Wolfe, B.
　1977　"A Cost-Effectiveness Analysis of Reductions in School Expenditures: An Application of an Educational Production Function." Journal of Education Finance 2 (Spring): 407-418.

Wortman, P. M., C. S. Reichardt, and R. G. St. Pierre
　1978　"The First Year of the Education Voucher Demonstration: A Secondary Analysis of Student Achievement Test Scores." Evaluation Quarterly 2 (May): 193-214.

Wright, J. D., P. H. Rossi, K. Daly, and E. Weber-Burdin
　1981　Weapons, Crime and Violence in America. Amherst, MA: Social and Demographic Research Institute.

Wright, J. D., P. H. Rossi, S. R. Wright, and E. Weber-Burdin
　1979　After the Clean-Up: Long-Range Effects of Natural Disasters. Beverly Hills, CA: Sage Publications.

Zaidan, G. C.
　1971　The Costs and Benefits of Family Planning Programs. Washington, DC: World Bank.

Zeckhauser, R.
　1975　"Procedures for Valuing Lives." Public Policy 23 (Fall): 419-464.